ENGLISH LOCAL STUDIES HANDBOOK

ENGLISH LOCAL STUDIES HANDBOOK

A guide to resources for each county
including libraries, record offices,
societies, journals and museums.

Compiled by Susanna Guy

University of Exeter Press

First published in 1992 by
University of Exeter Press
Reed Hall
Streatham Drive
Exeter EX4 4QR
UK

British Library Cataloguing in Publication Data
English local studies handbook : a guide to
 resources for each county including libraries,
 record offices, societies, journals and museums.
 1. England. Local history
 I. Guy, Susanna
 942

ISBN 0 85989 369 3

Printed in the UK by Short Run Press Ltd, Exeter

CONTENTS

INTRODUCTION

Purpose

The idea for the Handbook occurred to me when, as happened frequently, I was asked where to go for information about a locality (which library, the name of the county local history journal, which local society) and encountered considerable difficulty in finding the answers.

The names and addresses of local studies libraries, societies, journals and record offices are scattered throughout half-a-dozen or more directories and guides: the present publication attempts to list them under one cover, and county by county. The entries are deliberately brief, as the Handbook is intended to be a place of first resort for local studies information. More information can be found in the various directories and guides listed on pp. xiii–xiv, but enquirers should go to the libraries and information centres listed under each county and ask for the expert help and guidance of the local studies librarians and information officers.

Acknowledgements

The material for the Handbook was most patiently and courteously supplied and checked by local studies librarians and museum curators up and down the country. It supplements that which can already be found in the various published sources. It is as accurate as possible but I shall be glad to have my mistakes pointed out to me!

Notes on the general arrangement of the Handbook

The decision to use the pre-1974 county names and boundaries was taken mainly because this is a local <u>history</u> handbook: an enquirer asking for information about Rutland is not greatly helped by being told that there is no such county! Cross-referencing and the provision of 'before' and 'after' maps will help, I hope, to lead readers from the old to the new areas. The London boundaries were fixed ten years earlier in 1965, and I have perversely used these in preference to the old London boundaries.

Notes on the Sections

A. Nearly all the local studies libraries maintain a register of the local history societies in their area, down to the small village history/ amenity societies. I had originally intended to add a note to this effect to the appropriate entries but the practice is so universal that it seemed unnecessary to mention these registers individually.

B. The information in this section is taken mainly from the excellent HMSO publication *Record Repositories in Great Britain*, 8th edition, which lists opening times and details of collections.

C. The abbreviation (sec.) indicates that the society's address given is actually that of the present secretary. As implied in the notes for Section A, only major county societies are given here; details of the smaller societies can be obtained from the area local studies library.

D. The + after an entry indicates that the journal is still being issued.

E. It was not always easy to decide which museums to include in this section as the line between museums proper and theme parks, leisure centres or craft centres is a thin one. I have added notes about a museum's collections only where I thought it was not obvious from its title what subjects it covered.

NATIONAL SOCIETIES AND JOURNALS COVERING LOCAL HISTORY TOPICS

Societies

Local history

British Association for Local History, Shopwyke Hall, Chichester, West Sussex P020 6B

Archaeology

Association for Industrial Archaeology, The Wharfage, Iron Bridge, Telford TF8 7AW.
British Archaeological Association, Admont, Dancers End, Tring, Herts HP23 6JT.
Royal Archaeological Institute, c/o Society of Antiquaries, Burlington House, Piccadilly, London W1V OHS.
Society of Antiquaries of London, Burlington House, Piccadilly, London W1V 0HS.
Society for Medieval Archaeology, The Lawn, Union Road, Lincoln LN1 3BL.

History

British Agricultural History Society, Department of Geography, The University, Newcastle upon Tyne NE1 7RU.
Economic History Society, P.O.Box 190, 1 Greville Road, Cambridge CB1 3QG.
Historical Association, 59a Kennington Park Road, London SE11 4JH.
(There are local branches of the Association for Cambridge, Cheltenham and Gloucester, Chester, Cleveland, Derby, Durham, Essex, Hampstead and North West London, Hertfordshire, Humberside, Huntingdon, Isle of Wight, Liverpool and District, Matlock, Newcastle upon Tyne, Norfolk and Norwich, North London, North Staffs, Northampton, Oxford, Reading, South West London, West Cheshire and Clwyd, West Wilts, Windsor and Eton).

Oral History Society, c/o Department of Sociology, University of Essex, Colchester CO4 3SQ.
Social History Society of the United Kingdom, Centre for Social History, Lancaster University, Bailrigg, Lancaster LA1 4YG.

Family history and population studies

Federation of Family History Societies, 5 Mornington Close, Copthorne, Shrewsbury SY3 8XN.
Institute of Heraldic and Genealogical Studies, Northgate, Canterbury CT1 1BA.
Local Population Studies Society, 302 Prescot Road, Aughton, Ormskirk, Lancs L39 6RR.
Society of Genealogists, 14 Charterhouse Buildings, Goswell Road, London EC1M 7BA.

Journals: a national selection

Agricultural History Review (British Agricultural History Society), Vol.1, 1953 +

Antiquaries Journal (Society of Antiquaries of London), Vol.1, 1921 +

Archaeologia (Society of Antiquaries of London), Vol.1, 1770 +

Archaeological Journal (Royal Archaeological Institute), Vol.1, 1844 +

Economic History Review (Economic History Society), Vol.1, 1927 +

Family History News and Digest (Federation of Family History Societies), 1977 +

Genealogists' Magazine (Society of Genealogists), Vol.1, 1925 +

History: Journal of the Historical Association, Vol.1, 1916 +

Industrial Archaeology Review (Association for Industrial Archaeology), Vol.1, 1976 +

Journal of the British Archaeological Association, Vol.1, 1845 +

Local Historian (British Association for Local History), 1952 +

Local History News (British Association for Local History), 198? +

Medieval Archaeology (Society for Medieval Archaeology), Vol.1, 1957 +

Oral History: Journal of the Oral History Society, Vol.1, 1972 +

Regional history journals

Bulletin of Local History, East Midland Region, Vol.1, 1966 +
Midland History, Vol.1, 1971 +
Northern History, Vol.1, 1966 +
Southern History, Vol.1, 1979 +

SOME USEFUL DIRECTORIES AND HANDBOOKS

The titles listed here provided the basis of much of the information in the Handbook. Readers who want to know more about some of the entries in a particular county section may find it in one of these directories or guides.

Aslib Directory of Information Sources in the United Kingdom, 6th edition, London, Aslib, 1990.

British Archives: a guide to archive resources in the United Kingdom. Edited by Janet Foster and Julia Sheppard. 2nd edition, London, Macmillan, 1989.

Cambridge Guide to the Museums of Britain and Ireland. Edited by Kenneth Hudson and Ann Nicholls. Cambridge, C.U.P., 1987.

Directory of British Associations and Associations in Ireland. Edited by G.P. and S.P.A.Henderson. 10th edition, Beckenham, CBD Research, 1990.

Directory of Rare Book and Special Collections in the United Kingdom and the Republic of Ireland. Edited by Moelwyn I.Williams. London, Library Association, 1985.

Federation of Family History Societies publications: pamphlets (regularly updated) on topics of interest to local historians, including Census data, electoral registers, interviewing elderly relatives, Latin for local historians, militia lists, reading old handwriting, record offices.

Original Parish Registers in record offices and libraries. Original volume plus 4 supplements. Cambridge, Local Population Studies, 1974-82.

Record Repositories in Great Britain. 8th edition, London, H.M.S.O., 1987.

Texts and Calendars: an analytical guide to serial publications 1957-1982. Edited by E.L.C.Mullins. London, Royal Historical Society, 1958-1982. 2 vols.
Lists the publications of national and local record societies "wholly or partly devoted to the printing - in transcript or calendar form - of sources for the history of England and Wales" (e.g. parish registers, ecclesiastical registers, militia lists, records of local law courts, etc.)

GENERAL INDEXES TO ARTICLES IN LOCAL HISTORY JOURNALS

Many local history societies issue cumulative indexes to their own journals. There are, however, two indispensable general subject indexes:

A guide to the historical and archaeological publications of societies in England and Wales, 1901-1933. Edited by E.C.L.Mullins. London, Athlone Press, 1968.

British Humanities Index (formerly Subject Index to Periodicals), 1919 +

AVON

See GLOUCESTERSHIRE
SOMERSET AND BRISTOL

BEDFORDSHIRE: old county

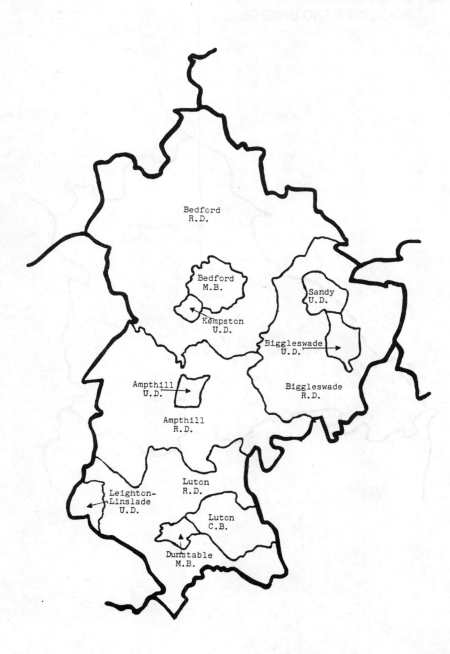

BEDFORDSHIRE: new county

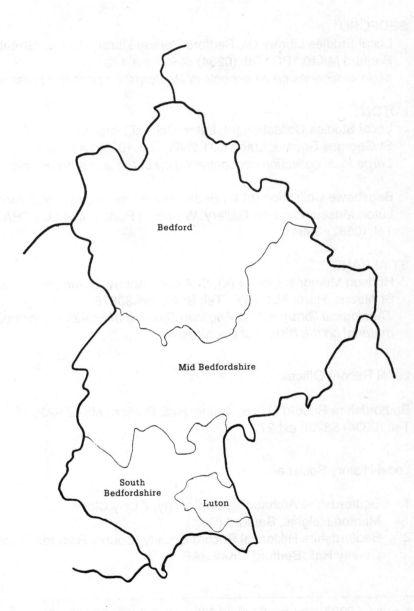

Bedford

Mid Bedfordshire

South
Bedfordshire

Luton

BEDFORDSHIRE

A. Local Studies Libraries and Collections

BEDFORD
Local Studies Library (c), Bedford Central Library, Harpur Street, Bedford MK40 1PG. Tel: (0234) 50931 ext.123.
Main collections on all aspects of Bedfordshire past and present.

LUTON
Local Studies Collection (b), Luton Central Library, St Georges Square, Luton LU1 2NG. Tel: (0582) 454580.
Large local collection concentrating on Luton and surrounding area.

Bagshawe Collection (b) on Bedfordshire topography and folklore, Luton Museum and Art Gallery, Wardown Park, Luton LU2 7HA. Tel: (0582) 36941.

ST ALBANS
Hudson Memorial Library (a), St Albans Abbey, 2 Sumpter Yard, St Albans, Herts AL1 1BY. Tel: St Albans 30576.
Theological library for the Anglican Diocese of St Albans, including material on the history of Bedfordshire.

B. Local Record Offices

Bedfordshire Record Office, County Hall, Bedford MK42 9AP. Tel: (0234) 53222 ext.277.

C. Local History Societies

1. Bedfordshire Archaeological Society, 7 Lely Close, Manton Heights, Bedford (Sec.)
2. Bedfordshire Historical Record Society, County Records Office, County Hall, Bedford MK42 9AP.

---

a = under 2000 vols; b = 2000-20,000 vols; c = over 20,000 vols.

3. Bedfordshire Natural History Society, 2 Ivel Close, Barton-Le-Clay, Bedfordshire MK45 4NT.
4. Bedfordshire Family History Society, 17 Lombard Street, Lidlington, Bedford MK43 0RP (Sec.).
5. Luton and District Historical Society, 7 Shingle Close, Barton Hills, Luton (Sec.).
6. South Bedfordshire Archaeological Society, 27 Lords Lane, Bradwell, Great Yarmouth, Norfolk (Sec.).

D. Local History Journals

1. Bedfordshire Archaeological Journal, Vol.1, 1962 +
2. Bedfordshire Historical Record Society Publications, No.1, 1913 +
3. Bedfordshire Magazine, Vol.1, 1947 +
4. Bedfordshire Naturalist, Vol.1, 1947 +
5. Bedfordshire Family History Society Journal, Vol.1, 1977 +
6. Northamptonshire and Bedfordshire Life, Vol.2(13), 1971 +

E. Museums with Local Studies Collections

1. Bedford Museum, Castle Lane, Bedford, Bedfordshire MK40 3XD. Tel: (0234) 53323.
   Archaeology, industrial and rural history, geology and natural history of North Bedfordshire area.
2. Luton Museum and Art Gallery, Wardown Park, Luton, Bedfordshire LU2 7HA. Tel: (0582) 36941.
   Natural and social history, archaeology of the area. Large newspaper cuttings collection. Houses the Bagshawe Collection (See Section A above)
3. Pitstone Green Farm Museum, Pitstone, Leighton Buzzard, Bedfordshire LU7 9EY. Tel: (0296) 668223.
   Run by the Pitstone Local History Society; archaeology, agricultural and social history of the area.

BERKSHIRE: old county

BERKSHIRE: new county

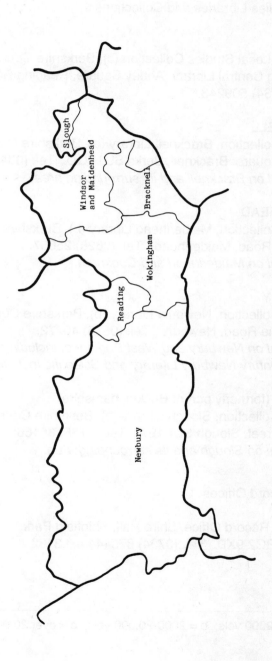

BERKSHIRE

A.   Local Studies Libraries and Collections

READING
County Local Studies Collection (c), Berkshire County Library,
Reading Central Library, Abbey Square, Reading RG1 3BQ.
Tel: (0734) 509243.

BRACKNELL
Local Collection, Bracknell Library (b), Berkshire County Library,
Town Square, Bracknell, Berks SL6 1QU. Tel: (0344) 423149.
Material on Bracknell and its surrounding area.

MAIDENHEAD
Local Collection, Maidenhead Library (b), Berkshire County Library,
St Ives Road, Maidenhead. Tel: (0628) 25657.
Material on Maidenhead and Cookham.

NEWBURY
Local Collection, Newbury Library (b), Berkshire County Library,
Carnegie Road, Newbury. Tel: (0635) 40972.
*Material on Newbury and West Berkshire, including items from the
19th century Newbury Literary and Scientific Institute.*

SLOUGH (formerly part of Buckinghamshire)
Local Collection, Slough Library (b), Berkshire County Library,
High Street, Slough SL1 1EA. Tel: (0735) 35166.
Material on Slough and its surrounding area.

B.   Local Record Offices

Berkshire Record Office, Shire Hall, Shinfield Park,
Reading RG2 9XD. Tel: (0734) 875444 ext.3182.

---

a = under 2000 vols; b = 2000-20,000 vols; c = over 20,000 vols.

C.   Local History Societies

1.   Berkshire Archaeological Society, 43 Laburnham Road,
      Maidenhead, Berks SL6 4DE (Sec.).
2.   Berkshire Family History Society, 87 Finchampstead Road,
      Wokingham, Berks RG11 2PE (Sec.).
3.   Berkshire Industrial Archaeology Group, 25 Andrews Road,
      Earley, Reading RG6 2PT (Sec.).
4.   Berkshire Local History Association, 43 Bannard Road,
      Maidenhead, Berks SL6 4NP (Sec.).
5.   Maidenhead Archaeological and Historical Society, 118 Hag Hill
      Rise, Taplow, Bucks SL6 0LT (Chairman's private address).
      *The Maidenhead Collection of material about the area is in the
      care of the Society.*
6.   Newbury District Field Club, 30 Butson Close,
      Newbury RG14 5JQ (Sec.).

D.   Local History Journals

1.   Berkshire Archaeological Journal, Vol.1, 1895 +
2.   Berkshire Family History Society Magazine, Vol.1, No.1, 1975 +
3.   Berkshire Local History Association Newsletter, 1976 +
4.   Biascope: the newsletter of the Berkshire Industrial Archaeology
      Group, Issue 1, 1976 +
5.   Newbury District Field Club Transactions, Vol.1, 1871 +

E.   Museums with Local Studies Collections

1.   Blake's Lock Museum, Gas Works Road, off Kenavon Drive,
      Reading, Berkshire RG1 3DH. Tel: (0734) 5900630.
      *Trades and industries of Reading; waterways section on
      boatbuilding, history of the rivers and canals.*
2.   Newbury District Museum, The Wharf, Newbury,
      Berkshire RG14 5AS. Tel: (0635) 30511.
      *Local archaeology, history, natural history, trades and industries
      of West Berkshire, canals and shipping.*

3. Reading: Museum and Art Gallery, Blagrave Street, Reading,
   Berkshire RG1 1QH. Tel: (0734) 55911.
   History and natural history of the Reading area.
4. Slough Museum, 23 Bath Road, Slough SL1 3UF.
   Tel: Slough 26422.
5. Windsor: Royal Borough Collection, Madame Tussaud's Royalty
   and Empire Exhibition, Windsor and Eton Central Station,
   Windsor, Berkshire SL4 1PJ. Tel: (0735) 857837.
   Victorian Windsor, commercial and social.

BRISTOL

See SOMERSET AND BRISTOL

BUCKINGHAMSHIRE: old county

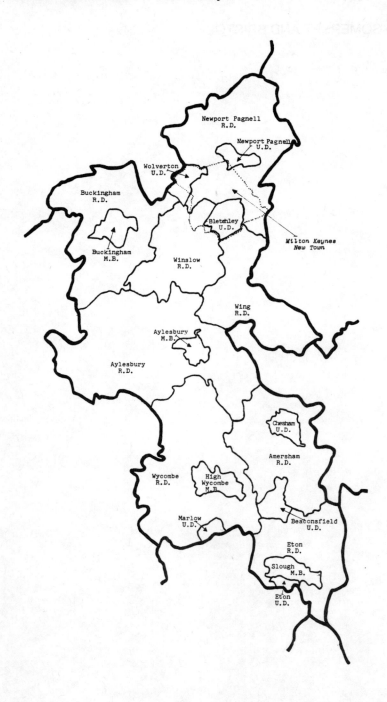

Newport Pagnell
R.D.

Newport Pagnell
U.D.

Wolverton
U.D.

Buckingham
R.D.

Buckingham
M.B.

Bletchley
U.D.

Milton Keynes
New Town

Winslow
R.D.

Wing
R.D.

Aylesbury
M.B.

Aylesbury
R.D.

Chesham
U.D.

Amersham
R.D.

Wycombe
R.D.

High
Wycombe
M.B.

Marlow
U.D.

Beaconsfield
U.D.

Eton
R.D.

Slough
M.B.

Eton
U.D.

BUCKINGHAMSHIRE: new county

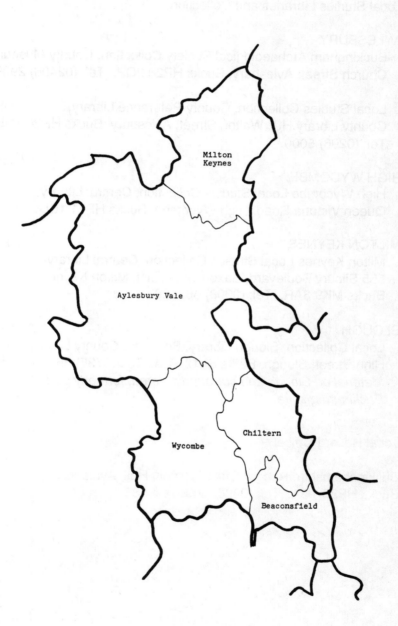

BUCKINGHAMSHIRE

A.   Local Studies Libraries and Collections

AYLESBURY
Buckingham Archaeological Society Collection, County Museum, Church Street, Aylesbury, Bucks HP20 2QP. Tel: (02406) 2909.

Local Studies Collection, County Reference Library, County Library HQ, Walton Street, Aylesbury, Bucks HP20 1UU. Tel: (0296) 5000.

HIGH WYCOMBE
High Wycombe Local Studies Collection, Central Library, Queen Victoria Road, High Wycombe, Bucks HP11 1BD.

MILTON KEYNES
Milton Keynes Local Studies Collection, Central Library, 555 Silbury Boulevard, Saxon Gate East, Milton Keynes, Bucks MK9 3AR. Tel: (0908) 663130.

SLOUGH
Local Collection, Slough Library, Berkshire County Library, High Street, Slough, Berks SL12 1EA. Tel: (0735) 35166. *Material on Slough and surrounding area, formerly part of Buckinghamshire.*

B.   Local Record Office

Buckinghamshire Record Office, County Hall, Aylesbury, Bucks HP20 1UA. Tel: (0296) 5000, ext.588.

C.   Local History Societies

1.   Beaconsfield and District Historical Society, Cerddbrenni, Channer Drive, Penn, Bucks HP10 8HT (Sec.).
2.   Buckingham Archaeological and Historical Society, 7 Chervil, Beanhill, Bletchley MK6 4LG (Sec.).
3.   Buckinghamshire Archaeological Society, 65 Camborne Avenue, Aylesbury HP21 7UE. (Sec.).
4.   Buckinghamshire Family History Society, 18 Rudds Lane, Haddenham, Aylesbury, Bucks (Sec.).
5.   Buckinghamshire Record Society, County Record Office, County Hall, Aylesbury HP20 1UA.
6.   Chess Valley Archaeological and Historical Society, 9 Westwood Close, Little Chalfont, Amersham HP6 6RP (Sec.).
7.   Middle Thames Archaeological and Historical Society, Pandora, Scotlands Drive, Farnham Common SL2 3ES (Sec.).

D.   Local History Journals

1.   Buckinghamshire Record Society, Records Branch Publications, No.1, 1937 +
2.   Chess Valley, 1981 +
3.   Records of Buckinghamshire, Vol.1, 1854 +

E.   Museums with Local Studies Collections

1.   Buckinghamshire County Museum, Church Street, Aylesbury, Bucks HP20 2QP. Tel: (0296) 82158/88849. Partially relocated, until 1992, at: Tring Road, Halton, Aylesbury, Bucks HP22 5PJ. Tel: (0296) 623166. Aylesbury history and special exhibitions galleries remain at main Museum site.
     History of Aylesbury. Sites and Monuments Record, Biological Data Centre (on computer and card files).
2.   Olney: Cowper and Newton Museum, Orchard Side, Market Place, Olney, Bucks MK46 4AJ. Tel: (0234) 711516. *Local collection about the Olney district.*

3.   Stacey Hill Collection of Industry and Rural Life,
      Stacey Hill Farm, Southern Way, Wolverton, Milton Keynes,
      Bucks MK12 5EJ. Tel: (0908) 316222.
      *Life in North Buckinghamshire in the 19th and early 20th
      centuries.*
4.   Wycombe Chair Museum, Castle Hill House, Priory Avenue,
      High Wycombe, Bucks HP13 6PX. Tel: (0494) 23879.
      *History of the High Wycombe chair and furniture industries.
      Books and articles covering the history of furniture, the country
      chair and its manufacture.*

CAMBRIDGESHIRE: old county

CAMBRIDGESHIRE: new county

CAMBRIDGESHIRE

A.   Local Studies Libraries and Collections

CAMBRIDGE
Cambridge Collection (c), University Library, West Road,
Cambridge CB3 9DR. Tel: (0223) 3333000.
*Contains the J.W.Clark Bequest of books and papers relating to the
University, town and county of Cambridge.*

The Cambridgeshire Collection (c), Cambridge City Central Library,
7 Lion Yard, Cambridge CB2 3QD. Tel: (0233) 65252 ext.30.
*Major collection on Cambrigeshire and Isle of Ely, including
newspapers, illustrations, maps and ephemera.*

LODE
Anglesey Abbey Library, Lode, Cambridgeshire CB5 9EJ.
Tel: (022020) 257.
*National Trust Library containing works on Cambridgeshire and the
Fens.*

WISBECH
Wisbech and Fenland Museum Library (b), Museum Square,
Wisbech, Cambs PE13 1ES. Tel: (0945) 3817.
*Good collection of material relating to Wisbech and surrounding
areas, including Muniment Room (legal documents, indexed by
parish), Corporation records from 1369, photographic collections,
newspapers.*

B.   Local Record Offices

1.   Cambridgeshire Record Office, Shire Hall, Cambridge CB3 0AP.
     Tel: (0233) 317281.
2.   Cambridgeshire Record Office, Grammar School Walk,
     Huntingdon PE18 6LF. Tel: (0480) 425842.

---

a = under 2000 vols; b = 2000-20,000 vols; c = over 20,000 vols.

C.   Local History Societies

1.   Cambridge Antiquarian Society, c/o Emmanuel College,
       Cambridge CB2 3AP (Sec.).
2.   Cambridge Society for Industrial Archaeology, Engineers House,
       Riverside, Cambridge CB5 8HN.
3.   Cambridgeshire Family History Society, 32 Ladywalk,
       Long Stanton, Cambs CB4 5ED (Sec.).
4.   Cambridgeshire Local History Society, County Record Office,
       Shire Hall, Castle Hill, Cambridge CB3 0AP
5.   Cambridgeshire Records Society, c/o County Record Office,
       Shire Hall, Cambridge CB3 0AP.
6.   Ely and District Archaeological Society, 13 Granta Close,
       Witchford, Ely CB6 2HR (Sec.).

D.   Local History Journals

1.   Cambridge Antiquarian Society Octavo Publications, Nos.1-55,
       1851-1942.
2.   Cambridge Antiquarian Society Proceedings (Antiquarian
       Communications), Vol.1, 1851/9 +
3.   Cambridge Antiquarian Society Quarto Publications, Nos.1-15,
       1840-49; New Series 1-6, 1908-51.
4.   Cambridgeshire and Huntingdonshire Archaeological Society
       Transactions, 1900-1952.
       *From 1953 included in Cambridge Antiquarian Society
       Proceedings.*
5.   Cambridgeshire Local History Society Bulletin, 1951 +
6.   Cambridgeshire Records Society Publications, 1974 +

E.   Museums with Local Studies Collections

1.   Cambridge and County Folk Museum, Castle Street, Cambridge
      CB3 0AQ. Tel: (0223) 355159.
      *Maintains files of information on Cambridgeshire agriculture,
      folklore, and Fenland history.*
2.   Wisbech and Fenland Museum, Museum Square, Wisbech,
      Cambridgeshire PE13 1ES. Tel: (0945) 583817.
      *Local and natural history, archaeology, decorative art. (For more
      details of holdings see entry in Section A above.*

CHANNEL ISLANDS

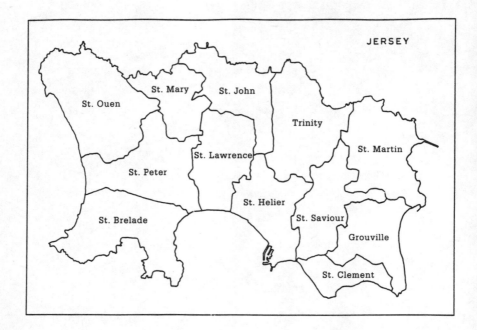

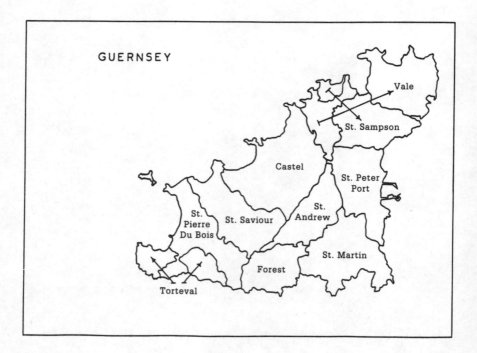

CHANNEL ISLANDS

A.   Local Studies Libraries and Collections

ALDERNEY

Alderney Society Museum Library, Old School House, High Street,
St Anne, Alderney. Tel: (048182) 3222.
*Reference collection of photographs, prints, postcards and
documents.*

GUERNSEY

Local Studies Library (b), Guille-Allès Library, Market Street,
St Peter Port, Guernsey. Tel: (0481) 20392.
*Current Island affairs, complete file of Guernsey Evening Press
newspaper.*

Channel Islands Collection, Priaulx Library, Candie Road,
St Peter Port, Guernsey. Tel: (0481) 20392.
Main local studies library for Guernsey.

JERSEY

Jersey States Library Service (b), Halkett Place, St Helier, Jersey.
*Subject coverage includes Channel Islands bibliography and
history, particularly the Bailiwick of Jersey.*

Société Jersiaise Library, Lord Coutanche Memorial Library,
9 Pier Road, St Helier, Jersey. Tel: (0534) 30538.
*Manuscript, archive and book collections, natural history
specimens and records for Jersey.*

---

a = under 2000 vols; b = 2000-20,000 vols; c = over 20,000 vols.

B.   Local Record Offices

Guernsey
  The Greffe, Royal Court House, St Peter Port, Guernsey.
  Tel: (0481) 25277.
Jersey
  Judicial Greffe, 10 Hill Street, St Helier, Jersey. Tel: (0534) 75472.

C.   Local History Societies

1.   Channel Islands Family History Society, PO Box 507, St Helier,
      Jersey.
2.   Channel Islands Occupation Society, Gladclift, St Peter's Lane,
      Ruette Braye, St Peter Port, Guernsey (Sec.)
3.   Guernsey Society. (Address as given for Société Guernesiaise
      below).
4.   Société Guernesiaise, Courtil à l'Herbe, Route des Bas Courtils,
      St Saviour, Guernsey (Sec.).
5.   Société Jersiaise, 9 Pier Road, St Helier, Jersey.

D.   Local History Journals

1.   Channel Islands Family History Society Journal, No.1, 1978/9 +
2.   Channel Islands Occupation Review, 1967 +
3.   Guernsey Society Bulletin, Vols.1-2, 1945-6. *Continued as No.5
      below)*
4.   Jersey Society in London Bulletin, May 1941 +
5.   Quarterly Review of the Guernsey Society, Vol.3, 1947 +
6.   Société Guernesiaise Reports and Transactions, Vol.1, 1882 +
7.   Société Jersiaise Annual Bulletin, Vol.1, 1875/84 +

E.   Museums with Local Studies Collections

Alderney
   Alderney Society Museum, High Street, Alderney.
   Tel: (048182) 3222.
   *History of Alderney from prehistoric times to the present, including
   photographs, geological and botanical manuscripts, 16th century
   charters. Files on Iron Age site at Les Huguettes, Victorian
   regiments stationed on Alderney.*

Guersey
   1. Guernsey Folk Museum, Saumarez Park, Catel, Guernsey.
      Tel: (0481) 55384.
      Rural activities, industries, domestic life, costume.
   2. Guernsey Museum and Art Gallery, Candie Gardens,
      St Peter Port, Guernsey. Tel: (0481) 26518.
      *Archaeology, geology, local and natural history. Lukis
      manuscript collection on local archaeological sites. Sites and
      Monuments Record for Guernsey.*

Jersey
   1. Jersey Museum, 9 Pier Road, St Helier, Jersey.
      Tel: (0534) 30511.
      Extensive art, print, and photographic collections about Jersey.
   2. La Hougue Bie Museum, Grouville, Jersey. Tel: (0534) 53823.
      Archaeology, geology, military and agricultural history of Jersey.

CHESHIRE: old county

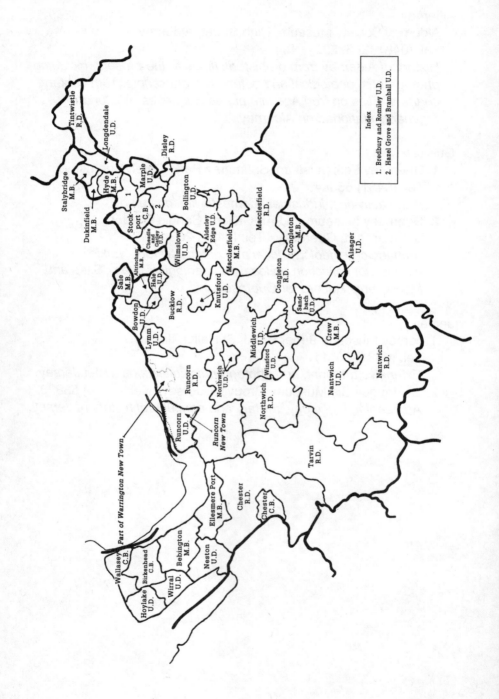

Index

1. Bredbury and Romiley U.D.
2. Hazel Grove and Bramhall U.D.

CHESHIRE: new county

CHESHIRE

A.   Local Studies Libraries and Collections

Cheshire Libraries are building up a Local Studies Database, available at 10 of their libraries.

ALSAGER
Local History and Antiquarian Collection on the History of Cheshire (a), Dr Annie Parkes Library, Crewe Alsager College of Higher Education, Hassall Road, Alsager, Stoke-on-Trent ST7 2HL. Tel: (0782) 882500.

ALTRINCHAM
Altrincham Library (b), 20 Stamford New Road, Altrincham, Cheshire WA14 1EJ. Tel: (061) 928 0317.

CARDIFF
Salisbury Library, University College Cardiff Library, PO Box 78, Cathays Park, Cardiff CF1 1XL. Tel: (0222) 44211
Contains material relating to the Welsh Border counties, especially Cheshire and Shropshire.

CHESTER
Chester Archaeological Society Library (a), Chester City Record Office, Town Hall, Chester CH1 2HJ. Tel: (0244) 324324 ext.2108.

Local Collection (b), Cheshire Libraries and Museums, Chester Library, Northgate Street, Chester CH1 2EF. Tel: (0244) 312935.

Local Collection (b), Cheshire Record Office, Duke Street, Chester CH1 1RL. Tel: (0244) 602574.
Large collection of material relating to Cheshire and surrounding counties.

---

a = under 2000 vols; b = 2000-20,000 vols; c = over 20,000 vols.

MACCLESFIELD
Macclesfield Museums Research Library, Heritage Centre,
Roe Street, Macclesfield, Cheshire SK11 6UT. Tel: (0625) 613210.
Collections on Macclesfield silk industry, mills and dyehouses,
outweavers, churches and Sunday Schools.

NORTHWICH
Local History Collection (a), Brunner Library, Witton Street,
Northwich, Cheshire. Tel: (0606) 44221.
Special section covering the salt industry of the area.

SALE
Sale Library (b), Tatton Road, Sale, Cheshire M33 1YS.
Tel: (061) 973 3142 and 872 2101.

STALYBRIDGE
Tameside Local Studies Library (b), Stalybridge Library,
Trinity Street, Stalybridge, Cheshire SK15 2BN. Tel: (061) 338
708.
Contains material on background history of Lancashire and
Cheshire.

STOCKPORT
Stockport Local Studies Library (c), Stockport Central Library,
Wellington Road South, Stockport SK1 3RS. Tel: (061) 474 4530.

WARRINGTON
Local History Library (b), Warrington Library, Museum Street,
Warrington, Cheshire.
Contains special collection of books and papers concerning Joseph
Priestley.

---

a = under 2000 vols; b = 2000-20,000 vols; c = over 20,000 vols.

B.   Local Record Offices

1.   Cheshire Record Office, Duke Street, Chester CH1 1RL.
      Tel: (0244) 602574.
2.   Chester City Record Office, Town Hall, Chester CH1 2HJ.
      Tel: (0244) 324324 ext.2108.
3.   Stockport Archives Service, Central Library,
      Wellington Road South, Stockport SK1 3RS.
      Tel: (061) 474 4530.

C.   Local History Societies

1.   Chester Archaeological Society, Bryn Gwyn Fford,
      Nant Rhuddlan, Clwyd LL18 2SW (Sec.).
2.   Chetham Society for the Publication of Remains Historical and
      Literary connected with the Palatine Counties of Lancaster and
      Chester, c/o Manchester University Press, Oxford Road,
      Manchester M13 9PL.
3.   County Palatine of Chester Local History Committee, Cheshire
      Community Council, 96 Lower Bridge Street, Chester CH1 1RU.
4.   Family History Society of Cheshire, 5 Henbury Rise, Henbury,
      Macclesfield, Cheshire SK11 9NW (Sec.).
5.   Historic Society of Lancashire and Cheshire, Liverpool Institute
      of Higher Education, Stand Park Road, Liverpool L16 9JD.
6.   Lancashire and Cheshire Antiquarian Society,
      59 Malmesbury Road, Cheadle Hume, Cheadle,
      Cheshire SK8 7QL.
7.   North Cheshire Family History Society, 2 Denham Drive,
      off Ack Lane East, Bramhall, Stockport, Cheshire SK7 2AT
      (Sec.).
8.   Record Society of Lancashire and Cheshire, c/o Lancashire
      Record Office, Bow Lane, Preston PR1 8ND.

D.   Local History Journals

1.   Cheshire Archaeological Bulletin, Vol.1, 1973 +
2.   Cheshire Historian (*then Cheshire Round*), Vol.1, nos.1-10,
      1951-1969.
3.   Cheshire History, Vol.1, 1978 +
4.   Cheshire History Newsletter, Vol.1, 1971 +
5.   Chester Archaeological Society Journal, Vols.1-3, 1849-85;
      New Series, Vol.1, 1887 +
6.   Chetham Society (Remains Historical and Literary connected
      with the Palatine Counties of Lancaster and Chester)
      Publications, Old Series Vols.1-114, 1844-83; New Series
      Vols.1-110, 1883-1947; Third Series Vol.1, 1949 +
7.   Historic Society of Lancashire and Cheshire Transactions
      (Proceedings and Papers), Vol.1, 1848 +
8.   Lancashire and Cheshire Antiquarian Society Transactions,
      Vol.1, 1883 +
9.   Record Society of Lancashire and Cheshire Publications,
      No.1, 1879 +

E.   Museums with Local Studies Collections

1.   Chester: Grosvenor Museum, 27 Grosvenor Street, Chester,
      Cheshire CH1 2DD. Tel: (0244) 321616.
      Local and natural history and archaeology of Chester and
      Cheshire.
2.   Compstall: Athenaeum, Andrew Street, Compstall,
      Cheshire SK6 5HN. Tel: (061) 427 2041.
3.   Macclesfield: Paradise Mill Museum, Old Park Lane,
      Macclesfield. Tel: (0625) 618228.
      Working silk mill.
4.   Macclesfield: The Silk Museum, Roe Street,
      Macclesfield SK11 6UT. Tel: (0625) 613210.
5.   Macclesfield: West Park Museum, Prestbury Road, Macclesfield,
      Cheshire.
      Local history and topography of Macclesfield.
6.   Nantwich Museum, Pillory Street, Nantwich, Cheshire CW5 5BQ.
      Tel: (0270) 627104.

7.   Northwich: The Salt Museum, 162 London Road, Northwich,
      Cheshire CW9 8AB. Tel: (0606) 41331.
      History of the local salt industry and of the area.
8.   Stockport Museum, Vernon Park, Turncroft Lane, Stockport,
      Greater Manchester SK1 4AR. Tel: (061) 480 3668.
      Includes material on the local hatting industry.
9.   Warrington Museum and Art Gallery, Bold Street, Warrington,
      Cheshire WA1 1JG. Tel: (0925) 30550
      *Archaeology, geology, local and natural history, including
      railways, waterways, Manchester Ship Canal.*

CLEVELAND

See DURHAM
YORKSHIRE (North Riding)

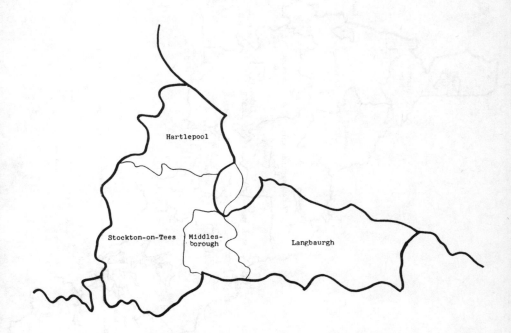

CORNWALL: old county

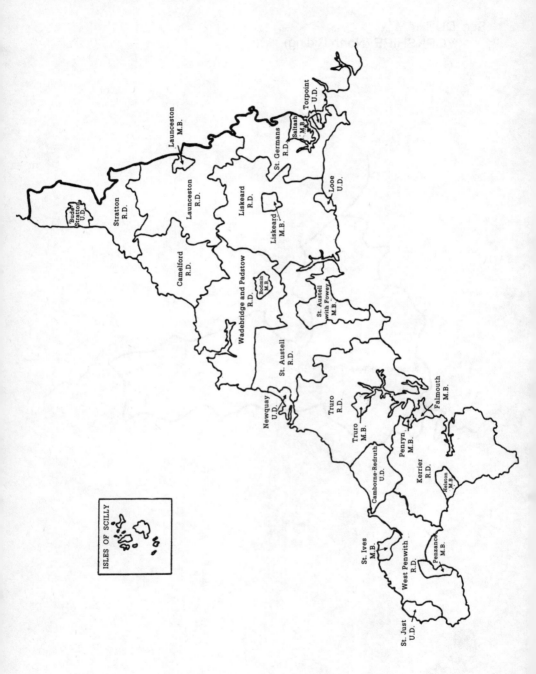

CORNWALL: new county

North Cornwall

Caradon

Restormel

Carrick

Kerrier

Penwith

Isles of Scilly

CORNWALL

A.   Local Studies Libraries and Collections

EXETER
West Country Studies Library (c), Castle Street, Exeter EX4 3PQ.
Tel: (0392) 273422.
Material on Cornwall, Devon, Dorset and Somerset, emphasis on Devon and Exeter.

PENZANCE
The Penzance Library, Morrab Gardens, Penzance TR18 4DQ.
Tel: (0736) 4474.
Important collection of Cornish material, including the Borlase Papers.

PLYMOUTH
Plymouth Athenaeum Library (b), Derry's Cross, Plymouth
PL1 2SW. Tel: (0752) 266079. (Private Library).
Collection covers Devon and Cornwall, with special emphasis on Plymouth.

REDRUTH
Cornish Studies Library (c), Cornwall County Library, Clinton Road,
Redruth TR15 2QE. Tel: (0209) 216760.
There are small local collections at Bodmin, Bude, Callington, Camborne, Falmouth, Fowey, Helston, Launceston, Liskeard, Newquay, Penzance, St Austell, St Ives, Saltash, and Truro Branch Libraries.

SCILLY ISLES
Isles of Scilly Museum, Church Street, St Mary's, Isles of Scilly,
Cornwall TR21 0JT. Tel: (0720) 22337.
Collection of books, manuscripts, parish register transcripts, court record books, about the Isles of Scilly.

---

a = under 2000 vols; b = 2000-20,000 vols; c = over 20,000 vols.

TRURO
County Reference and Information Library, Union Place,
Truro TR1 1EP. Tel: (0872) 72702.

Courtney Library, Royal Institution of Cornwall, River Street,
Truro TR1 2SJ. Tel: (0872) 72205.

B.   Local Record Offices

1.   Cornwall Record Office, County Hall, Truro TR1 3AY.
      Tel: (0872) 73698/74282 ext.3127.
2.   Royal Institution of Cornwall, County Museum, River Street,
      Truro TR1 2SJ. Tel: (0872) 72205.

C.   Local History Societies

1.   Centre for South-Western Historical Studies, c/o Devon and
      Exeter Institution, 7 The Close, Exeter EX1 1EZ.
2.   Cornish Methodist Historical Association, Lambourne,
      Mt.Ambrose, Redruth (President's private address).
3.   Cornwall Archaeological Society, Trezeres, Harleigh Road,
      Bodmin PL31 1AQ (Sec.).
4.   Cornwall Association of Local Historians, Mill House, Rilla Mill,
      Callington (Sec.).
5.   Cornwall Family History Society, 11 Penrose Road, Falmouth,
      Cornwall TR11 2DU (Sec.).
6.   Devon and Cornwall Record Society, c/o The Close,
      Exeter EX1 1EZ.
7.   Federation of Old Cornwall Societies, Tremarsh, Launceston,
      Cornwall (Sec.).
8.   Royal Institution of Cornwall, County Museum, River Street,
      Truro TR1 2SJ.
9.   Trevithick Society, Salakee Cottage, Lelant Downs, Hayle
      TR27 6NH(Sec.).
10.   South-West Maritime History Society, Yellow Ribbon, Weston,
      Honiton, Devon EX14 0NZ

D.   Local History Journals

1.   Cornish Archaeology, Vol.1, 1962 + *(continuation of the Proceedings of the West Cornwall Field Club).*
2.   Cornish Methodist Historical Association Journal, Vol.1, 1960 +
3.   Cornish Studies, Vol.1, 1973 +
4.   Cornwall Association of Local Historians Newsletter, No.1, 1984 +
5.   Cornwall Family History Society Journal, No.1, 1976 +
6.   Devon and Cornwall Notes and Queries, Vol.1, 1901 +
7.   Devon and Cornwall Record Society Publications, 1906-1954; New Series Vol.1, 1955 + ; Extra Series Vol.1, 1973 +
8.   Old Cornwall, Vol.1, 1924 +
9.   Royal Cornwall Polytechnic Society Annual Reports, 1833 +
10. Royal Institution of Cornwall Journal, Vols.1-25, 1864-1942; New Series Vol.1, 1946 +
11. Trevithick Society Journal, No.1, 1973 +
12. Trevithick Society Newsletter, No.1, 1973 +
13. West Cornwall Field Club Proceedings, Vols.1-2, 1936-61 *(continued as Cornish Archaeology).*

E.   Museums with Local Studies Collections

1.   Bodmin Town Museum, Mount Folly Square, Bodmin, Cornwall PL31 2DQ. Tel: (0208) 5516.
2.   Bude Historical and Folk Exhibition, The Wharf, Bude, Cornwall EX23 8LG. Tel: (0288) 3576.
     Including the tug-boat canal, the local lifeboat, and shipwrecks.
3.   Camborne Museum, The Cross, Camborne, Cornwall TR14 8HA. Tel: Helston 564027.
     Emphasis on mining and minerals.
4.   Cornwall County Museum, Royal Institution of Cornwall, River Street, Truro, Cornwall TR1 2SJ. Tel: (0872) 72205.
     Archaeology and history of Cornwall.
5.   Cotehele Quay Museum, St Dominick, nr Saltash, Cornwall PL12 6TA. Tel: (0579) 50830.
     Local shipping, shipbuilding and related industries.

6.   Duke of Cornwall's Light Infantry Museum, The Keep,
      Bodmin PL31 IE6.
7.   Falmouth Maritime Museum, 2 Bell's Court , Falmouth, and
      Steam Tug St Denys, Custom House Quay, Falmouth.
      Tel: (0326) 250507 (Hon.Secretary's number; correspondence
      to Hon.Secretary, Higher Penpol House, Mawnan Smith,
      Falmouth).
      *Maritime history of Cornwall, especially southwest Cornwall,
      including small photographic archives.*
8.   Geevor Tin Mining Museum, Pendeen, Penzance,
      Cornwall TR19 7EW. Tel: (0736) 788662.
      History of tin mining in West Cornwall.
9.   Helston Folk Museum, The Old Butter Market, Church Street,
      Helston, Cornwall TR13 8TH. Tel: Helston 564027.
      *Crafts and industries of Helston in the 19th and early 20th
      centuries.*
10.   Isles of Scilly Museum, Church Street, St Mary's, Isles of Scilly,
      Cornwall TR231 0JT. Tel: (0720) 22337.
      *Geology, archaeology, history, flora and fauna of the Isles of
      Scilly. Collection of books, manuscripts, parish register
      transcripts, court record books.*
11.   Lanreath Farm and Folk Museum, Churchtown, Lanreath, Looe,
      Cornwall PL13 2NX. Tel: (0503) 20321/20349.
      Social, domestic and agricultural history of the area.
12.   Mevagissey Folk Museum, Frazier House, East Quay,
      Mevagissey, Cornwall. Tel: (0726) 843568.
      *Traditional life and occupations of the district. Comprehensive
      photographic archive of the area.*
13.   North Cornwall Museum and Gallery, The Clease, Camelford,
      Cornwall PL35 9PL. Tel: (0840) 212954.
      *History of rural and domestic crafts and agriculture in North
      Cornwall.*
14.   Penlee House Museum and Art Gallery, Penlee Park, Penzance,
      Cornwall TR18 4HF. Tel: (0736) 63625.
15.   St Agnes Museum, 45 Lawrence Road, St Agnes.
      *Archaeology of Cornwall, local, natural, and social history of the
      area. Paintings of the Newlyn School.*

16. St Ives Museum, Wheal Dream, St Ives, Cornwall.
     Tel: (0736) 796005.
17. Wheal Martyn Museum, Carthew, nr St Austell, Cornwall.
     Tel: (0726) 850362.
     *History of the Cornish china clay industry including photographic
     collection.*

CUMBERLAND: old county

Border
R.D.

Carlisle
C.B.

Wigton
R.D.

Penrith
R.D.

Alston with
Garrigill
R.D.

Maryport
U.D.

Cockermouth
U.D.

Penrith
U.D.

Workington
M.B.

White-
haven
M.B.

Keswick
U.D.

Cockermouth
R.D.

Ennerdale
R.D.

Millom
R.D.

CUMBERLAND: new county

CUMBRIA

Carlisle

Allerdale

Eden

Copeland

South Lakeland

Barrow-in-Furness →

CUMBERLAND

A.   Local Studies Libraries and Collections

BARROW-IN-FURNESS
Barrow Library (Cumbria County Library) (b), Ramsden Square,
Barrow-in-Furness. Tel: (0229) 20650.
*Contains Furness Library of material relating to the North West of
England, with special emphasis on Furness, Cartmel, and South
Lakeland.*

CARLISLE
Carlisle Library (Cumbria County Library) Local Studies Collection:
the Bibliotheca Jacksoniana (b), Gloke Lane, Carlisle CA3 8NX.
Tel: (0228) 24166.
Material on Cumberland, Westmorland and Furness.

KENDAL
Kendal Library (b), Stricklandgate, Kendal, Cumbria LA9 4PY.
Tel: (0539) 20254.
*Local collection with special emphasis on the Lake District and the
old county of Westmorland.*

WHITEHAVEN
Local Studies Collection (b), Daniel Hay Library, Lowther Street,
Whitehaven, Cumbria CA28 7QZ. Tel: (0946) 695611/2.
Special collections on coalmining and shipbuilding.

WORKINGTON
Local Studies Collection (b), Workington Library, Vulcans Lane,
Workington, Cumbria CA14 2ND. Tel: (0900) 603744/5311.
Material on Allerdale district.

---

a = under 2000 vols; b = 2000-20,000 vols; c = over 20,000 vols.

B.   Local Record Offices

1.   Cumbria Record Office, The Castle, Carlisle CA3 8UR.
      Tel: (0228) 23456 ext.2416.
2.   Cumbria Record Office, 140 Duke Street, Barrow-in-Furness
      LA14 1XW. Tel: (0229) 31269.
3.   Cumbria Record Office, County Offices, Kendal LA9 4RQ.

C.   Local History Societies

1.   Cumberland and Westmorland Antiquarian and Archaeological
      Society, 2 High Tenterfell, Kendal, Cumbria LA9 4PG (Sec.).
2.   Cumbria Family History Society, 32 Granada Road, Denton,
      Manchester M34 2LJ (Sec.).

D.   Local History Journals

1.   Cumberland and Westmorland Antiquarian and Archaeological
      Society:
      Transactions, Vols.1-16, 1866-1900; New Series Vol.1, 1901 +
      Transactions, Extra Series, Nos.1-8, 1877-1937.
      Record or Chartulary Series, Nos.1-8, 1897-1932.
      Tract Series, No.1, 1882 +

E.   Museums with Local Studies Collections

1.   Carlisle Museum and Art Gallery, Tullie House, Castle Street,
      Carlisle, Cumbria CA3 8TP. Tel: (0228) 34781.
2.   Furness Museum, Ramsden Square, Barrow-in-Furness,
      Cumbria LA14 1LL. Tel: (0229) 20650.
3.   Kendal: Museum of Lakeland Life and Industry, Kirkland, Kendal,
      Cumbria LA9 5AL. Tel: (0539) 22464.
4.   Kendal Museum, Station Road, Kendal, Cumbria LA9 6BT.
      Tel: (0539) 21374.

5.   Keswick Museum and Art Gallery, Fitz Park, Keswick,
     Cumbria CA12 4NF. Tel: (0596) 73263.
     *Important collection of literary manuscripts of Lake District
     authors. Flintoft's 1867 model of the Lake District.*
6.   Maryport: Maritime Museum, 1 Senhouse Street, Shipping Brow,
     Maryport, Cumbria CA15 6AB. Tel: (0900) 813738.
7.   Millom Folk Museum, St George's Road, Millom,
     Cumbria LA18 4DD. Tel: (0675) 2555.
     *Traditional life and occupations of the area. Comprehensive
     photographic collection on the local iron and steel industry.*
8.   Penrith Museum, Robinson's School, Middlegate, Penrith,
     Cumbria CA11 7PT. Tel: (0768) 64671.
     *Archaeology, history and geology of the Eden Valley and Penrith
     town.*
9.   Whitehaven Museum, Civic Hall, Lowther Street, Whitehaven,
     Cumbria CA28 7SH. Tel: (0946) 3111 ext.307.

CUMBRIA

See CUMBERLAND
    LANCASHIRE
    WESTMORLAND
    YORKSHIRE (West Riding)

DERBYSHIRE: old county

DERBYSHIRE: new county

High Peak

Chesterfield

Bolsover

North East
Derbyshire

West
Derbyshire

Amber Valley

Derby

Erewash

South
Derbyshire

DERBYSHIRE

A.   Local Studies Libraries and Collections

DERBY
Derby Local Studies Library (c), 25b Irongate, Derby.
Tel: Derby 31111 ext.2184.
Oldest and largest collection of local material in the county.

BUXTON
Buxton Library (b), The Crescent, Buxton SK17 6DJ.
Tel: Buxton 5331/2.
Coverage of High Peak area.

CHESTERFIELD
Chesterfield Library (b), New Beetwell Street, Chesterfield
SS0 1QN. Tel: Chesterfield 209292 ext.38.
Covers county in general as well as Chesterfield area.

GLOSSOP
Glossop Library (a), Victoria Hall, Glossop SK13 9DQ.
Tel: Glossop 2616.
Extensive manuscript collections on Glossop and area.

HEANOR
Heanor Library (a), Ilkeston Road, Heanor, Derby DE7 7DX.
Tel: Langley Mill 712482.
Small collection covering the Heanor area.

ILKESTON
Ilkeston Library (a), Market Place, Ilkeston, Derbyshire DE7 5RN.
Tel: Ilkeston 301104 ext.10.
Small collection covering the Ilkeston area.

---

a = under 2000 vols; b = 2000-20,000 vols; c = over 20,000 vols.

LONG EATON

Long Eaton Library (a), Tamworth Road, Long Eaton,
Derbyshire NG10 1JG. Tel: Long Eaton 5426.
*General collection on East Midlands, with comprehensive coverage
of Long Eaton area.*

MATLOCK

Derbyshire Local Studies Library (b), Derbyshire Library Services,
County Offices, Matlock, Derbyshire DE4 3AG.
Tel: (0629) 580000 ext. 6480.
*Books, pamphlets and periodicals relating to the county. Houses
the collection of the Peak District Mines Historical Society.*

NEW MILLS

New Mills Library (a), Hall Street, New Mills, via Stockport,
Derbyshire SK12 3BR. Tel: New Mills 43508.
*Collection of general Derbyshire interest, also contains material
relating specifically to New Mills area.*

NOTTINGHAM

East Midlands Collection (b), University of Nottingham Library,
University Park, Nottingham NG7 2RD. Tel: (0602) 484848.
*Covers Derbyshire, Leicestershire, Lincolnshire, Nottinghamshire
and Rutland.*

B.   Local Record Offices

Derbyshire Record Office, County Offices,
Matlock DE4 3AG (postal address only; materials housed
in New Street, Matlock). Tel: (0629) 580000 ext.7347.

---

a = under 2000 vols; b = 2000-20,000 vols; c = over 20,000 vols.

C.   Local History Societies

1.   Arkwright Society, Tawney House, Matlock Green, Matlock.
      Industrial archaeology society.
2.   Derbyshire Archaeological Society, 12 Wilne Road, Draycott,
      Derby (Sec.).
3.   Derbyshire Family History Society, 15 Elmhurst Road,
      Forest Town, Mansfield, Notts NG19 0EV (Sec.).
4.   Derbyshire Record Society, 9 Caernarvon Close, Walton,
      Chesterfield, Derbyshire S40 3DY.
5.   Peak District Mines Historical Society Ltd., Peak District Mining
      Museum, The Pavilion, South Parade, Matlock Bath, Matlock,
      Derbyshire DE4 3NR.
6.   Peakland Archaeological Society, 3 Hallsteads Close,
      Dove Holes, Buxton, Derbyshire SK17 8BS Sec.).

D.   Local History Journals

1.   Bulletin of the Peak District Mines Historical Society,
      Vol.1, 1959 +
2.   Derbyshire Archaeological Society Journal (Derbyshire
      Archaeological Journal), Vol.1, 1879 +
3.   Derbyshire Archaeological Society Record Series, Nos.1-7,
      1965-1972/3
      continued as Publications of the Derbyshire Record Society.
4.   Derbyshire Life and Countryside, 1931 +
5.   Derbyshire Miscellany,Vol.1,1956 +
6.   East Derbyshire Field Club Transactions, 1903-17, 1922-3,
      1931.
7.   Peakland Archaeological Society Newsletter, 1959 +
8.   The Reliquary, 1860-1909

E.   Museums with Local Studies Collections

1.   Buxton Museum and Art Gallery, Terrace Road, Buxton,
      Derbyshire SK17 6DU. Tel: (0298) 4658.
      Archaeology, history, and natural history of the Peak District and
      Buxton.
2.   Derby Industrial Museum, The Silk Mill, off Full Street, Derby
      DE1 3AR. Tel: (0332) 293111 ext.740.
      Industrial history of Derby and Derbyshire. Files kept on
      extractive sites for leadmining, coalmining, brickworks, etc.
      Extensive collection of photographs, drawings, plans, relating to
      Midland and LMS Railways, Rolls Royce Engines material.
3.   Derby Museum and Art Gallery, The Strand, Derby DE1 1BS.
      Tel: (0332) 2931111.
      Archaeology, history and natural history of Derby.
4.   Derbyshire Museum Service, John Turner House, The Parkway,
      Darley Dale, Matlock, Derbyshire DE4 2FW.
      Tel: Matlock 733226.
      Collections of local photographs, slides, maps, prints, drawings
      and paintings. Douglas Collection Archive of Randolph Douglas
      material.
5.   Erewash Museum, High Street, Ilkeston, Derbyshire DE7 5JA.
      Tel: (0602) 303361 ext.331.
6.   Eyam Private Museum, "Le Roc", Lydgate, Eyam,
      Derbyshire S30 1QU. Tel: (0433) 31010.
7.   Peak District Mining Museum, The Pavilion, South Parade,
      Matlock Bath, Matlock, Derbyshire DE4 3PS.
      Tel: (0629) 583834.
      History of lead mining in the Peak. Library of Peak District Mines
      Historical Society kept in Derbyshire Local Studies Library,
      County Offices, Matlock - see Section A.

DEVON: old county

Ilfracombe U.D.

Lynton U.D.

Barnstaple R.D.

Northam U.D.

Barnstaple M.B.

Bideford R.D.

Bideford M.B.

Great Torrington M.B.

South Molton R.D.

Torrington R.D.

Tiverton M.B.

Tiverton R.D.

Crediton R.D.

Holsworthy R.D.

Okehampton R.D.

Crediton U.D.

Honiton R.D.

Honiton M.B.

Okehampton M.B.

Exeter C.B.

Ottery St. Mary U.D.

Axminster R.D.

Sidmouth U.D.

St. Thomas R.D.

Seaton U.D.

Tavistock R.D.

Newton Abbot R.D.

Budleigh Salterton U.D.

Dawlish U.D.

Exmouth U.D.

Teignmouth U.D.

Ash-burton U.D.

Buckfast-leigh U.D.

Newton Abbot U.D.

Plympton St. Mary R.D.

Totnes M.B.

Torbay C.B.

Plymouth C.B.

Totnes R.D.

Kingsbridge R.D.

Kingsbridge U.D.

Dartmouth M.B.

Salcombe U.D.

DEVON: new county

North Devon

Torridge

Tiverton

East Devon

Exeter

West Devon

Teignbridge

Torbay

Plymouth

South Hams

DEVON

A.   Local Studies Libraries and Collections

BARNSTAPLE
North Devon Athenaeum Library (b), North Devon Library and
Record Office, July Street, Barnstaple, Devon EX32 7EJ.
Tel: (0271) 42174.
Emphasis on North Devon and Exmoor.

North Devon Local Studies Library (b), North Devon Library and
Record Office, July Street, Barnstaple EX32 7EJ.
Tel: (0271) 47068.
Emphasis on North Devon and Exmoor.

BIDEFORD
Pearse-Chope Collection (b), Bideford Library, New Road,
Bideford EX39 2HW. Tel: (02372) 76075.
Emphasis on North Devon.

EXETER
Devon and Exeter Institution Library (b), 7 The Close,
Exeter EX1 1EZ. Tel: (0392) 51017. (Private library, access
restricted to members).
Material on Devon, especially local newspapers.

West Country Studies Library (c), Castle Street, Exeter EX4 3PQ.
Tel: (0392) 273422.
*Material on Cornwall, Devon, Dorset and Somerset, emphasis on
Devon and Exeter.*
*The Devon Sites and Monuments Register is kept in the Property
Department, County Hall, Topsham Road, Exeter EX2 4QQ.
Tel: (0392) 272266.*

---

a = under 2000 vols; b = 2000-20,000 vols; c = over 20,000 vols.

PLYMOUTH

Plymouth Athenaeum Library (b), Derry's Cross, Plymouth
PL1 2SW. Tel: (0752) 266079. (Private library).
*Collection covers Devon and Cornwall, with special emphasis on
Plymouth.*

Plymouth Local History Library (b), Central Library, Drake's Circus,
Plymouth PL4 8AL. Tel: (0752) 264676.
Emphasis on history of Plymouth.

TORQUAY

Torquay Central Library Local Collection (b), Lymington Road,
Torquay TQ1 3DT. Tel: (0803) 217673.
Emphasis on South Devon. Some Cornish material.

Torquay Natural History Society Library (b), The Museum,
Babbacombe Road, Torquay. Tel: (0803) 23975. (Private library).
Material on history of Torquay and Torbay area.

B.   Local Record Offices

1.   Devon Record Office, Castle Street, Exeter EX4 3PU.
     Tel: (0392) 273509.
2.   Exeter Dean and Chapter Archives, Cloister Library,
     Diocesan House, Palace Gate, Exeter EX1 1HX.
     Tel: (0392) 72894/273063.
3.   North Devon Record Office, July Street, Barnstaple EX32 7EJ.
     Tel: (0271) 47068.
4.   West Devon Record Office, Unit 3, Clare Place, Coxside,
     Plymouth PL4 0JW. Tel: (0752) 264685.

---

a = under 2000 vols; b = 2000-20,000 vols; c = over 20,000 vols.

C.   Local History Societies

1.   Centre for South Western Historical Studies, c/o 7 The Close, Exeter EX1 1EZ.
2.   Devon and Cornwall Record Society, c/o Devon and Exeter Institution, 7 The Close, Exeter EX1 1EZ.
3.   Devon Archaeological Society, Royal Albert Memorial Museum, Queen Street, Exeter EX4 3RX.
4.   Devon Buildings Group, c/o 48 Park Street, Crediton, Devon EX17 3ET.
5.   Devon Family History Society, Court Barton, Higher Cheriton, Payhembury, Honiton, Devon EX14 0JL.
6.   Devon History Society, c/o 82 Hawkins Avenue, Torquay TQ2 6ES.
7.   Devonshire Association for the Advancement of Science, Literature and Art, 7 The Close, Exeter EX1 1EZ.
8.   Nautical Archaeology Society (South West Branch), c/o 27 Prideaux Road, Ivybridge, Devon.
9.   South-West Maritime History Society, Yellow Ribbon, Weston, Honiton, Devon EX14 0NZ.
10.   Torquay Natural History Society, The Museum, Babbacombe Road, Torquay TQ1 1HG.

D.   Local History Journals

1.   Devon and Cornwall Notes and Queries, Vol.1, 1901 +
2.   Devon and Cornwall Record Society Publications, 1906-1954; New Series Vol.1, 1955 + ; Extra Series Vol.1, 1973 +
3.   Devon Archaeological Society (formerly Devon Archaeological Exploration Society) Proceedings, Vol.1, 1929/32 + ; News Bulletin, Nos.1-49, 1962-75; DAES Newsletter, Nos.1-18, 1962-67; Newsletter, New Series No.1, 1975 +
4.   Devon Archaeology, Vol.1, 1983 +
5.   Devon Family Historian, Vol.1, 1977 +
6.   Devon Historian, No.1, 1970 +
7.   Devon's Origins, No.1, 1987 +
8.   Devonian Yearbook, 1910-1938.

9. Devonshire Association for the Advancement of Science, Literature and Art Report and Transactions, Vol.1, 1863 +
10. Exeter Diocesan Architectural and Archaeological Society Transactions, Vols.1-7, 1843-57; 2nd Series Vols.1-5, 1867-78; 3rd Series Vols.1-5, 1894-1933.
11. Plymouth Athenaeum Proceedings, Vol.1, 1961/62 +
12. Plymouth Institution and Devon and Cornwall Natural History Society Transactions, 1830-1960/1
13. Torquay Natural History Society Journal, Vols.1-3, 1909-22; Transactions and Proceedings, Vol.1, 1922 +

E. Museums with Local Studies Collections

1. Ashburton Museum, 1 West Street, Ashburton, Devon TQ13 7DT. Tel: (0364) 53278 (Hon.Curator's private number).
2. Axe Valley Heritage Museum, Town Hall, Seaton, Devon.
3. Axminster Museum, The Old Court House, Church Street, Axminster, Devon. Tel: (0297) 24386.
    History of Axminster, especially the carpet industry.
4. Barnstaple: St Anne's Chapel Museum, Church Lane, Barnstaple, Devon. Tel: (0271) 78709.
    History of Barnstaple.
5. Barnstaple: Museum of North Devon, The Square, Barnstaple EX32 8LN. Tel: (0271) 46747.
6. Braunton and District Museum, Church Street, Braunton EX33 2EL. Tel: Braunton 812131.
7. Brixham Museum, Bolton Cross, Brixham, South Devon TQ5 8LZ. Tel: (08045) 6267.
    Files of information on Berry Head area.
8. Budleigh Salterton: Fairlynch Museum, 27 Fore Street, Budleigh Salterton, Devon EX9 6NG. Tel: (03954) 2666.
    Local and natural history of the town and area to the present day, mainly 19th century.
9. Dartmouth Town Museum, The Butterwalk, Dartmouth, Devon TQ6 9PZ. Tel: (08043) 2923.

10. Dawlish Museum, The Knowle, Barton Terrace, Dawlish, Devon.
11. Exeter: Royal Albert Memorial Museum, Queen Street, Exeter,
    Devon EX4 3RX. Tel: (0392) 265858.
    Archaeology, local and natural history of Devon and Exeter.
12. Exmouth Museum, Sheppard Row, Exmouth, Devon.
13. Great Torrington Museum, Town Hall, Torrington,
    Devon EX38 8HN. Tel: (0805) 24324.
14. Hartland Quay Museum, Hartland, nr Bideford, North Devon.
    Tel: (028883) 353.
    *Natural environment and history of the North-West Devon
    coastal region.*
15. Holsworthy Museum, Manor Offices, Holsworth, Devon.
16. Honiton: Allhallows Museum, High Street, Honiton,
    Devon EX14 8PE.
    *Includes the Honiton lace industry. Extensive collection of
    printed handbills, notices, etc., covering all aspects of Honiton's
    affairs throughout the 19th century.*
17. Ilfracombe Museum, Wilder Road, Ilfracombe, Devon EX34 8AF.
    Tel: (0271) 63541.
    Archaeology, local and natural history of the area.
18. Kingsbridge: Cookworthy Museum, The Old Grammar School,
    108 Fore Street, Kingsbridge, Devon TQ7 1AW.
    Tel: Kingsbridge 3235.
    *History of rural life in Devon. Computer files of information by
    name, property and event about Kingsbridge and surrounding
    area; subject files on shipping, agriculture, etc.*
19. Morwellham Quay, Morwellham, Tavistock, Devon PL19 8JL.
    Tel: (0822) 832766.
    *History of Morwellham and the copper mining industry of the
    Tamar Valley.*
20. Newton Abbot Town Museum, 2a St Paul's Road,
    Newton Abbot, Devon.TQ12 2HP. Tel: (0626) 334675.
21. North Devon Maritime Museum, Odun House, Odun Road,
    Appledore, Devon EX39 1PT. Tel: (02372) 74852.
    North Devon shipbuilding and maritime history.

22. Okehampton and District Museum of Dartmoor Life,
    3 West Street, Okehampton, Devon EX20 1HQ.
    Tel: (0837) 3020.
    *Okehampton and District Photographic Archive and Oral History
    Archive.*

23. Plymouth: Merchant's House Museum, 33 St Andrew's Street,
    Plymouth, Devon.
    Social, economic and maritime history of Plymouth to 1670.

24. Plymouth City Museum and Art Gallery, Drake Circus,
    Plymouth PL4 8AJ. Tel: (0752) 668000 ext.4878.
    *Natural history of the South-West area, archaeology of Dartmoor
    and Plymouth area, social history of the South-West.*

25. Salcombe Maritime and Local History Museum, Customs House,
    The Quay, Salcombe.

26. Sidmouth Museum, Hope Cottage, Church Street, Sidmouth,
    Devon EX10 8LY. Tel: Sidmouth 516139.

27. South Molton Museum, Town Hall, Market Street, South Molton,
    Devon. Tel: (07695) 2951.
    *Agriculture, mineral mining, woollen industry, town trades and
    social history of the district.*

28. Tavistock Museum, Parish Council Chamber, Drake Road,
    Tavistock, Devon.

29. Teignmouth Museum, 29 French Street, Teignmouth,
    South Devon TQ14 8ST.

30. Tiverton Museum, St Andrew's Street, Tiverton,
    Devon EX16 6PH. Tel: (0884) 256295.
    *Life and history of Tiverton and mid-Devon from prehistoric times
    to present.   History of the firm of Heathcoat.*

31. Topsham Museum, Holman House, 25 The Strand, Topsham,
    Exeter EX3 0AX. Tel: (0392) 873244.

32. Torquay Museum, 529 Babbacombe Road, Torquay,
    South Devon TQ1 1HG. Tel: (0803) 293975.
    *Archaeology, geology, natural history of Torbay and South
    Devon.*

33. Totnes Museum, 70 Fore Street, Totnes, Devon TQ9 5RU.
    Tel: (0803) 863821.
    Library of local material.

DORSET: old county

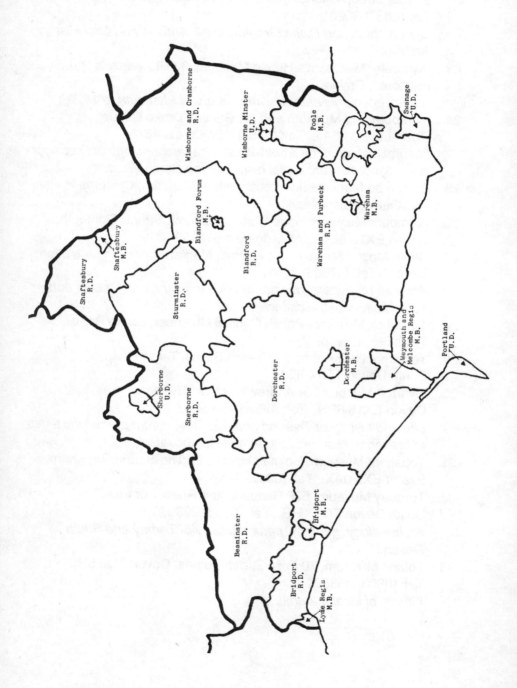

DORSET: new county

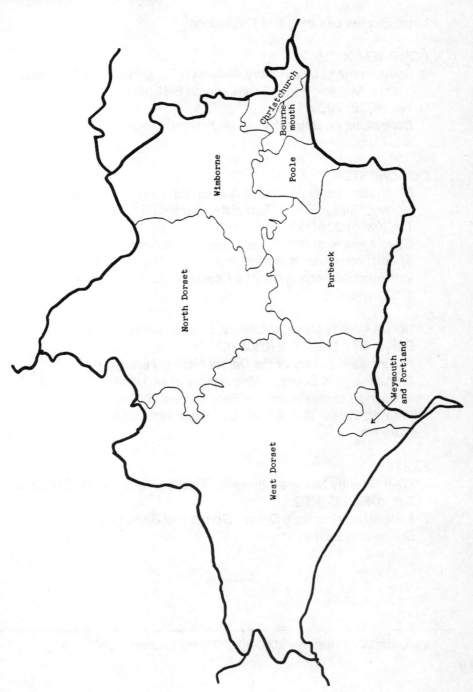

Christchurch

Bournemouth

Wimborne

Poole

North Dorset

Purbeck

Weymouth and Portland

West Dorset

DORSET

A.   Local Studies Libraries and Collections

BOURNEMOUTH
Bournemouth Local History Collection (b), Lansdowne Reference
Library, Meyrick Road, Bournemouth BH1 3DJ.
Tel: (0202) 292021.
*Collections on Bournemouth and surrounding districts of Dorset
and Hampshire.*

DORCHESTER
Dorchester Local Studies Collection (b), Dorchester Reference
Library, Colliton Park, Dorchester, Dorset DT1 1XJ.
Tel: (0305) 204442.
*Covers whole of Dorset, with special emphasis on West Dorset.
Special collection of printed material relating to Thomas Hardy,
smaller collections on Powys Family, William Barnes, and
T.E.Lawrence.*

Dorset County Museum Library, High Street West, Dorchester,
Dorset DT1 1XA. Tel: (0305) 62735.
*Includes the Library of the Dorset Natural History and
Archaeological Society. Manuscripts of various local authors,
including Thomas Hardy, William Barnes, Sylvia Townsend
Warner, Valentine Ackland. C.D.Drew Index of Medieval Dorset
(card file).*

EXETER
West Country Studies Library (c), Castle Street, Exeter EX4 3PQ.
Tel: (0392) 273422.
*Material on Cornwall, Devon, Dorset and Somerset, emphasis on
Devon and Exeter.*

---

a = under 2000 vols; b = 2000-20,000 vols; c = over 20,000 vols.

POOLE
Poole Local Studies Collection (b), Poole Central Reference
Library, Dolphin Centre, Poole BH15 1QE.
*Collections on Poole, Brownsea and other islands, Wimborne and
the Purbecks.*

WEYMOUTH
Weymouth Local Studies Collection (b), Weymouth Library,
Westwey Road, Weymouth, Dorset DT4 8SU. Tel: (0305) 786498.
Collections on Weymouth and Portland.

B.   Local Record Office

Dorset County Record Office, Bridport Road, Dorchester.

C.   Local History Societies

1.   Centre for South-West Historical Studies, c/o 7 The Close,
      Exeter EX1 1EZ.
2.   Dorset Natural History and Archaeological Society, c/o Dorset
      County Museum, High West Street, Dorchester DT1 1XA.
3.   Dorset Record Society, 16 Melcombe Avenue, Weymouth,
      Dorset (Sec.).
4.   Dorchester Association for Research into Local History and
      Archaeology, Camelot, Sutton Poyntz, Weymouth, Dorset (Sec.).
5.   East Dorset Antiquarian Society, 2 Wigbeth Cottage, Horton,
      Dorset (Sec.).
6.   Somerset and Dorset Family History Society, PO Box 170,
      Taunton TA1 1HF.

D.   Local History Journals

1.   Dorset Natural History and Archaeological Society Proceedings,
      Vol.1, 1876/77 +
2.   Dorset Record Society Publications, No.1, 1964 +
3.   Dorset Yearbook, 1904/5 +
4.   Notes and Queries for Somerset and Dorset, Vol.1, 1890 +

E.   Museums with Local Studies Collections

1.   Blandford: Park Farm Museum, Milton Abbas, Blandford,
       Dorset DT11 0AX. Tel: (0258) 880216.
       Large photographic collection.
2.   Blandford Forum Museum, The Old Coach House, Bere's Yard,
       Market Place, Blandford Forum, Dorset DT11 7HU.
       Tel: (0258) 51115
3.   Dorset County Museum, High Street West, Dorchester,
       Dorset DT1 1XA. Tel: (0305) 62735.
       *Archaeology, geology, local literary, artistic and natural history of
       Dorsetshire.*
4.   Gillingham Local History Museum, Church Walk, Gillingham,
       Dorset.
5.   Langton Matravers: Coach House Museum, St George's Close,
       Langton Matravers, Swanage, Dorset. Tel: (0929) 423168.
       *Includes history of the local stone industry, including Purbeck
       stone and "marble", and Portland stone.*
6.   Lyme Regis Philpot Museum, Bridge Street, Lyme Regis,
       Dorset DT7 3QA. Tel: (02974) 3370.
       Geology and local history of the Lyme Regis area.
7.   Poole: Guildhall Museum, Market Street, Poole,
       Dorset BH15 1NP. Tel: (0202) 675151.
       History of Poole.
8.   Poole: Maritime Museum, Paradise Street, The Quay, Poole,
       Dorset. Tel: (0202) 675151.
9.   Poole: Scaplen's Court, High Street, Poole, Dorset.
       Tel: (0202) 675151.
       History of the domestic life of Poole.
10.   Portland Museum, 217 Wakeham, Portland, Dorset.
       Tel: (0305) 821804.
11.   Shaftesbury Local History Museum, Gold Hill, Shaftesbury,
       Dorset SP7 4JW. Tel: (0747) 2157.
12.   Sherborne Museum, Abbey Gate House, Sherborne,
       Dorset DT9 3BP. Tel: (0935) 812252.
13.   Swanage: Tithe Barn Museum and Art Centre, Church Hill,
       Swanage, Dorset. Tel: (0929) 424546.
       *Archaeology, architecture and social history of Swanage and
       Purbeck.*

14. Wareham Town Museum, East Street, Wareham,
    Dorset BH20 4NP. Tel: (0295) 3006.
15. Wimborne Minster: Priest's House Museum, 23 High Street,
    Wimborne Minster, Dorset BH21 1HR.

DURHAM: old county

DURHAM: new county

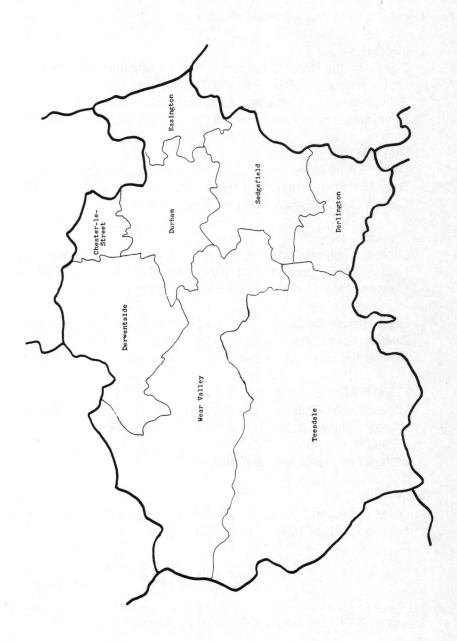

DURHAM
(including parts of the new districts of Cleveland and Tyne and Wear)

A.   Local Studies Libraries and Collections

BEAMISH
Beamish: the North of England Open Air Museum, Beamish,
Co.Durham DH9 0RG. Tel: (0207) 231811.
*Reference Library including specialist collection of books on
agriculture, mining, trade and domestic life. Sound Archive.*

DARLINGTON
Local History Collection, Durham County Library Darlington
Branch, Crown Street, Darlington. Tel: (0325) 462034 or 469858.
Covers South Durham and Darlington, with parts of N.Yorkshire.

DURHAM
Local Collection, Durham University Library: Special Collections,
Palace Green, Durham DH1 3RN. Tel: (0385) 61262/3 or 64466.
Concentrates on older material, especially manuscripts.

Local History Collection, Durham County Library Durham City
Branch, South Street, Durham. Tel: (0385) 64003.
Covers the whole of the old County of Durham.

GATESHEAD
Local Studies Collection (c), Gateshead Public Libraries, Central
Library, Prince Consort Road, Gateshead, Tyne and Wear
NE8 4LN. Tel: (091) 4773478.
Material on Gateshead and surrounding area.

HARTLEPOOL
Local Collection (b), Hartlepool Reference Library, Clarence Road,
Hartlepool TS24 7GW. Tel: (0429) 272905.

---

a = under 2000 vols; b = 2000-20,000 vols; c = over 20,000 vols.

SOUTH SHIELDS
Local Collection (b), South Tyneside Library, Central Library,
Prince Georg Square, South Shields, Tyne and Wear NE33 2PE.
Tel: (091) 4271818 ext.2135.
Material on South Tyneside.

STOCKTON
Local Collection (b), Stockton Reference Library, Church Road,
Stockton-on-Tees TS18 1TU. Tel: (0642) 672680.

SUNDERLAND
Local Collection (b), Sunderland Central Library, Borough Road,
Sunderland SR1 1PP. Tel: Sunderland 5141235.
*Covers Sunderland and surrounding area, and the old County of
Durham in less detail.*

B.   Local Record Offices

1.   Cleveland County Archives Department, Exchange House,
     6 Marton Road, Middlesbrough TS1 1DB. Tel: (0642) 248321.
2.   Durham County Record Office, County Hall, Durham DH1 5UL.
     Tel: (091) 3864411 ext.2474/2235.
3.   Durham County Record Office, Local History Section,
     Darlington Library, Crown Street, Darlington DL1 IND.
     Tel: (0325) 469858.
4.   Tyne and Wear Joint Archives Service, Blandford House, West
     Blandford Street, Newcastle upon Tyne NE1 4JA. Tel: (091) 232
     6789.

---

a = under 2000 vols; b = 2000-20,000 vols; c = over 20,000 vols.

C.   Local History Societies

1.   Architectural and Archaeological Society of Durham and
     Northumberland, Department of Archaeology, University of
     Durham, 46 Saddler Street, Durham DH1 3NU.
2.   Cleveland and Teesside Local History Society,
     11a Orchard Road, Linthorpe, Middlesbrough, Cleveland (Sec.).
3.   Cleveland Family History Society, 1 Oxgang Close, Redcar,
     Cleveland TS10 4ND.
4.   Durham County Local History Society, c/o County Record Office,
     County Hall, Durham DH1 5UA.
5.   Northumberland and Durham Family History Society,
     10 Melrose Grove, Jarrow, Tyne and Wear NE32 4HP (Sec.).
6.   Society of Antiquaries of Newcastle upon Tyne, The Black Gate,
     Newcastle upon Tyne.
7.   Surtees Society, The Prior's Kitchen, The College, Durham
     DH1 3EQ.

D.   Local History Journals

1.   Archaeologia Aeliana, Vol.1, 1822 +
2.   Architectural and Archaeological Society of Durham and
     Northumberland Transactions, Vols.1-11, 1862-1965;
     New Series 1-6, 1968-82.
     Continued as Durham Archaeological Journal.
3.   Cleveland and Teesside Local History Society Bulletin, 1979 +
4.   Durham and Northumberland Parish Register Society
     Publications, Nos.1-3,6, 1898-1926.
5.   Durham Archaeological Journal, Vol.1, 1984 +
6.   Durham County Local History Society Bulletin, Vol.1, 1964 +
7.   Northumberland and Durham Family History Society Journal,
     1975 +
8.   Society of Antiquaries of Newcastle upon Tyne Proceedings,
     Vol.1, 1855-5th Series Vol.1, 1956.
9.   Society of Antiquaries of Newcastle upon Tyne Records
     Committee Publications, Nos.1-12, 1920-33.
10. Surtees Society Publications, Vol.1, 1835 +

E.   Museums with Local Studies Collections

1.   Beamish: The North of England Open Air Museum, Beamish,
      Co.Durham DH9 0RG. Tel: (0207) 231811.
      *Social history of North East England in 19th and early 20th
      centuries. Maintains a card file of listed buildings in counties of
      Northumberland, Durham, Cleveland and Tyne and Wear.*
2.   Durham: Museum of Archaeology, The Old Fulling Mill,
      The Banks, Durham DH1 3EB. Tel: (091) 374 3623.
      Archaeology of the city and county of Durham.
3.   Durham Heritage Centre, St Mary-le-Bow, North Bailey,
      Durham DH1 3ET.
      History of Durham and district.
4.   Hartlepool: Gray Art Gallery and Museum, Clarence Road,
      Hartlepool, Cleveland TS24 8BT. Tel: (0429) 266522, ext.259.
      History of Hartlepool.
5.   Hartlepool Maritime Museum, Northgate, Hartlepool,
      Cleveland TS24 0LT. Tel: (0429) 272814.
      *Hartlepool's shipbuilding, marine engineering, shipping and
      fishing industries.*
6.   South Shields Museum and Art Gallery, Ocean Road,
      South Shields, Tyne and Wear NE33 2AU. Tel: (091) 4568740.
7.   Stockton Museum and Galleries, Museum Administration,
      PO Box 116, Gloucester House, 72 Church Road, Stockton-on-
      Tees, Cleveland TS18 1AT. Tel: (0642) 674308.
      Card file of listed buildings of the Stockton district.
8.   Sunderland: Grindon Museum, Grindon Lane, Sunderland,
      Tyne and Wear SR4 8HW. Tel: (0783) 284942.
      Edwardian life in Sunderland.
9.   Sunderland Museum and Art Gallery, Borough Road,
      Sunderland, Tyne and Wear SR1 1PP. Tel: (091) 5141235.
      *Archaeology and history of Wearside, natural history and
      geology of North East England between Tyne and Tees.*

EAST SUSSEX

See SUSSEX

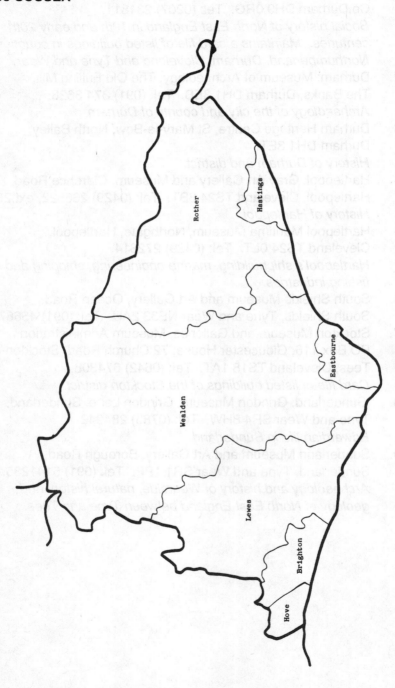

ESSEX: old county

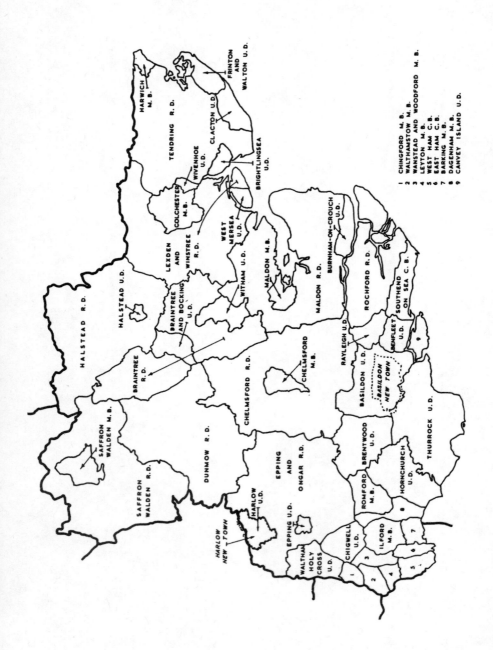

ESSEX: new county

ESSEX

A.   Local Studies Libraries and Collections

BASILDON
Basildon Library (a), Fodderwick, Basildon SS14 1DP.
Tel: (0268) 22446.
Small collection on Basildon area.

BRENTWOOD
Brentwood Library (a), Coptfold Road, Brentwood CM14 4BN.
Tel: (0277) 221818.
Small collection on Brentwood area.

CHELMSFORD
Chelmsford Library (b), PO Box 882, Market Road,
Chelmsford CM1 1LH. Tel: (0245) 4992758.
Collection on Chelmsford area.

CLACTON
Clacton Library (a), Station Road, Clacton-on-Sea CO15 1SF.
Tel: (0255) 421207.
Small collection on Clacton area.

COLCHESTER
Local Studies Department (b), Essex Libraries, Central Library,
Trinity Square, Colchester CO1 1JR. Tel: (0206) 562243 ext.209.

DAGENHAM
Essex, Barking and Dagenham Collection (b), Valence Reference
Library, (Barking Public Libraries), Becontree Avenue, Dagenham,
Essex RM8 3HT. Tel: (081) 592 6537.

---

a = under 2000 vols; b = 2000-20,000 vols; c = over 20,000 vols.

GRAYS

Grays Library (b), Orsett Road, Grays RM17 5DX.
Tel: (0375) 383611.
Collection on Grays area.

HARLOW

Harlow Library (a), The High, Harlow CM20 1HA.
(Tel: (0279) 413772.
Small collection on Harlow area.

ILFORD

Local History Collection and Brand Collection on Essex (Redbridge Public Libraries), Central Reference Library, 112B High Road, Ilford, Essex IG1 1BY. Tel: (081) 478 0017/8.

LOUGHTON

Loughton Library (b), Traps Hill, Loughton IG10 1HD.
Tel: (081) 502 0181.
Collection on Loughton area.

RAYLEIGH

Rayleigh Library (b), 132/4 High Street, Rayleigh SS6 7BX.
Tel: (0268) 775830.
Small collection on Rayleigh area.

ROMFORD

Local History Collection, Havering Public Libraries, Central Reference Library, St Edward's Way, Romford, Essex RM1 3AR.
Tel: (0708) 46040 ext.3169/3174.
Materials on the former county of Essex.

SAFFRON WALDEN

Saffron Walden Library (a), 2 King Street,
Saffron Walden CB10 1ES. Tel: (0799) 23178.
Small collection on Saffron Walden area.

---

a = under 2000 vols; b = 2000-20,000 vols; c = over 20,000 vols.

SOUTHEND
Southend Library (b), Victoria Avenue, Southend SS2 6EX.
(Tel: (0702) 612612.
Collection on Southend area.

STRATFORD
Essex Field Club Collection, Passmore Edwards Museum Library,
Romford Road, Stratford, London E15 4LZ.
Tel: (081) 534 4545 ext.376.

Local Studies Library, Newham Public Libraries, Stratford
Reference Library, Water Lane, Stratford E15 4NJ.
Tel: (081) 534 4544 ext.25662.

WALTHAM ABBEY
Waltham Forest Archives and Local History Library, Vestry House
Museum, Vestry Road, Walthamstow E17 9NH.
Tel: (081) 527 5544.
*Contains Walthamstow Collection built round the collections formed
by the Walthamstow Antiquarian Society, and the Essex Collection
on the former County of Essex, including Waltham Forest area,
Epping Forest, Lea Valley.*

WITHAM
Witham Library (a), 18 Newland Street, Witham CM8 2AQ.
Tel: (0376) 519625.
Small Collection on Witham area.

B.   Local Record Offices

1.   Essex Record Office, County Hall, Chelmsford SM1 1LY.
      Tel: (0245) 267222 ext.2104.
2.   Essex Record Office, Colchester and North East Essex Branch,
      Stanwell House, Stanwell Street, Colchester CO2 7DL.
      Tel: (0206) 572099.

---

a = under 2000 vols; b = 2000-20,000 vols; c = over 20,000 vols.

3. Essex Record Office, Southend Branch, Central Library, Victoria Avenue, Southend-on-Sea SS2 6EX. Tel: (0702) 612621.
4. Redbridge Central Library, Local History Room, Clements Road, Ilford EG1 1EA. Tel: (081) 478 7145.
5. Waltham Forest Archives, Vestry House Museum, Vestry Road, Walthamstow, London E17 9NH. Tel: (081) 509 1917 or 527 5544 ext.4391.

C. Local History Societies

1. Essex Archaeological and Historical Congress, 10 Alloa Road, Goodmayes, Ilford, Essex IG3 9SP. (Sec.).
2. Essex Archaeological Society, The Holly Trees, High Street, Colchester CO1 1UG.
3. Essex Historic Buildings Group, Rose Cottage, Marsh Road, Tillingham, Southminster, Essex CM0 7SZ (Sec.).
4. Essex Mills Group, Paycockes, West Street, Coggeshall, Colchester, Essex CO6 1NS. (Sec.).
5. Essex Society for Family History. The Cottage, Boyton Cross, Roxwell, Chelmsford, Essex CM1 4LP (Sec.).
6. Friends of Historic Essex, 43 Vicarage Road, Chelmsford, Essex CM2 9BS (Sec.).
7. Mid-Essex Archaeological and Historical Group, 6 Pottery Lane, Chelmsford (Sec.).
8. South-East Essex Archaeological Society, 33 Sundown Avenue, Westcliff on Sea (Sec.).
9. Waltham Forest Family History Society, 1 Gelsthorpe Road, Romford, Essex RM5 2NB (Sec.).
10. West Essex Archaeological Group, 102 Malford Grove, South Woodford, London E18 2DQ. (Sec.).

D. Local History Journals

1. East Anglian, Vols.1-4, 1864-71; New Series Vols.1-13, 1885-1910.
2. Essex Archaeological News, 1972-1984.
    Continued as Essex Archaeology and History News (see below).

3.   Essex Archaeological Society Transactions,Vols.1-5, 1858-73; New Series Vols.1-25, 1878-1952; 3rd Series 1961-1971.
       Continued as Essex Archaeology and History.
4.   Essex Archaeology and History, 1971 +
5.   Essex Archaeology and History News, No.89, 1984 +
6.   Essex Family Historian.
7.   Essex Field Club Bulletin, Vol.1, 1970 +
8.   Essex Journal, Vol.1, 1966 +
9.   Essex Life, Vol.1, Nos.1-13, 1966-67.
10.   Essex Naturalist, Vols.1-33, 1887-1976; New Series, 1977 +
11.   Essex Record Office Publications, No.1, 1946 +
12.   Essex Review, Vols.1-66, 1892-1957.
13.   Mid-Essex Archaeological and Historical Group Newsletter, No.1, 1971 +
14.   Roots in the Forest (Waltham Forest Family History Society), 1979 +
15.   West Essex Archaeological Group Bulletin, Nos.1-49, 1958-72; Newsletter, Nos.50-53, 1972-73; Newsletter New Series, 1980 +

E.   Museums with Local Studies Collections

1.   Bardfield Cottage Museum, Cage Cottage, Great Bardfield, Braintree, Essex CM7 4ST.
2.   Billericay: Cater Museum, 74 High Street, Billericay, Essex CM12 9BS. Tel: (0277) 622023.
       Local bygones, large collection of 19th and early 20th century photographs of the district.
3.   Burnham Museum, 4 Providence, Burnham-on-Crouch, Essex (NB not postal address).
       Local history of Dengie Hundred, Essex.
4.   Colchester: Hollytrees Museum, High Street, Colchester CO1 1UG. Tel: (0206) 712481/2.
5.   Colchester: Social History Museum, Holy Trinity Church, Trinity Street, Colchester, Essex. Tel: (0206) 712481/2.
       Traditional rural life and handicrafts of Essex.
       Social history of Essex in the 18th and 19th centuries.

6.   Colchester and Essex Museum, The Castle, Colchester,
     Essex CO1 1TJ. Tel: (0206) 712481/2.
     Archaeology of Colchester and Essex.
7.   Dagenham: Valence House Museum, Becontree Avenue,
     Dagenham, Essex RM8 3HT. Tel: (081) 592 4500 ext.4293.
     *Archaeology and history of the area. Essex Collection arranged
     by parish: prints, photographs, maps, plans, documents.*
8.   Epping Forest District Museum, 39-41 Sun Street,
     Waltham Abbey, Essex EN9 1EL. Tel: (0992) 716882.
     Social history of Epping Forest District.
9.   Epping Forest Museum and Queen Elizabeth's Hunting Lodge,
     Rangers Road, Chingford, London E4 7QH.
     Tel: (081) 529 6681.
     Natural history and local history of Epping Forest.
10. Finchingfield Guildhall Museum, Church Hill, Finchingfield,
     nr Braintree, Essex.
11. Halstead: Brewery Chapel Museum, Adams Court, off Colne
     Valley Close, Halstead, Essex CO9 1JQ.
12. Harlow Museum, Passmores House, Third Avenue, Harlow,
     Essex CMN18 6YL. Tel: (0279) 446422.
13. Maldon Museum, 71 High Street, Maldon, Essex.
14. Mersea Museum, High Street, West Mersea, Colchester,
     Essex CO5 8QD.
15. Saffron Walden Museum, Museum Street, Saffron Walden,
     Essex CO10 1JL.
     *Collection of local topographical prints and photographs of North
     West Essex.*
16. Southend: Central Museum, Victoria Avenue, Southend-on-Sea,
     Essex SS2 6EX. Tel: (0702) 330214.
     *Natural and social history of South-East Essex. Padgett
     Collection of photographs. Sites and Monuments Records and
     Biological Records for South East Essex.*
17. Stratford: Passmore Edwards Museum, Romford Road,
     Stratford, London E15 4LZ. Tel: (081) 534 4545 ext.5670.
     *Biology, geology, archaeology and local history of the county of
     Essex.*
18. Thurrock Local History Museum, Central Complex, Orsett Road,
     Grays, Essex RM17 5DX. Tel: (0375) 33325.

19. Thurrock Riverside Museum, Civic Square, Tilbury, Essex.
    Tel: (03752) 79216.
    History of Tilbury's riverside area and docks.
20. Upminster Tithe Barn Agricultural and Folk Museum, Hall Lane,
    Upminster, Essex RM14 1AU. Tel: (0708) 44297.
21. Walthamstow: Vestry House Museum, Vestry Road,
    Walthamstow E17 9NH.
    Local history of Waltham Forest area.

GLOUCESTERSHIRE: old county

Cheltenham
R.D.

Tewkesbury
M.B.

Newent
R.D.

North Cotswold
R.D.

Cheltenham
M.B.

Charlton Kings
U.D.

East
Dean
R.D.

Gloucester
C.B.

Northleach
R.D.

West Dean
R.D.

Gloucester
R.D.

Stroud
R.D.

Cirencester
R.D.

Stroud
U.D.

Lydney
R.D.

Nailsworth
U.D.

Cirencester
U.D.

Dursley
R.D.

Thornbury
R.D.

Tetbury
R.D.

Sodbury
R.D.

Mangotsfield
U.D.

Bristol
C.B.

Kingswood
U.D.

Warmley
R.D.

GLOUCESTERSHIRE: new county

GLOUCESTERSHIRE
(including parts of the new county of Avon)

A.   Local Studies Libraries and Collections

CHELTENHAM
Local History Collection (b), Cheltenham Divisional Library,
Clarence Street, Cheltenham, Glos GL50 3JT.
Tel: (0242) 515636, 512131.
Material mainly on Cheltenham.

CIRENCESTER
Cirencester Collection (b), Bingham Library, The Waterloo,
Cirencester GL7 2PN. Tel: (0285) 659813.
Material on Cirencester town.

GLOUCESTER
Gloucestershire Collection (c), Gloucester Library,
Brunswick Road, Gloucester GL1 1HT. Tel: (0452) 426979.

B.   Local Record Office

Gloucestershire Record Office, Clarence Row, off Alvin Street,
Gloucester GL1 3DW. Tel: (0452) 425295.

C.   Local History Societies

1.   Bristol and Gloucestershire Archaeological Society,
      22 Beaumont Road, Gloucester (Sec.).
2.   Cotteswold Naturalists' Field Club, Spring House, Ball's Green,
      Minchinhampton GL6 9AR (Sec.).
3.   Forest of Dean Local History Society, Albion House,
      Parkend Walk, Coalway, Coleford, Glos . (Sec.).
4.   Gloucester and District Archaeological Research Group,
      11 Trowscoed Avenue, Cheltenham GL53 7BP (Sec.).

---

a = under 2000 vols; b = 2000-20,000 vols; c = over 20,000 vols.

5. Gloucestershire Family History Society, 2 The Lake, Elton,
    nr Newnham, Glos GL14 1JO (Sec.).
6. Gloucestershire Local History Committee, Community House,
    15 College Green, Gloucester GL1 2LKZ.
7. Gloucestershire Society for Industrial Archaeology, Oak House,
    Hamshill, Coaley, Dursley, Glos GL11 5EH (Sec.).

D. Local History Journals

1. Avon Past, No.1, 1979 +
2. Bristol and Gloucestershire Archaeological Society Records
    Section Publications, Vol.1, 1952 +
3. Bristol and Gloucestershire Archaeological Society
    Transactions,Vol.1, 1876 +
4. Cotteswold Naturalists' Field Club Proceedings, Vol.1, 1847/53 +
5. Glevensis: Gloucester and District Archaeological Research
    Group Review, 1968 +
6. Gloucestershire Society for Industrial Archaeology
    Journal, 1964 +

E. Museums with Local Studies Collections

1. Cheltenham Art Gallery and Museum, Clarence Street,
    Cheltenham, Glos GL50 3JT. Tel: (0242) 237431.
    *Local History, archaeology, geology, traditional rural life, Arts
    and Crafts Movement in the Cotswolds.*
2. Cirencester: Corinium Museum, Park Street, Cirencester, Glos
    GL7 2BX. Tel: (0285) 655611.
    *Prehistory and Roman history of the Cotswolds. History of
    Cotswold wool trade. History of Cirencester from Tudor times.
    Archive files from local archaeological excavations.*
3. Cotswold Countryside Collection, Northleach, Cheltenham,
    Glos GL54 3JH. Tel: (0451) 60715.
    Social and agricultural history of Gloucestershire.
4. Dean Heritage Museum, Camp Hill, Soudley, Cinderford,
    Glos GL14 7UG. Tel: (0594) 22170.
    *History, traditions, and natural environment of the Forest of
    Dean.*

5.   Gloucester: City Museum and Art Gallery, Brunswick Road,
     Gloucester, GL1 1HP. Tel: (0452) 24131.
     Archaeology and natural history of city and county of Gloucester.
6.   Gloucester Folk Museum, 99-103 Westgate Street,
     Gloucester GL1 2PG. Tel: (0452) 26467.
7.   Stroud District Museum, Lansdown, Stroud, Glos GL5 1BB.
     Tel: (04536) 763394.
     Local history and archaeology of South Gloucestershire.
8.   Tewkesbury Museum, 64 Barton Street, Tewkesbury,
     Glos GL20 5PX.
9.   Winchcombe Folk Museum, Town Hall Museum, Winchcombe,
     Glos. Tel: (0242) 602925.

GREATER MANCHESTER

See CHESHIRE
     LANCASHIRE
     YORKSHIRE

HAMPSHIRE: old county

HAMPSHIRE: new county

Basingstoke

Hart

Rushmoor

Test Valley

East Hampshire

Winchester

East-
leigh

Southampton

New Forest

Fareham

Havant

Ports-
mouth

Gos-
port

HAMPSHIRE

A.   Local Studies Libraries and Collections

BASINGSTOKE
Local Studies Collection (a), Basingstoke Central Library,
Westminster House, Potters Walk, Basingstoke RG21 1LS.
Tel: (0256) 473901.
Material on north and north-east Hampshire.

PORTSMOUTH
Local Studies Library (b), Portsmouth Central Library,
Guildhall Square, Portsmouth PO1 2DX.
Tel: (0705) 819311-7 ext.57.
*Material on Portsmouth and south-east Hampshire areas. Naval
Collection, Genealogical Collection.*

Portsmouth Polytechnic Central Library (b), Cambridge Road,
Portsmouth PO1 2ST. Tel: (0705) 827681.

SOUTHAMPTON
Cope Collection (b), Southampton University Library, Highfield,
Southampton SO9 5NH. Tel: (0703) 559122.
Includes 2500 maps and prints.

Local Studies Library (b), Southampton Central Library,
Civic Centre, Southampton SO9 4XP. Tel: (0703) 832462.
*Material on Southampton and south-west Hampshire areas.
Maritime Collection.*

WINCHESTER
Local Studies Library (b), Winchester Library, Jewry Street,
Winchester, Hants SO23 8RX. Tel: (0962) 841408.
*Material on Winchester and central Hampshire areas. Railway
Collection.*

---

a = under 2000 vols; b = 2000-20,000 vols; c = over 20,000 vols.

B.   Local Record Offices

1.   Hampshire County Record Office, ~~20 Southgate Street,~~
      SUSSEX ST (handwritten annotation)
      SO23 8TH (handwritten annotation)   Winchester ~~SO23 9EF.~~ Tel: (0962) 846154.
2.   Portsmouth City Records Office, 3 Museum Road,
      Portsmouth PO1 2LE. Tel: (0705) 829765.
3.   Southampton City Records Office, Civic Centre,
      Southampton SO9 4XL. Tel: (0703) 832251/223855 ext.251.

C.   Local History Societies

1.   Hampshire Field Club and Archaeological Society,
      King Alfred's College, Winchester, Hants SO22 4NR.
      Tel: (0962) 841515.
2.   Hampshire Geneaological Society, 37 Russell Road,
      Lee-on-Solent, Hants PO13 9HR (Sec.).

D.   Local History Journals

1.   Hampshire Archaeology and Local History Newsletter
      *(Hampshire Field Club and Archaeological Society Newsletter for
      first 3 issues)*, Old Series Vols.1-10, 1965-75; New Series
      Vols.1-12, 1975-80.
2.   Hampshire Field Club and Archaeological Society,
      Archaeological Section Newsletter, Vol.1 (1-5), 1980-83.
3.   Hampshire Field Club and Archaeological Society, Geological
      Section Newsletter, Nos.1-3, 1980-81.
4.   Hampshire Field Club and Archaeological Society, Historic
      Buildings Newsletter, Vols.1-2, 1983.
5.   Hampshire Field Club and Archaeological Society, Local History
      Section Newsletter, Vol.1 (1-8), 1980-83.
6.   Hampshire Field Club and Archaeological Society Papers and
      Proceedings, Vol.1, 1985 +
7.   Hampshire Field Club and Archaeological Society, Section
      Newsletters, New Series 1, 1984 + *(continues all previous
      section newsletters)*.

8.   Hampshire Record Series, Vol.1, 1976 +
9.   Hampshire Record Society Publications, Vols.11-13, 1889-1897.
10.   Portsmouth Archives Review, No.1, 1976 +
11.   Portsmouth Record Series, No.1, 1971 +
12.   Portsmouth Papers, No.1, 1967 +
13.   Southampton Record Society Publications, Nos.1-41, 1905-41.
      (Continued as Southampton Records Series)
14   Southampton Records Series Publications, No.1, 1951 +

E.   Museums with Local Studies Collections

1.   Hampshire County Museum Service, Chilcomb House,
      Chilcomb Lane, Bar End, Winchester SO23 8RD.
      Tel: (0962) 66242.
      Reserve material, study collections, archive collections,
      reference book collection and local topographical photographs
      held centrally here. Museums in the Service, which are
      essentially display units:

      A.   Andover Museum, 6 Church Close, Andover,
            Hants SP10 1DP. Tel: (0264) 66283.
            Local geology, natural history, archaeology, industrial
            history of Tasker firm.
      B.   Curtis Museum, High Street, Alton, Hants GU34 1BA.
            Tel: (0420) 82802.
            Archaeology, social and industrial history of Alton and
            district, especially brewing.
      C.   Havant Museum and Art Gallery, East Street, Havant,
            Hants PO9 1BS.
            Archaeology, history and natural history of the Havant area.
      D.   Museum of the Iron Age, 6 Church Close, Andover,
            Hants SP10 1DP. Tel: (0264) 66283.
            Archaeological material from excavations of Danebury Iron
            Age hillfort, Hants.
      E.   Red House Museum, Art Gallery and Gardens, Quay Road,
            Christchurch, Dorset BH23 1BU. Tel: (0202) 482860.
            Local and natural history of Christchurch and district.

F.   Rockbourne Roman Villa, Rockbourne, nr Fordingbridge,
     Hants SP6 3PG. Tel: (07253) 445.
     Thematic display of Roman archaeology.
G.   Willis Museum, Old Town Hall, Market Place, Basingstoke,
     Hants. Tel: (0256) 465902
     Archaeology, history and natural history of the area.

2.   Gosport Museum, Walpole Road, Gosport, Hants PO12 1ED.
     Tel: (0705) 588035.

3.   Manor Farm, Upper Hamble Country Park, Brook Lane, Botley,
     Hants SO3 2ER (postal address only). Tel: (04892) 787055.

4.   Portsmouth Museums Service:

A.   City Museum and Art Gallery, Museum Road,
     Portsmouth PO1 2LJ. Tel: (0705) 827261.
     History of Portsmouth.
B.   Cumberland House and Aquarium, Eastern Parade,
     Southsea, Hants PO4 9RF.
     *History of Portsmouth and the Hampshire Basin during the
     last 200 years.*
C.   Southsea Castle, Clarence Esplanade, Southsea,
     Hants PO5 3PA.
     Local archaeology.

5.   Southampton City Museum Service, Holyrood Chambers,
     125 High Street, Southampton SO1 0AA. Tel: (0703) 224216.
     *General enquiries should be directed here in the first place,
     except for archaeological enquiries - see God's House Tower
     entry below. Museums include:*

A.   God's House Tower Museum, Winkle Street, Town Quay,
     Southampton. Tel: (0703) 220007.
     Archaeological history of Southampton.
B.   Southampton Maritime Museum, Ocean Village.

C.   Tudor House Museum, Bugle Street, St Michael's Square
Southampton SO1 0AD. Tel: (0703) 224216.
*Local and social history of Southampton. Large collection
of photographs, including Associated British Ports
photographs of docks and shipping. Oral History Section
tapes, topographical paintings and drawings of
Southampton.*

6.   Winchester Museums Service, Hyde Historic Resources Centre
75 Hyde Street, Winchester SO23 7DW. Tel: (0962) 848269.
*Archaeology and history of Winchester. Sites, Monuments and
Buildings Record for whole of Winchester district on card and
computer files.*

HEREFORD AND WORCESTER

See HEREFORDSHIRE
WORCESTERSHIRE

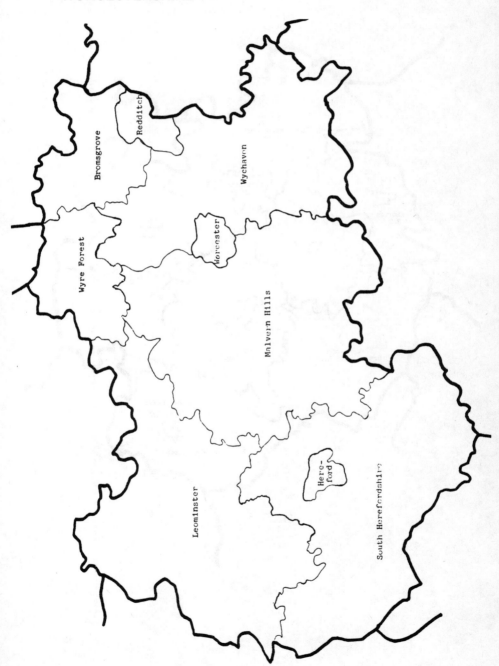

HEREFORDSHIRE: old county

HEREFORDSHIRE: new status

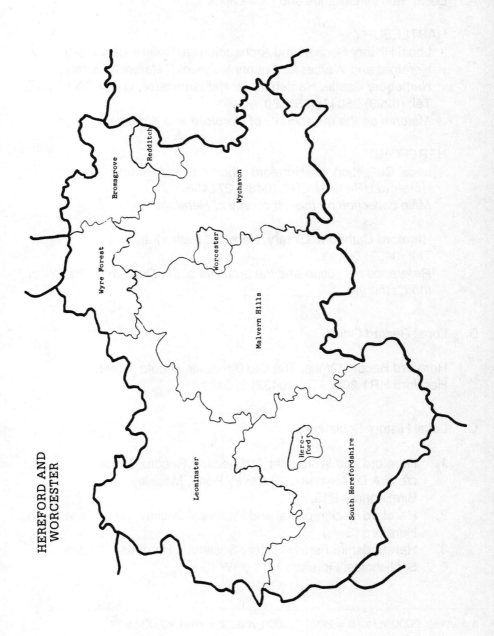

HEREFORDSHIRE

A.   Local Studies Libraries and Collections

HARTLEBURY
Local History Section and Archaeological Reference Library,
Hereford and Worcester County Museum Reference Library,
Hartlebury Castle, Hartlebury, nr Kidderminster, Worcs DY11 7XZ.
Tel: (0299) 250416/250560.
Material on the new county of Hereford and Worcester.

HEREFORD
Local Collection (b), Hereford Library, Broad Street,
Hereford HR4 9AU. Tel: (0432) 272456.
Main collection on the old county of Hereford.

Hereford Cathedral Library, Hereford Cathedral.
Tel: (0432) 58403.
*Reference collection and the archives of the Dean and Chapter of
the Cathedral.*

B.   Local Record Office

Hereford Record Office, The Old Barracks, Harold Street,
Hereford HR1 2QX. Tel: (0432) 265441.

C.   Local History Societies

1.   Hereford and Worcester Architecture Record Group,
c/o N.A.D.Molyneux, 56 Dovey Road, Moseley,
Birmingham B13.
2.   Hereford Geographical and Historical Society, 59 College Road,
Hereford (Sec.).
3.   Herefordshire Family History Society, 4 Burmarsh, Sutton
St Nicholas, Hereford HR1 3BW (Sec.).

---

a = under 2000 vols; b = 2000-20,000 vols; c = over 20,000 vols.

4.   Woolhope Naturalists' Field Club, Chy an Whyloryon, Wigmore, Leominster HR6 9UD (Sec.).

D.   Local History Journals

1.   Woolhope Naturalists' Field Club (Woolhope Natural History and Archaeological Society) Transactions, 1852/65 +

E.   Museums with Local Studies Collections

1.   Hereford: Old House Museum, High Town, Hereford.
Tel: (0432) 268121 ext.207/334.
Hereford during the Civil War.
2.   Hereford: St John and Coningsby Medieval Museum, Widemarsh Street, Hereford HR4 9HN. Tel: (0432) 272837.
History of the Order of the Knights of St John, of the Coningsby Pensioners, and of Nell Gwynne, famous native of Hereford.
3.   Hereford City Museum and Art Gallery, Broad Street, Hereford, HR4 9AU. Tel: (0432) 268121 ext.207.
Local and natural history, archaeology of Hereford and surrounding area. Sites and Monuments Record for Hereford, Biological Records Centre for Hereford, card files of Hereford information: military, agricultural, social history.
4.   Hereford and Worcester County Museum, Hartlebury Castle, Hartlebury, nr Kidderminster DY11 7XZ. Tel: (0299) 250416.
Life in Herefordshire and Worcestershire from prehistoric times. County social history files, Archaeological Sites and Monuments Record, County Excavation Archive, parish files.
5.   Herefordshire Rural Heritage Museum, Doward, Symonds Yat, Ross-on-Wye. Tel: (0600) 890474.
Displays of farm machinery and byegones illustrating the agricultural and rural life of Herefordshire.
6.   Leominster Folk Museum, Etnam Street, Leominster, HR6 8AN.
Tel: (0568) 5186.

HERTFORDSHIRE: old county

1 HARPENDEN U.D.
2 CHORLEYWOOD U.D.
3 RICKMANSWORTH U.D.
4 BUSHEY U.D.
5 ELSTREE R.D.
6 WELWYN GARDEN CITY U.D.
7 WELWYN NEW TOWN
8 HODDESDON U.D.
9 SAWBRIDGEWORTH U.D.
10 BISHOP'S STORTFORD U.D.

HERTFORDSHIRE: new county

HERTFORDSHIRE

A.   Local Studies Libraries and Collections

HENDON
Barnet Archives and Local Studies Department, Central Library,
Ravensfield House, The Burroughs, Hendon, London NW4 4BE.
Tel: (081) 202 5625.

HERTFORD
Hertford Museum Collection, Hertford Museum, 18 Bull Plain,
Hertford SG14 1DT. Tel: (0992) 582686.
Incorporates books belonging to East Herts Archaeological Society.

Hertfordshire Record Office Library, County Hall,
Hertford SG13 8DE. Tel: (0992) 555105.

Hertfordshire Local Studies Collection (c),
Room 100, Register Office Block, County Hall, Hertford SG13 8EJ.
Tel: (0992) 556624.

ST ALBANS
Hudson Memorial Library (a), St Albans Abbey, 2 Sumpter Yard,
St Albans, Herts AL1 1BY. Tel: St Albans 30576.
*Theological Library of the Anglican Diocese of St Albans, covers
history of St Albans city and abbey, county history of Hertfordshire
and Bedfordshire, Beardsmore Collection of Hertfordshire material.*

Local History Collection, St Albans City Library, Maltings,
St Albans, Herts AL1 3JQ. Tel: (0727) 60000.

WATFORD
Local History Collection (b), Watford Central Library,
Hampstead Road, Watford WD1 3EU. Tel: (0932) 226230.
Contains Hertford Collection and Watford Collection.

---

a = under 2000 vols; b = 2000-20,000 vols; c = over 20,000 vols.

B.   Local Record Offices

1.   Barnet Archives and Local Studies Department, Ravensfield
House, The Burroughs, London NW4 4BE. Tel: (081) 202 5625.
2.   Hertfordshire Record Office, County Hall, Hertford SG13 8DE.
Tel: (0992) 555105.

C.   Local History Societies

1.   Barnet Local History Society, Barnet Museum, Wood Street,
Barnet, Herts.
2.   East Herts Archaeological Society, 1 Marsh Lane,
Stanstead Abbotts, Ware, Herts SG12 8HH (Sec.).
3.   Hertfordshire Family and Population History Society,
6 The Crest, Ware, Herts SG12 0RR (Sec.).
4.   Hertfordshire Local History Council, Bengeo Rectory, Hertford
(Sec.).
5.   Hertfordshire Natural History Society and Field Club,
14 Roughdown Road, Boxmoor, Herts (Sec.).
6.   North Hertfordshire Archaeological Society, Letchworth Museum,
Broadway, Letchworth, Herts.
7.   North Herts Villages Research Group, Foxhall, Kelshall, Herts.
(Chairperson's private address).

D.   Local History Journals

1.   East Hertfordshire Archaeological Society Transactions, Vols. 1-
14(2), 1899-1965. *(continued as Hertfordshire Archaeology)*.
2.   Hertfordshire Archaeology, Vol.1, 1968 +
3.   Hertfordshire Natural History Society and Field Club
Transactions, Vol.1, 1879 +
4.   Hertfordshire's Past, 1976 +
5.   Hertfordshire People: the journal of the Hertfordshire Family and
Population History Society, Vol.1, 1977 +
6.   Rickmansworth Historian, Vol.1, 1954 +
7.   St Albans and Hertfordshire Architectural and Archaeological
Society Transactions, 1884-1961. *(continued as Hertfordshire
Archaeology)*.

E.   Museums with Local Studies Collections

1.   Ashwell Village Museum, Swan Street, Ashwell, Baldock,
     Herts BG7 5NY.
2.   Barnet Museum, 31 Wood Street, Barnet, Herts.
     Tel: (081) 449 8066.
     *History of the district represented by the collections of the Barnet
     Local History Society.*
3.   Bishop's Stortford and District Local History Museum,
     Cemetary Lodge, Apton Road, Bishop's Stortford.
4.   Broxbourne Museum, Lowewood, High Street, Hoddesdon.
     Tel: Hoddesdon 445596.
     Archaeology and local history of Hoddesdon and Cheshunt.
5.   Hertford Museum, 18 Bull Plain, Hertford, SG14 1DT.
     Tel: (0992) 52686.
     Material covering East Hertfordshire.
6.   Hitchin Museum and Art Gallery, Paynes Park, Hitchin.
     Tel: Hitchin 34476.
     Contains Hines Local History Collection.
7.   Letchworth: First Garden City Heritage Museum,
     296 Norton Way South, Letchworth, Herts SG6 1SU.
     Tel: (0462) 683149.
     Extensive archives and records of the building of Letchworth.
8.   Mill Green Museum and Mill, Mill Green, Hatfield,
     Herts AL9 5PD. Tel: (07072) 71362.
     *Social history and archaeology of the Welwyn-Hatfield area.
     Sites and Monuments Record for Welwyn and Hatfield area.*
9.   Royston and District Museum, Lower King Street, Royston,
     Herts SG8 7AL. Tel: (0763) 42587.
10. St Albans: Museum of St Albans, Hatfield Road, St Albans,
     Herts AL1 3RR. Tel: (0727) 56679.
     Contains the Evans Local History Collection.
11. Stevenage Museum, St George's Way, Stevenage,
     Herts SG1 1XX. Tel: (0438) 354292.
     *Large photographic archive on the building of Stevenage New
     Town.*
12. Ware Museum, The Priory Lodge, High Street, Ware.
13. Watford Museum, 194 High Street, Watford, Herts WD1 2HG.
     Tel: (0923) 32297.

HUMBERSIDE

See LINCOLNSHIRE
    YORKSHIRE (East and West Ridings)

HUNTINGDONSHIRE: old county

HUNTINGDONSHIRE: new status

CAMBRIDGESHIRE

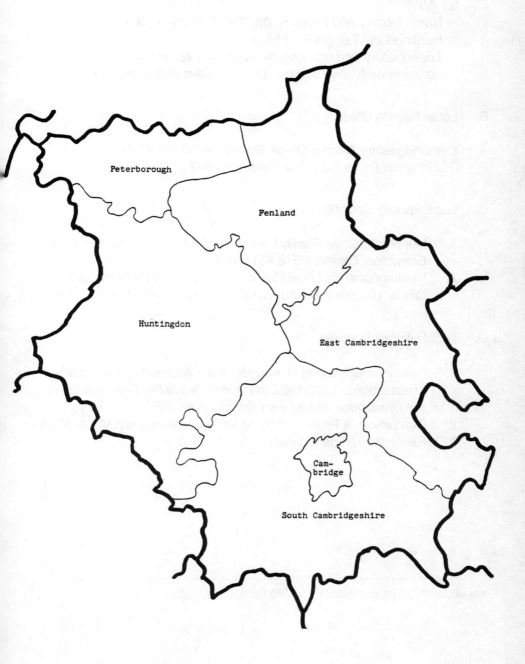

HUNTINGDONSHIRE

A.   Local Studies Libraries and Collections

ST IVES
Norris Library and Museum (b), The Broadway, St Ives,
Huntingdon. Tel: (0480) 65101.
*Local history and topography, especially religion and
nonconformity, civil war pamphlets, Pepys and Cromwell.*

B.   Local Record Office

Cambridgeshire Record Office, Grammar School Walk,
Huntingdon PE18 6LF. Tel: (0480) 425842.

C.   Local History Societies

1.   Huntingdonshire Family History Society, 14 Horseshoes Way,
Brampton, Cambs PE18 8TN (Sec.).
2.   Huntingdonshire Local History Society, c/o County Record
Office, Grammar School Walk, Huntingdon PE18 6LF.

D.   Local History Journals

1.   Cambridgeshire and Huntingdonshire Archaeological Society
Transactions, 1900-1952 *(then included in the Proceedings of
the Cambridge Antiquarian Society from 1953).*
2.   Durobrivae, a Review of Nene Valley Archaeology, Vol.1, 1973 +
3.   Records of Huntingdonshire, Vol.1, 1965 +

---

a = under 2000 vols; b = 2000-20,000 vols; c = over 20,000 vols.

E.   Museums with Local Studies Collections

1.   Longsands Museum, Longsands Community College,
      Longsands Road, St Neots, Huntingdon PE19 1LQ.
      Tel: (0480) 72229 Ext.48.
      Life in the district since Roman times.
2.   Norris Museum, The Broadway, St Ives, Huntingdon PE17 4BX.
      Tel: (0480) 65101.
      History of the County of Huntingdon from earliest times to
      present, including geology, archaeology.
3.   Ramsey Rural Museum, Woodyard, Ramsey, Huntingdon.
      Tel: (0487) 813223.

ISLE OF MAN

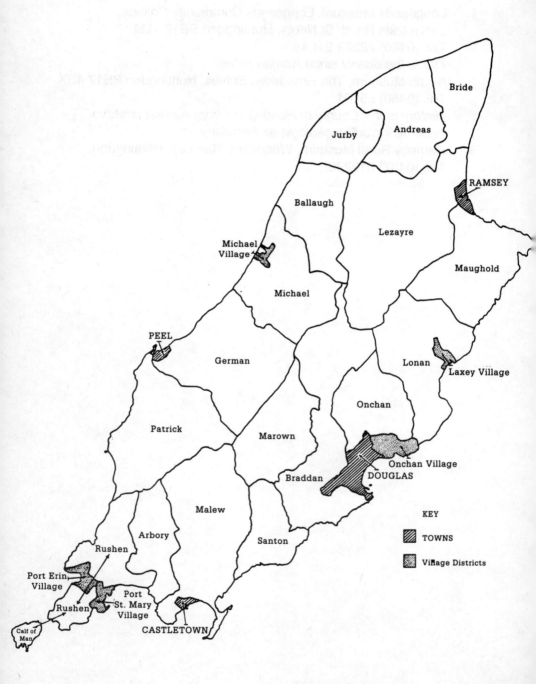

ISLE OF MAN

A.   Local Studies Libraries and Collections

CASTLETON
King William's College Library (a), King William's College, Castletown, Isle of Man. Tel: (0624) 2552.

DOUGLAS
Manx Collection, Douglas Public Library, Ridgway Street, Douglas, Isle of Man. Tel: (0624) 23021.

Manx Museum and National Trust Library (b), Douglas, Isle of Man. Tel: (0624) 75522.
Manx National Reference Library, includes archives and published works relating to the Isle of Man.

B.   Local Record Office

Manx Museum and National Trust Library, Kingswood Grove, Douglas, Isle of Man. Tel: (0624) 25125 ext.133.

C.   Local History Societies

1.   Isle of Man Family History Society, 3 Wesley Terrace, Douglas, Isle of Man (Sec.).
2.   Isle of Man Natural History and Antiquarian Society, 4 Peveril Terrace, Peel, Isle of Man (Sec.).

---

a = under 2000 vols; b = 2000-20,000 vols; c = over 20,000 vols.

D.   Local History Journals

   1.   Isle of Man Natural History and Antiquarian Society Proceedings,
         Vols.1-4, 1880-1906; New Series Vol.1, 1906 +
   2.   Mannin, Vols.1-9, 1913-1918.
   3.   Manx Museum Journal, 1924-1980.
   4.   Manx Society Publications, Nos.1-33, 1859-1894.

E.   Museums with Local Studies Collections

   1.   Castletown Maritime Museum, Bridge Street, Castletown,
         Isle of Man. Tel: (0624) 75522.
         Maritime history of the Isle of Man.
   2.   Cregneash Folk Museum, Cregneash, Isle of Man.
         Manx crofting and fishing life.
   3.   The Grove Rural Life Museum, Andreas Road, Ramsey,
         Isle of Man. Tel: (0624) 75522.
   4.   Manx Museum and National Trust, Douglas, Isle of Man.
         Tel: (0624) 75522.
         *Manx archaeology, history and natural history. Sites and
         Monuments Record on computer file. Card files of information
         on natural and social history*

ISLE OF WIGHT

PRE-1974

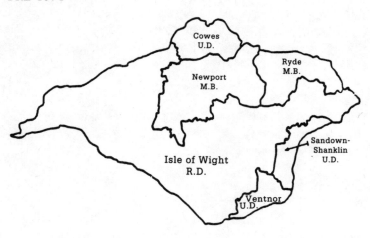

POST-1974

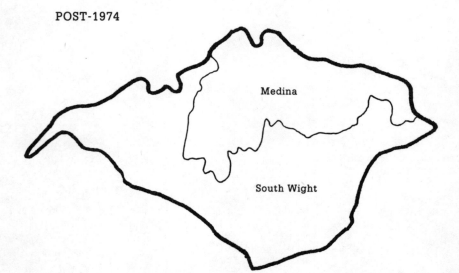

ISLE OF WIGHT

A.   Local Studies Libraries and Collections

NEWPORT
Isle of Wight County Library (b), County Record Office, 26 Hillside
Street, Newport, Isle of Wight PO30 1LL. Tel: (0983) 823800.
*Covers local and maritime history, geology and archaeology of the
Island.*

OXFORD
Old Dominion Collection, Oxford University School of Geography
Library, Mansfield Road, Oxford OX1 3TB. Tel: (0865) 46139.
Books on the Isle of Wight.

SOUTHAMPTON
Cope Collection, Southampton University Library, University Road,
Highfield, Southampton SO9 5NH. Tel: (0703) 559122.
Collection covers Hampshire and the Isle of Wight.

B.   Local Record Office

Isle of Wight County Record Office, 26 Hillside, Newport,
Isle of Wight, PO3 2EB. Tel: (0983) 823820.

C.   Local History Societies

1.   Isle of Wight Family History Society, 37 James Avenue,
     Lake Sandown, Isle of Wight (Sec.).
2.   Isle of Wight Natural History and Archaeological Society,
     Ivy Cottage, New Barn Lane, Shorwell, Newport, Isle of Wight
     (Sec.).

---

a = under 2000 vols; b = 2000-20,000 vols; c = over 20,000 vols.

D.   Local History Journals

Isle of Wight Natural History and Archaeological Society Proceedings, Vol.1, 1919 +

E.   Museums with Local Studies Collections

Carisbrooke Castle Museum, Carisbrooke Castle, Newport, Isle of Wight PO30 1XY. Tel: (0983) 523112.
History of the castle and social history of the Isle of Wight.

KENT: old county

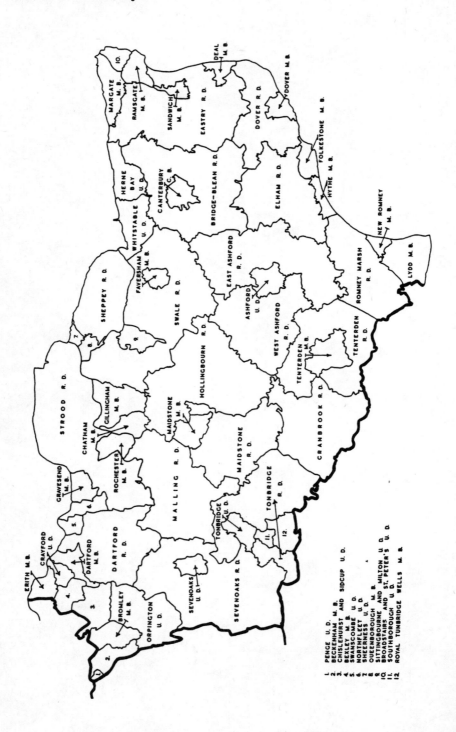

1. PENGE U. D.
2. BECKENHAM M. B.
3. CHISLEHURST AND SIDCUP U. D.
4. BEXLEY M. B.
5. SWANSCOMBE U. D.
6. NORTHFLEET U. D.
7. SHEERNESS U. D.
8. QUEENBOROUGH M. B.
9. SITTINGBOURNE AND MILTON U. D.
10. BROADSTAIRS AND ST. PETER'S U. D.
11. SOUTHBOROUGH U. D.
12. ROYAL TUNBRIDGE WELLS M. B.

KENT: new county

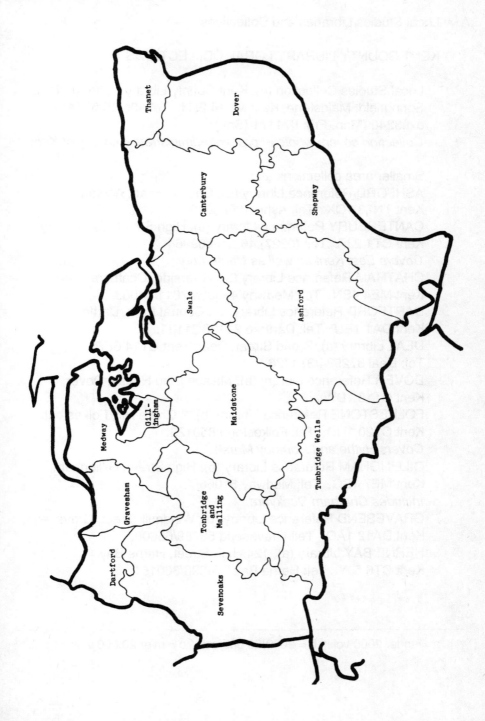

Thanet

Dover

Canterbury

Shepway

Swale

Ashford

Maidstone

Gillingham

Medway

Tunbridge Wells

Gravesham

Tonbridge and Malling

Dartford

Sevenoaks

KENT

A.   Local Studies Libraries and Collections

KENT COUNTY LIBRARY LOCAL COLLECTIONS

Local Studies Collection (b), Kent County Library Headquarters, Springfield, Maidstone, Kent ME14 2LH. Tel: (0622) 671411 ext.3240 (Mon.-Fri), 671171 (Sat.).
Collection covers whole of present administrative county of Kent.

Smaller area collections at:
ASHFORD Reference Library (b), Church Road, Ashford, Kent TN23 1QX. Tel: Ashford 620649.
CANTERBURY Reference Library (b), High Street, Canterbury, Kent CT1 2JF. Tel: (0227) 463608/69964.
Covers East Kent as well as Canterbury.
CHATHAM Reference Library (b), Riverside, Chatham, Kent ME4 4SN. Tel: Medway 43589/47811/44083.
DARTFORD Reference Library (b), Central Park, Dartford, Kent DA1 1EU. Tel: Dartford 21133/21134.
DEAL Library (a), Broad Street, Deal, Kent CT14 6ER. Tel: Deal 372984/374726.
DOVER Reference Library (b), Maison Dieu House, Dover, Kent CT16 1DW.
FOLKESTONE Reference Library (b), 2 Grace Hill, Folkestone, Kent CT20 1HD. Tel: Folkestone 850123.
Covers Hythe and Romney Marsh.
GILLINGHAM Reference Library (b), High Street, Gillingham, Kent ME7 1BG. Tel: Medway 51066/7.
Includes Chatham Dockyard.
GRAVESEND Reference Library (b), Windmill Street, Gravesend, Kent DA12 1AQ. Tel: Gravesend 52758/65600.
HERNE BAY Library (a), 124 High Street, Herne Bay, Kent CT6 5JY. Tel: Herne Bay 374896/360151.

---

a = under 2000 vols; b = 2000-20,000 vols; c = over 20,000 vols.

MAIDSTONE Reference Library (b), St Faith's Street, Maidstone, Kent ME14 1LH. Tel: (0622) 52344/677449.

MARGATE Reference Library (b), Cecil Square, Margate, Kent CT9 1RE. Tel: Thanet 223626/292895.

Covers Isle of Thanet.

RAMSGATE Library (b), Guildford Lawn, Ramsgate, Kent CT11 9AY. Tel: Thanet 593532.

ROCHESTER Reference Library (b), Northgate, Rochester, Kent ME1 1LKS. Tel: Medway 42415/43837.

Includes general material on Medway towns.

SEVENOAKS Reference Library (b), Buckhurst Lane, Sevenoaks, Kent TN13 1LQ. Tel: Sevenoaks 453118/452384.

SHEERNESS Library (a), 44 Trinity Road, Sheerness, Kent ME12 2PF. Tel: Sheerness 662618.

Includes Isle of Sheppey.

SITTINGBOURNE Reference Library (a), Central Avenue, Sittingbourne, Kent ME10 4AH. Tel: Sittingbourne 76545/77041.

TONBRIDGE Reference Library (b), Avebury Avenue, Tonbridge, Kent TN9 1TG. Tel: Tonbridge 352754/350479.

TUNBRIDGE WELLS Reference Library (b), Mount Pleasant, Tunbridge Wells, Kent TN1 1NS. Tel: Tunbridge Wells 22352/3.

BEXLEY

Local Studies Section Library (b), Bexley Libraries and Museums Department, Hall Place, Bourne Road, Bexley, Kent DA5 1PQ. Tel: (03225) 26574.

BROMLEY

London Borough of Bromley Local Studies Library (b), Bromley Central Library, High Street, Bromley, Kent BR1 1EX. Tel: (081) 460 9955 ext.261 or 262.

Special collections on Crystal Palace, Walter de la Mare, and H.G.Wells.

Branch local studies collections at:

ANERLEY Library (a), Anerley Town Hall, Anerley Road, Anerley, London SE20.

a = under 2000 vols; b = 2000-20,000 vols; c = over 20,000 vols.

BECKENHAM Library (b), Beckenham Road, Beckenham,
Kent BR3 4PE.
ORPINGTON Library (b), The Priory, Church Hill, Orpington,
Kent BR6 0HH.

GREENWICH

Kent Collection (b), Greenwich Public Libraries, Greenwich Local
History Library, Woodlands, 90 Mycenae Road, Blackheath,
London SE3 7SE. Tel: (081) 858 4631.

LAMBETH

Kent Collection, Lambeth Palace Library, Lambeth Palace Road,
London SE1 7JU. Tel: (071) 928 6222.

B.   Local Record Offices

1.   Bexley Libraries and Museums Department, Local Studies
      Section, Hall Place, Bourne Road, Bexley, Kent DA5 1PQ.
      Tel: (0322) 526574 ext.217 & 218.
2.   London Borough of Bromley Archives Department, Central
      Library, High Street, Bromley, Kent BR1 1EX.
      Tel: (081) 460 9955 ext.261.
3.   Canterbury Cathedral, City and Diocesan Record Office,
      The Precincts, Canterbury, Kent CT1 2EG. Tel: (0227) 463510.
4.   Kent Archives Office, County Hall, Maidstone, Kent ME14 1XQ.
      Tel: (0622) 671411 ext.3363.
5.   Kent Archives Office, North East Kent Area, Ramsgate Library,
      Guildford Lawn, Ramsgate, Kent CT11 9AI.
      Tel: (0843) 593532 ext.3
6.   Kent Archives Office, South East Kent Area, Central Library,
      Grace Hill, Folkestone, Kent CT20 1HD. Tel: (0303) 57583.
7.   West Kent Area Archives Office, Central Library, The Drive,
      Sevenoaks, Kent. Tel: (0732) 452384.

---

a = under 2000 vols; b = 2000-20,000 vols; c = over 20,000 vols.

C.   Local History Societies

1.   Association of Men of Kent and Kentish Men, Cantium Lodge, Terrace Road, Maidstone, Kent ME16 8HU. (Sec.).
2.   Bexley Historical Society,7 Meadowview Road, Bexley, Kent (Sec.).
3.   Bromley and West Kent Archaeological Society, 5 Harvest Bank Road, West Wickham, Kent (Sec.).
4.   Bromley Borough Local History Society, 24 Suningdale Road, Bromley, Kent (Sec.).
5.   Bromley Heritage, 62 Harvest Bank Road, West Wickham, Kent (Sec.).
6.   Croydon Natural History and Scientific Society Ltd., 96a Brighton Road, Croydon, Surrey CR2 6AD.
       Covers parts of North West Kent.
7.   Folkestone and District Family History Society, 69 Cudworth Road, Ashford, Kent TN24 OBE (Sec.).
8.   Kent Archaeological Society, The Museum, St Faith's Street, Maidstone, Kent ME14 1LH.
9.   Kent Family History Society, 8 Malvern Road, Ashford, Kent TN24 8HP (Sec.).
10.   Kent History Federation, 4 Castle Hill, Rochester, Kent ME1 1QQ.
       Body to which most of the local history societies in Kent are affiliated. Produces the Journal of Kent Local History.
11.   North West Kent Family History Society, 190 Beckenham Road, Beckenham, Kent BR3 4RJ (Sec.).

D.   Local History Journals

1.   Archaeologia Cantiana, Vol.1, 1858 +
2.   Beckenham Historian, No.1, 1967 +
3.   Bromley Local History, No.1, 1976 +
4.   Bygone Kent, 1979 +
5.   Cantium, Vol.1-Vol.6(4), 1974.
6.   Greenwich and Lewisham Antiquarian Society Transactions, Vols.1-10(1), 1905-85.
7.   Home Counties Magazine, Vols.1-14, 1899-1912.

8.   Invicta Magazine, Vols.1-3(3), 1913.
9.   Journal of Kent Local History, No.1, 1975 +
10.   Kent (Association of Men of Kent and Kentish Men),
      No.1, 1920 +
11.   Kent Archaeological Review, 1965 +
12.   Kent Archaeological Society Newsletter, No.1, 1981 +
13.   Kent Archaeological Society Records Branch Publications,
      No.1, 1912 +
14.   Kent Family History Society Journal, No.1, 1974 +
15.   Kent Life, No.1, 1962 +
16.   Kentish Yesterdays, Nos.1-3, 1908.
17.   North West Kent Family History, No.1, 1978 +

E.   Museums with Local Studies Collections

1.   Kent County Museums Service, West Malling Air Station,
      West Malling, Kent ME19 6QE. Tel: (0732) 845845 ext.2147.
      *Enquiries about the following eight museums, which the Service
      looks after, should be addressed to Kent County Museums
      Service in the first instance.*
      A.   Ashford Local History Museum, Ashford Central Library,
            Church Road, Ashford, Kent. Tel: (0233) 20649.
      B.   Deal Archaeological Collection, Deal Library, Broad Street,
            Deal, Kent. Tel: (0304) 374726.
      C.   Folkestone Museum and Art Gallery, Grace Hill,
            Folkestone, Kent CT20 1HD. Tel: (0303) 57583.
      D.   Gravesham Museum, High Street, Gravesend, Kent.
            Tel: (0474) 323159.
      E.   Herne Bay Museum, High Street, Herne Bay, Kent.
            Tel: (0227) 360151.
            *Records of the Herne Bay Record Society housed in the
            same building.*
      F.   Hythe Local History Room, Oaklands, Stade Street, Hythe,
            Kent CT21 6BG. Tel: (0303) 66152.
            Includes the history of the Cinq Ports.

G.   Ramsgate Museum, Ramsgate Library, Guildford Lawn,
      Ramsgate, Kent. Tel: (0843) 593532.
H.   Sevenoaks Museum, Sevenoaks Library and Museum,
      Buckhurst Lane, Sevenoaks, Kent. Tel: (0732) 452384.

2.   Bexley Museum, Hall Place, Bourne Road, Bexley,
      Kent DA5 1PQ. Tel: (0322) 526574 ext.221.
3.   Bromley: London Borough of Bromley Museum, The Priory,
      Church Hill, Orpington, Kent BR6 0HH.
      *Slide collection of archaeological sites and buildings in the
      Borough. Ordnance Survey record cards for the Borough.*
4.   Canterbury: Royal Museum and Art Gallery, High Street,
      Canterbury, Kent CT1 2JE. Tel: (0227) 452747.
5.   Canterbury Heritage, Poor Priests' Hospital, Stour Street,
      Canterbury, Kent. Tel: (0227) 452747.
6.   Deal Maritime and Local History Museum, 22 St George's Road,
      Deal, Kent. CT14 6BA. Tel: (0304) 362837.
      Honey Collection of photographs and negatives.
7.   Dover Museum, Ladywell, Dover, Kent CT16 1DQ.
      Tel: (0304) 201066.
8.   Erith Museum, Erith Library, Walnut Tree Road, Erith, Kent.
      Tel: (0322) 526574 ext.221.
9.   Faversham: Fleur de Lis Heritage Centre, 13 Preston Street,
      Faversham, Kent ME13 8NS. Tel: (0795) 534542.
10.   Maidstone Museum and Art Gallery, St Faith's Street, Maidstone,
      Kent ME14 ILH. Tel: (0622) 54497.
      *Archaeology, natural and social history of Kent. Houses the
      Kent Archaeological Society its Library.*
11.   Margate: Old Town Hall and Local History Museum,
      Market Place, Margate, Kent. Tel: (0843) 225511.
12.   Margate: Tudor House Museum, King Street, Margate,
      Kent CT9 1XZ. Tel: (0843) 225511.
      *Human occupation of Thanet from earliest times to the end of
      the Tudor period.*
13.   Museum of Kent Rural Life, Lock Lane, Sandling, Maidstone,
      Kent ME14 3AU. Tel: (0622) 63936.
      *Library of books relating to rural Kent, history of agriculture and
      gardening. Card file of agricultural sites.*

14. Rochester: Guildhall Museum, High Street, Rochester, Kent ME1 1QU. Tel: (0634) 48717.
15. Sandwich Town Museum, The Guildhall, Sandwich,Kent. Tel: (0304) 617197.
    William Boyer collection of Victorian photographs.
16. Sittingbourne: The Court Hall, High Street, Milton Regis, Sittingbourne, Kent.
17. Tenterden and District Museum, Station Road, Tenterden, Kent TN30 6HN. Tel: (05806) 3605.
    Includes material on the Cinq Ports, and Col.Stephens' collection of light railway material.
18. Tunbridge Wells Museum and Art Gallery, Civic Centre, Tunbridge Wells, Kent TN1 1NS. Tel: (0892) 26121 ext.3171.

LANCASHIRE: old county

Index

1. Abram U.D.
2. Accrington M.B.
3. Adlington U.D.
4. Aspull U.D.
5. Atherton U.D.
6. Billinge-and-Winstanley U.D.
7. Blackrod U.D.
8. Chadderton U.D.
9. Church U.D.
10. Clayton-le-Moors U.D.
11. Eccles M.B.
12. Farnworth M.B.
13. Haydock U.D.

14. Hindley U.D.
15. Ince-in-Makerfield U.D.
16. Kearsley U.D.
17. Little Lever U.D.
18. Orrell U.D.
19. Prestwich M.B.
20. Rishton U.D.
21. Royton U.D.
22. Standish-with-Langtree U.D.
23. Swinton and Pendlebury M.B.
24. Tottington U.D.
25. Tyldesley U.D.
26. Whitefield U.D.

LANCASHIRE: new county

Lancaster

Ribble Valley

Pendle

Wyre

Burnley

Blackpool→

Hyndburn

Preston

Fylde

South Ribble

Rossendale

Blackburn

Chorley

West Lancashire

LANCASHIRE
(including Manchester and Liverpool areas)

A.   Local Studies Libraries and Collections

BARROW-IN-FURNESS
Furness Library (b), Barrow Library (Cumbria County Library),
Ramsden Square, Barrow-in-Furness, Cumbria.
Tel: (0229) 20650.
*Collection relating to Northwest England in general and the
Furness and South Lakeland area in particular.*

BLACKBURN
Blackburn Library (b), Town Hall Street, Blackburn BB2 1AG.
Tel: Blackburn 661221.

BLACKPOOL
Blackpool Library (b), Queen Street, Blackpool FY1 1PX.
Tel: Blackpool 23977.

BOLTON
Local Studies Collection (c), Bolton Reference Library, Bolton
Central Library, Le Mans Crescent, Bolton BL1 1SE.
Tel: (0204) 22311 ext.2173.

BURNLEY
Burnley Library (b), Grimshaw Street, Burnley BB11 2BD.
Tel: Burnley 37115.

BURY
Local Studies Collection (b), Reference Library, Manchester Road,
Bury, Lancs BL9 0DR.

KNOWSLEY
Knowsley Library Service (b), Derby Road, Huyton,
Merseyside L36 9UJ. Tel: (051) 443 3740.

---

a = under 2000 vols; b = 2000-20,000 vols; c = over 20,000 vols.

LANCASTER
Lancaster Library (b), Market Square, Lancaster LA1 1HY.
Tel: Lancaster 63266/7.

LEIGH
Dootson Collection (b), Leigh Library (Wigan Metropolitan Borough
Reference Libraries), Civic Square, Leigh, Lancs WN7 1EB.
Tel: (0942) 604131.

LIVERPOOL
Local Collection, The Athenaeum, Church Alley, Liverpool L1 3DD.
Tel: (051) 709 0418.

Local History Collection (c), Liverpool City Libraries,
William Brown Street, Liverpool L3 8EW. Tel: (051) 207 2147;
direct line: 051 225 5417.
*Major repository of material for all aspects of the history of
Liverpool.*

Ryland Collection, Liverpool University Library, Sydney Jones
Library, PO Box 123, Liverpoool L69 3DA. Tel: (051) 709 6022.

MANCHESTER
Chetham's Library (c), Long Millgate, Manchester M3 1SB.
Tel: (061) 834 7961.
*Includes the Tonge Collection on the history of Lancashire,
Cheshire and Yorkshire.*

Local History Library (c), Manchester Central Library,
St Peter's Square, Manchester M2 5PD. Tel: (061) 236 9422.
Covers the area within, broadly, a 23-mile radius of Manchester.

OLDHAM
Oldham Local Studies Library (a), 84 Union Street,
Oldham OL1 1DN. Tel: (061) 678 4654.

---

a = under 2000 vols; b = 2000-20,000 vols; c = over 20,000 vols.

PRESTON

Preston Library (b), Harris Library, Market Square,
Preston PR1 2PP. Tel: Preston 531291.
Covers mainly the Preston area.

Headquarters Library (b), 143 Corporation Street,
Preston PR1 2TB. Tel: Preston 264021.
Main source for history of the old county of Lancaster.

ROCHDALE

Local Studies Section (Rochdale Public Libraries), Area Central
Library, The Esplanade, Rochdale, Lancs OL16 1AQ.
Tel: (0706) 47474 (49116 in evenings); direct line: 514915.
*Local history collections dispersed among the three local authority
libraries which were amalgamated in 1974: Rochdale, Middleton,
Heywood.*

SALFORD

Salford Local History Library (b), Peel Park, Salford M5 4WU.
Tel: (061) 736 2649.
*Collection relates to the Salford, Eccles, Irlam, Swinton and Worley
areas.*

ST HELENS

St Helens Local History and Archives Library (b), Central Library,
Gamble Institute, Victoria Square, St Helens WA10 1DY.
Tel: (0744) 24061 ext.2952.

STALYBRIDGE

Tameside Local Studies Library (b), Tameside Metropolitan
Borough, Stalybridge Library, Trinity Street, Stalybridge,
Cheshire SK15 2BN. Tel: (061) 338 3831.

STRETFORD

Stretford Library (b), Kingsway, Stretford, Manchester M32 8AP.
Tel: (061) 865 2218/9.

---

a = under 2000 vols; b = 2000-20,000 vols; c = over 20,000 vols.

URMSTON
Urmston Library (b), Croft Bank Road, Urmston M31 1TZ.
Tel: (061) 748 0774.

WESTHOUGHTON
Local Collection (b), Westhoughton Library, Library Street,
Westhoughton BL5 3AU. Tel: (0942) 811939.

WIGAN
Local History Collection (b), Wigan Library, Rodney Street,
Wigan WN1 1DG. Tel: (0942) 827619.

B.   Lancashire Record Offices

1.   Bolton Archive Service, Central Library, Civic Centre,
     Le Mans Crescent, Bolton BL1 1SE. Tel: (0204) 22311
     ext.2179.
2.   Bury Archive Service, 22a Union Arcade, Bury BL9 0QF.
     Tel: (061) 797 6697.
3.   Greater Manchester County Record Office, 56 Marshall Street,
     New Cross, Manchester M4 5FU. Tel: (061) 247 3383.
4.   Lancashire Record Office, Bow Lane, Preston PR1 8ND.
     Tel: (0772) 54868 ext.3039/3041.
5.   Liverpool Record Office, City Libraries, William Brown Street,
     Liverpool L3 8EW. Tel: (051) 207 2147 ext.34.
6.   Manchester Central Library Archives Department,
     St Peter's Square, Manchester M2 5PD.
     Tel: (061) ~~236 9422 ext.269.~~ 234 - 1980 (direct)
7.   Maritime Records Centre, Merseyside Maritime Museum,
     Albert Dock, Liverpool 1. Tel: (051) 207 0001.
8.   Merseyside County Archives, Maritime House, Mann Island,
     Pier Head, Liverpool L2 8DQ. Tel: (057) 236 8038.
9.   Salford Archives Centre, 658/662 Liverpool Road, Irlam,
     Manchester M30 5AD. Tel: (061) 775 5643.

---

a = under 2000 vols; b = 2000-20,000 vols; c = over 20,000 vols.

10. Stockport Archives Service, Central Library, Wellington Road, South Stockport SK1 3RS. Tel: (061) 480 7297/3038.
11. Tameside Archive Service, Tameside Local Studies Library, Stalybridge Library, Trinity Street, Stalybridge SK15 2BN. Tel: (061) 338 3831.
12. Wigan Record Office, Town Hall, Leigh WN7 2DY. Tel: (0942) 672421 ext.266.
13. Wirral Archives Service, Birkenhead Reference Library, Borough Road, Birkenhead L41 2XB. Tel: (051) 652 6106/7 ext.34.

C.   Local History Societies

1.   Chetham Society for the Publication of Remains Historical and Literary connected with the Palatine Counties of Lancaster and Chester, c/o Manchester University Press, Oxford Road, Manchester M13 9PL.
2.   Historic Society of Lancashire and Cheshire, 302 Prescot Road, Aughton, Ormskirk, Lancs L39 6RR (Sec.).
3.   Lancashire and Cheshire Antiquarian Society, 59 Malmesbury Road, Cheadle Hulme, Cheadle, Cheshire SK8 7QL.
4.   Lancashire Archaeological Society, Peacehaven, Lodge Lane, Little Singleton, Blackpool FY6 8LT (Sec.).
5.   Lancashire Family History and Heraldry Society, 183 Bolton Street, Ramsbottom, Lancs BL0 9JD (Sec.).
6.   Lancashire Local History Federation, 77 Arundel Drive, Poulton-le-Fylde, Lancs FY6 7TE (Sec.).
7.   Liverpool and District Family History Society, Ashlea, Station Road, Lydiate, Merseyside L31 4EY.
8.   Manchester and Lancashire Family History Society, Clayton House, 59 Piccadilly, Manchester M1 2AG.
9.   Manchester Region Industrial Archaeology Society, c/o 19 Gibsons Road, Stockport, Stockport SK4 4JX.
10.   Merseyside Archaeological Society, c/o Archaeological Services, Environmental Advisory Unit, University of Liverpool, PO Box 147, Liverpool L69 3BX.

11. North Western Society for Industrial Archaeology and History, Merseyside County Museums, William Brown Street, Liverpool L3 8EN.
12. Record Society of Lancashire and Cheshire, c/o Lancashire Record Office, Bow Lane, Preston PR1 8ND.
13. West Lancashire Archaeological Society, 34 Holly Close, Westhead, Ormskirk, Lancs L40 6HS (Sec.).

D.   Local History Journals

1.   Chetham Society (Remains Historical and Literary connected with the Palatine Counties of Lancaster and Cheshire) Publications, Old Series Vols.1-114, 1844-83; New Series Vols.1-110, 1883-1947; 3rd Series Vol.1, 1949 +
2.   Cumberland and Westmorland Antiquarian and Archaeological Society Transactions, Vol.1, 1844 +
3.   Historic Society of Lancashire and Cheshire Transactions (Proceedings and Papers), Vol.1, 1848+
4.   Lancashire: Journal of the Lancashire Family History and Heraldry Society, Vol.1, 1975 +
5.   Lancashire and Cheshire Antiquarian Society Transactions, Vol.1, 1883 +
6.   Lancashire Parish Register Society Publications, No.1, 1898 +
7.   Manchester Region History Review, Vol.1, 1987 +
8.   Record Society of Lancashire and Cheshire Publications, No.1, 1879 +

E.   Museums with Local Studies Collections

1.   Ashton-under-Lyne: Portland Basin Industrial Heritage Centre, 1 Portland Place, Portland Street South, Ashton-under-Lyne, Tameside OL6 7SY.
      Tameside's social and industrial history.
2.   Bacup Natural History Society and Folk Museum, 24 Yorkshire Street, Bacup, Lancs OL13 9AE.
3.   Bolton Local History Museum, Little Bolton Town Hall, St George's Street, Bolton, Greater Manchester B1 2EN. Tel: (0204) 22311 ext.6193.

4.   Burnley: Queen Street Mill, Harle Syke, Burnley, Lancs.
      BB10 2HX. Tel: (0282) 59996.
      History of the textile industry in Lancashire.
5.   Burnley: Weavers' Triangle Visitor Centre, 85 Manchester Road,
      Burnley, Lancs BB11 1JZ. Tel: (0282) 52403.
      History of Burnley, particularly textile industry and canal.
6.   Bury Art Gallery and Museum, Moss Street, Bury,
      Lancs BL9 0DR. Tel: (061) 705 5879.
      Social and industrial history of the Borough of Bury.
7.   Clitheroe Castle Museum, Castle House, Clitheroe,
      Lancs BB7 1BA. Tel: (0200) 24635.
8.   Darwen: Sunnyhurst Wood Centre, off Earnsdale Road, Darwen,
      Lancs Tel: (0254) 71545.
      Local and natural history of the area.
9.   Ellesmere Port: The Boat Museum, Dockyard Road,
      Ellesmere Port, South Wirral L65 4EF. Tel: (051) 355 5017.
      History of the Port of Manchester and of Ellesmere Port.
10.   Fleetwood Museum, Dock Street, Fleetwood, Lancashire
      FY7 6AQ. Tel: (03917) 6621.
      History of the Lancashire fishing industry.
11.   Fletcher Moss Museum, Didsbury, Manchester M20 8AU.
      Tel: (061) 445 1109.
12.   Furness Museum, Ramsden Square, Barrow-in-Furness,
      Cumbria LA14 1LL. Tel: (0229) 20650.
13.   Greater Manchester Museum of Science and Industry,
      Liverpool Road Station, Liverpool Road, Castleford,
      Manchester M3 4JP. Tel: (061) 832 2244.
      *History and development of Greater Manchester, the world's first
      industrial conurbation.*
14.   Helmshore Textile Museums, Higher Mill, Holcombe Road,
      Helmshore, Rossendale, Lancs BB4 4NP.
      Tel: (0706) 226459/18838.
      History of the development of the Lancashire textile industry.
15.   Lancaster City Museum, Market Square, Lancaster LA1 1HT.
      Tel: (0524) 64637.
16.   Lancaster Cottage Museum, 15 Castle Hill, Lancaster, Lancs.
      Tel: (0524) 64637.
      Cottage of c.1820 illustrating working-class home of the area.

17. Lancaster Maritime Museum, Custom House, St George's Quay,
     Lancaster LA1 1RB. Tel: (0524) 64637.
     *History of Lancaster's overseas trade, the Lancaster Canal,
     ecology and history of Morcambe Bay and its fishing industry.*
18. Leyland: South Ribble Museum and Exhibition Centre, The Old
     Grammar School, Church Road, Leyland, Preston, Lancs.
     Tel: (0772) 432041.
     History of Leyland town and area.
19. Liverpool Museum, William Brown Street, Liverpool,
     Merseyside L3 8EN. Tel: (051) 207 0001.
     *Natural history, including records, of Merseyside, Cheshire,
     Greater Manchester and Lancashire. Sites and Monuments
     Record for Merseyside. Archaeology of Merseyside.*
20. Liverpool: Museum of Labour History, Islington, Liverpool,
     Merseyside L3 8EE. Tel: (051) 227 5234.
     Includes the archives of Merseyside Unity Theatre.
21. Merseyside Maritime Museum, Albert Dock, Liverpool,
     Merseyside L3 4AA. Tel: (051) 207 0001.
     History of the Port of Liverpool.
22. Museum of Yorkshire Dales Leadmining, The Old Grammar
     School, School Lane, Earby, Colne, Lancs. Tel: (0282) 843210.
23. Oldham Local Interest Centre, Greaves Street, Oldham,
     Lancs OL1 1QN. Tel: (061) 678 4657.
24. Preston: Harris Museum and Art Gallery, Market Square,
     Preston, Lancs.PR1 2PP. Tel: (0772) 58248.
     Social history and archaeology of the area.
25. Rochdale Museum, Sparrow Hill, Rochdale, Greater Manchester
     OL16 1QT. Tel: (0706) 47474 ext.769.
26. Rossendale Museum, Whitaker Park, Haslingdon Road,
     Rawtenstall, Rossendale, Lancs BB4 6RE. Tel: (0706) 217777
     and 226509.
27. Rufford Old Hall, Rufford, nr Ormskirk, Lancs LA40 1SG.
     Tel: (0704) 821254.
     *Includes the Philip Ashcroft Folk Museum, illustrating the
     traditional life of the area.*
28. Saddleworth Museum and Art Gallery, High Street, Uppermill,
     Oldham, Lancs OL3 6HS. Tel: (04577) 4093.
29. St Helens Museum and Art Gallery, College Street, St Helens,
     Merseyside WA10 1TW. Tel: (0744) 24061.

30. Salford: Ordsall Hall Museum, Taylorson Street, Salford, Greater Manchester M5 3EX. Tel: (061) 872 0251. *History of the area. Includes a small Museum Library.*
31. Salford Museum and Art Gallery, Peel Park, The Crescent, Salford, Greater Manchester M5 4WU. Tel: (061) 736 2649..
32. Stockport Museum, Vernon Park, Turncroft Lane, Stockport, Greater Manchester SK1 4AR. Tel: (061) 480 3668.
33. Wigan Pier, Wigan, Lancs WN3 4EV. Tel: (0942) 323666. *Social and industrial life of the Wigan area.*

LEICESTERSHIRE: old county

Castle
Donington
R.D.

Ashby de la
Zouch
U.D.

Ashby
Woulds
U.D.

Ashby de la
Zouch
R.D.

Shep-
shed
U.D.

Lough-
borough
M.B.

Coalville
U.D.

Barrow upon Soar
R.D.

Melton and Belvoir
R.D.

Melton
Mowbray
U.D.

Market Bosworth
R.D.

Leicester
C.B.

Oadby
U.D.

Wigston
U.D.

Billesdon
R.D.

Hinckley
U.D.

Blaby
R.D.

Lutterworth
R.D.

Market Harborough
R.D.

Market Harborough
U.D.

LEICESTERSHIRE: new county

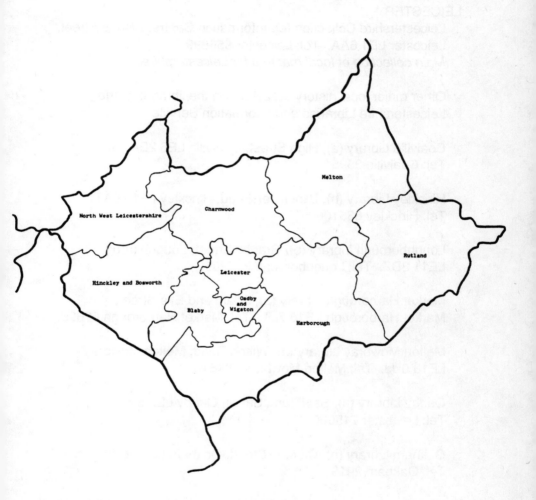

LEICESTERSHIRE

A.　Local Studies Libraries and Collections

LEICESTER
Leicestershire Collection (c), Information Centre, Bishop Street, Leicester LE1 6AA. Tel: Leicester 556699.
Main collection of local material for Leicestershire.

Other major local history collections in the libraries of the Leicestershire Libraries and Information Service:

Coalville Library (a), High Street, Coalville LE6 2EA.
Tel: Coalville 35951.

Hinckley Library (b), Lancaster Road, Hinckley LE10 0AT.
Tel: Hinckley 635106.

Loughborough Library (b), Granby Street, Loughborough LE11 3DZ. Tel: Loughborough 212985.

Market Harborough Library (a), Adam and Eve Street, Market Harborough LE16 7LT. Tel: Market Harborough 62699.

Melton Mowbray Library (b), Wilton Road, Melton Mowbray LE13 0UJ. Tel: Melton Mowbray 60161.

Oadby Library (a), Sandhurst Street, Oadby LE2 5AR.
Tel: Leicester 715066.

Oakham Library (b), Catmos Street, Oakham LE15 6HW.
Tel: Oakham 2918.

Wigston Magna Library (a), Bull Head Street, Wigston LE8 1PT.
Tel: Leicester 887381.

---

a = under 2000 vols; b = 2000-20,000 vols; c = over 20,000 vols.

Leicester University Department of English Local History,
Marc Fitch House, 5 Salisbury Road, Leicester LE1 7QR.
Tel: Leicester 522762 and 522522.
Contains Leicestershire material in its more general local history collections.

NOTTINGHAM
East Midlands Collection, University of Nottingham Library,
University Park, Nottingham NG7 2RD. Tel: (0602) 484848.

B.   Local Record Office

Leicestershire Record Office, 57 New Walk, Leicester LE1 7JB.
Tel: (0533) 544566.

C.   Local History Societies

1.   Leicestershire Archaeological and Historical Society,
      The Guildhall, Leicester LE1 5FQ.
2.   Leicestershire Family History Society, 25 Homecroft Drive,
      Packington, Ashby-de-la-Zouch LE6 5WG (Sec.).
3.   Leicester Literary and Philosophical Society, 3 Shirley Road,
      Leicester (Sec.).
4.   Leicestershire Industrial History Society, 54 Chapel Street,
      Measham, Burton-on-Trent, Staffordshire DE12 7JD (Sec.).
5.   Leicestershire Local History Council, c/o Leicestershire Record
      Office, 57 New Walk, Leicester LE1 7JB.
6.   Vaughan Archaeological and Historical Society,
      29 Walton Street, Leicester (Sec.).

D.   Local History Journals

1.   Leicestershire and Rutland Heritage, Vol.1, 1988/9 +
2.   Leicestershire and Rutland Magazine, Vols.1-2(3), 1948-50.
3.   Leicestershire and Rutland Notes and Queries, Vols.1-3, 1889-93.
4.   Leicestershire Archaeological and Historical Society Reports and Papers, 1857-1931 *(in Reports and Papers of the Associated Architectural Societies)*; Transactions, Vol.1, 1866 +
5.   Leicestershire Historian, Vol.1, 1967 +
6.   Leicestershire Industrial History Society Bulletin, Vol.1, 1976 +
7.   Leicester Literary and Philosophical Society Reports and Transactions, 1835 +

E.   Museums with Local Studies Collections

1.   Ashby-de-la-Zouch Museum, North Street, Ashby-de-la-Zouch, Leicestershire. Tel: (0530) 415603.
2.   Leicester: Jewry Wall Museum and Site, St Nicholas Circle, Leicester, LE1 4LB. Tel: (0533) 554100 ext.3020/1/3. *Archaeology of Leicester from earliest times to AD 1485. Sites and Monuments Record with computer index.*
3.   Leicester: Newarke Houses Museum, The Newarke, Leicester. *Social history of Leicestershire from 1500 onwards. Has a small working local history library.*
4.   Market Harborough Museum, Council Offices, Adam and Eve Street, Market Harborough. Tel: Market Harborough 32468.
5.   Melton Mowbray: Melton Carnegie Museum, Thorpe End, Melton Mowbray, Leicestershire. Tel: (0664) 69946. *Covers the 50 parishes of north-east Leicestershire administered by Melton Mowbray Borough Council.*

LINCOLNSHIRE: old county

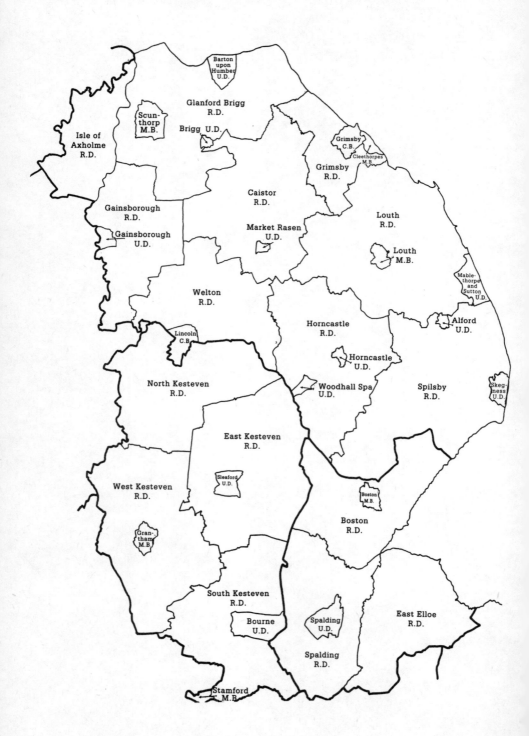

LINCOLNSHIRE: new county

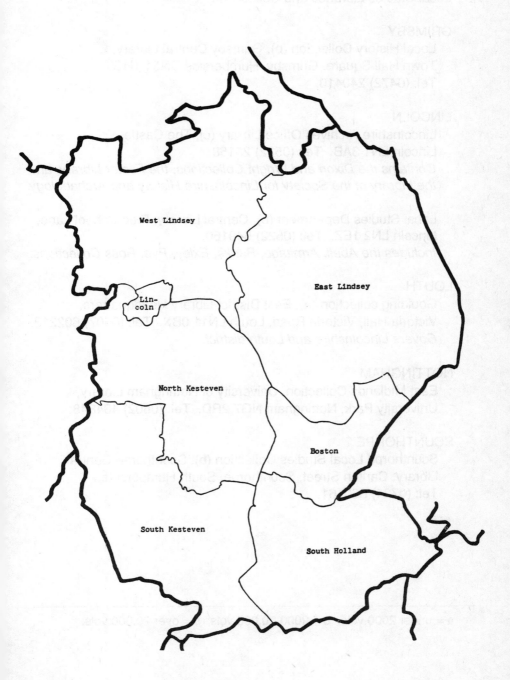

West Lindsey

East Lindsey

Lincoln

North Kesteven

Boston

South Kesteven

South Holland

LINCOLNSHIRE

A.   Local Studies Libraries and Collections

GRIMSBY
Local History Collection (b), Grimsby Central Library,
Town Hall Square, Grimsby, Humberside DN31 1HG.
Tel: (0472) 240410.

LINCOLN
Lincolnshire Archives Office Library (c), The Castle,
Lincoln LN1 3AB. Tel: (0522) 25158.
*Contains the Dixon and Wright Collections, the Foster Library, and
the Library of the Society for Lincolnshire History and Archaeology.*

Local Studies Department (b), Central Library, Free School Lane,
Lincoln LN2 1EZ. Tel: (0522) 549160.
Includes the Abell, Armitage, Banks, Exley, Pye, Ross Collections.

LOUTH
Goulding collection (a), East District Library Headquarters,
Victoria Hall, Victoria Road, Louth LN11 0BX. Tel: (0507) 602218.
Covers Lincolnshire and Louth district.

NOTTINGHAM
East Midlands Collection, University of Nottingham Library,
University Park, Nottingham NG7 2RD. Tel: (0602) 484848.

SCUNTHORPE
Scunthorpe Local Studies Collection (b), Scunthorpe Central
Library, Carlton Street, Scunthorpe, South Humberside.
Tel: (0724) 860161.

---

a = under 2000 vols; b = 2000-20,000 vols; c = over 20,000 vols.

SPALDING
Local History Collection (a), Spalding Gentlemen's Society Library,
The Museum, Broad Street, Spalding, Lincs PE11 1TB.
Tel: (0775) 4658.

B.   Local Record Offices

1.   Lincolnshire Archives Office, The Castle, Lincoln LN1 3AB.
Tel: (0522) 25158.
2.   South Humberside Area Record Office, Town Hall Square,
Grimsby DN31 1HX. Tel: (0472) 353481.

C.   Local History Societies

1.   Lincoln Record Society, Lincolnshire Archives Office,
The Castle, Lincoln LN1 3AB.
2.   Society for Lincolnshire History, Family History Section,
135 Baldertongate, Newark, Notts NG24 1RY.
3.   Society for Lincolnshire History and Archaeology, Jews Court,
Steep Hill, Lincoln LN2 1LS.
4.   Spalding Gentlemen's Society, The Museum, Broad Street,
Spalding, Lincs PE11 1TB.
5.   Trust for Lincolnshire Archaeology, 28 Boston Road, Sleaford,
Lincs. (Sec.).

D.   Local History Journals

1.   Archaeology in Lincolnshire, Vol.1, 1984/5 +
2.   Lincoln Record Society Publications, No.1, 1911 +
3.   Lincolnshire Architectural and Archaeological Society Reports
and Papers, Vols.1-42, 1850-1935 (*in Reports and Papers of the
Associated Architectural Societies*); New Series Vols.1-10,
1936-64.
4.   Lincolnshire Historian, Vols.1-2, 1947-65. *(replaced by
Lincolnshire History and Archaeology).*
5.   Lincolnshire History and Archaeology, Vol.1, 1966 +

6.   Lincolnshire Magazine, Vols.1-4, 1932-9. *(replaced by Lincolnshire History and Archaeology).*
7.   Lincolnshire Notes and Queries, Vols.1-24, 1888-1936.

E.   Museums with Local Studies Collections

1.   Alford: The Manor House, Alford and District Civic Trust Ltd., West Street, Alford, Lincs.
Traditional occupations, social and domestic life of rural Lincolnshire. Material on Lincolnshire and America. Nainby Collection of 19th century photographs.
2.   Baysgarth Museum, Baysgarth House, Baysgarth Park, Caistor Road, Barton-on-Humber, South Humberside DN18 6AH. Tel: (0652) 32318.
Geology, archaeology and history of the district.
3.   Boston: Guildhall Museum, South Street, Boston, Lincs. Tel: (0205) 65954.
4.   Gainsborough: Richmond Park Exhibition Centre, Richmond Park House, Morton Terrace, Gainsborough, Lincs. *Local social history.*
5.   Grantham Museum, St Peter's Hill, Grantham, Lincs NG31 6PY. Tel: (0476) 68783.
6.   Grimsby: Welholme Galleries, Welholme Road, Great Grimsby, South Humberside DN32 9PL. Tel: (0472) 242000 ext.1385.
History of Grimsby and the area. Fisheries archive of trawler plans, crew lists, etc.
7.   Immingham Museum and Gallery, Bluestone Corner, Immingham, South Humberside DN40 2DX. Tel: (0469) 75777.
8.   Lincoln: City and County Museum, Broadgate, Lincoln, LN2 1EZ. Tel: (0522) 26866.
History of Lincolnshire from prehistoric times to 1750. Sites and monuments Record for the county.
9.   Lincoln: Museum of Lincolnshire Life, Burton Road, Lincoln LN1 3LY. Tel: (0522) 28448.
Social history of Lincolnshire, mainly 19th and early 20th century. Lincolnshire Windmill Archive.

10. Scunthorpe Museum and Art Gallery, Oswald Road, Scunthorpe, South Humberside DN15 7BD. Tel: (0724) 843533.
    Reference Library of local material. Sites and Monuments Record for North Lincolnshire and South Humberside.
11. Scunthorpe: Normanby Park Farming Museum, Normanby Park, Scunthorpe DN15 9HU.
12. Skegness: Church Farm Museum, Church Road South, Skegness, Lincs. Tel: (0754) 66658.
    Agricultural history of Lincolnshire.
13. Stamford Museum, Broad Street, Stamford, Lincs PE9 1PJ. Tel: (0780) 55611.

LONDON AND MIDDLESEX: London pre-1965

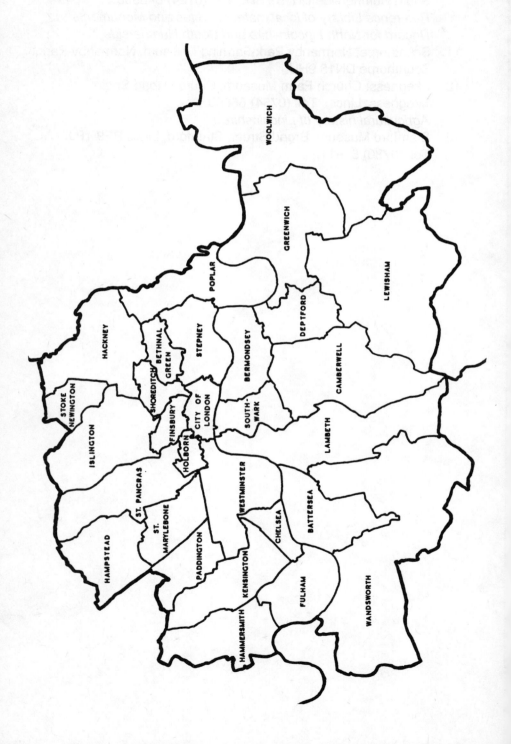

LONDON AND MIDDLESEX: Middlesex pre-1965

LONDON AND MIDDLESEX: Greater London post-1965

LONDON AND MIDDLESEX

Covers the Greater London area as constituted in 1965, which includes parts of the old counties of Essex, Hertfordshire, Kent and Surrey.

There are two recent publications of great help to London historians:
London Local Archives: a directory of local authority record offices and libraries; edited by Elizabeth Silverthorne. 2nd edition enlarged and revised. London, Guildhall Library and Greater London Archives Network, 1989.
Greater London Local History Directory and Bibliography; compiled by Peter Marcan. High Wycombe, Peter Marcan Publications, 1988.

Greater London area in general

A. Local Studies Libraries and Collections

1.   Bromhead Library, University of London Library, Senate House, Malet Street, London WC1E 7HU. Tel: (071) 636 4514.
2.   Greater London History Library, Greater London Record Office, 40 Northampton Road, London EC1R 0AB. Tel: (071) 633 6851.
      History of London local government and administration.
3.   Guildhall Library, Aldermanbury, London EC2P 2EJ.
      Tel: (switchboard) 071 606 3030
            (printed books) 071 260 1868/1870
            (manuscripts) (071) 260 1863
            (prints and maps) (071) 260 1839
4.   Highgate Literary and Scientific Institution, 11 South Grove, Highgate Village, London N6 6BS. Tel: (081) 340 3343.
5.   London Collection, Bishopsgate Institute Reference Library, 230 Bishopsgate, London EC2M 4QH. Tel: (071) 247 6844.
6.   London Collection, St Paul's Cathedral Chapter Library, St Paul's Cathedral, London EC4M 8AE.
7.   London Collection, and London Society Library, City University Library, Northampton Square, London EC1V 0HB.
      Tel: (071) 253 4399.

8.   London History Library, University College London,
      Gower Street, London WC1E 6BT. Tel: (071) 387 7050.
9.   Mayson Beeton Collection, Directorate of Ancient Monuments
      and Historic Buildings Library, Fortress House, 23 Saville Row,
      London W1X 2HE. Tel: (071) 6010 ext.323 325.
10.   Museum of London Library, London Wall, London EC2Y 5HN.
      Tel: (071) 600 3699.
      *Includes the London Collection, and the Library of the London
      and Middlesex Archaeological Society.*

B.   Record Offices

1.   Greater London Record Office, 40 Northampton Road,
      London EC1R 0HB. Tel: (071) 633 6851.
2.   Corporation of London Records Office, PO Box 270, Guildhall,
      London EC2P 2EJ. Tel: (071) 606 3030 ext.1251.
3.   Guildhall Library, Aldermanbury, London EC2P 2EJ.
      Tel: (071) 606 3030 ext.1863.

C.   Local History Societies

1.   Central Middlesex Family History Society, 155 Harrow View,
      Harrow, Middlesex HA1 4SX (Sec.).
2.   Centre for Metropolitan History, Institute of Historical Research,
      Senate House, Malet Street, London WC1E 7HU.
3.   City of London Historical Society, 172 Bishopsgate,
      London EC2M 4NQ (Chairperson's business address).
4.   East London History Society, 20 Brownfield Street,
      London E14 6NE (Sec.)
5.   East of London Family History Society, 178 Burrage Road,
      Plumstead, London SE18 (Sec.)
6.   East Surrey Family History Society, 15 Apeldoorn Drive,
      Wallington, Surrey SM6 9LE (Sec.).
7.   Essex Society for Family History, The Cottage, Boyton Cross,
      Roxwell, Chelmsford, Essex CM1 4LP (Sec.).
8.   Greater London Industrial Archaeology Society,
      30 Gaveston Drive, Berkhamstead, Herts HP4 1JF (Sec.).

9. Hertfordshire Family and Population History Society,
    6 The Crest, Ware, Herts SG12 0RR (Sec.).
10. London and Middlesex Archaeological Society,
    Museum of London, London Wall, London EC2Y 5HN.
11. London Natural History Society, 8 Crossfield Road,
    London NW3 4NS (Sec.)
12. London Record Society, c/o Institute of Historical Research,
    Senate House, Malet Street, London WC1E 7HU.
13. London Society, c/o City University, Northampton Square,
    London EC1V 0HB.
14. Middlesex Society, 64 Elm Drive, North Harrow,
    Middlesex HA2 7BY. (Sec.)
15. North Middlesex Family History Group, 6 Milton Court, 83/87
    Hoe Street, Walthamstow, London E17 4SA.
16. North West Kent Family History Society, 190 Beckenham Road,
    Beckenham, Kent BR3 4J (Sec.).
17. South London History Workshop, 58 Fearnley House,
    Vestry Road, London SE5.
18. Waltham Forest Family History Society, 1 Gelsthorpe Road,
    Romford, Essex RM5 2NB (Sec.).
19. West Middlesex Family History Society, 17 Croft Gardens,
    Ruislip, Middlesex HA4 8EY.
20. West Surrey Family History Society, Bradstone Garden Cottage,
    Christmas Hill, Shalford, Surrey GU4 8HR.
21. Woolwich and District Family History Society, 4 Church Road,
    Bexleyheath, Kent DA7 4DA.

D. Local History Journals

1. Cockney Ancestors (East of London Family History Society),
    1978 +
2. Greentrees (Central Middlesex Family History Society), 1978 +
3. Guildhall Miscellany, Vols.1-4, 1952/59-1971/73.
    (continued as Guildhall Studies in London History.)
4. Guildhall Studies in London History, Vols.1-5, 1973-1981.
5. London and Middlesex Archaeological Society Transactions,
    Vol.1, 1860 +
6. London and Middlesex Historian, Nos.1-4, 1965-67.

7. London Archaeologist, Vol.1, 1968 +
8. London Journal, Vol.1, 1975 +
9. London Natural History Society Transactions 1914-1920.
    (continued by London Naturalist - see below).
10. London Naturalist, Vol.1, 1921 +
11. London Record Society Publications, Vol.1, 1965 +
12. London Society Journal, Vol.1, 1913 +
13. London Topographical Record, Vol.21, 1900 +
14. London's Industrial Archaeology, Nos.1-3, 1979-84.
15. Middlesex Local History Countil Bulletin, Nos.1-18, 1952-64.
16. Middlesex Quarterly and London County Review, Nos.1-21, 1953-59.
17. North Middlesex (North Middlesex Family History Society), Vol.1, 1978/9 +
18. South London Record.
19. West Middlesex Family History Society Journal.
20. Woolwich and District Family History Society Journal.

E. Museums with Local Studies Collections

Museum of London, London Wall, London EC2Y 5NH.
    Tel: (071) 600 3699.
All aspects of the history of London.

London Boroughs

BARKING AND DAGENHAM
(part of the old county of Essex)

A.   Local Studies Libraries and Collections

Local History Collections (Barking Public Libraries), Valence
Reference Library, Becontree Avenue, Dagenham,
Essex RM8 3HT. Tel: (081) 592 2211.

B.   Local Record Office

Valence Reference Library, Becontree Avenue, Dagenham,
Essex RM8 3HT. Tel: (081) 592 4500 *ext.*4293.

C.   Local History Societies

1.   Barking (and District) Historical Society, 10 Crouch Avenue,
      Barking, Essex IG11 0QZ (Sec.).
2.   East of London Family History Society, 178 Burrage Road,
      Plumstead, London SE18.
3.   Essex Society for Family History, The Cottage, Boyton Cross,
      Roxwell, Chelmsford, Essex CM1 4LP (Sec.)

D.   Local History Journals

1.   Barking Historical Society Transactions, Vol.1(1-2), 1960/61.
2.   Cockney Ancestor (East of London Family History Society),
      1978 +
3.   Essex Family Historian.

E.   Museums with Local Studies Collections

Valence House Museum, Becontree Avenue, Dagenham,
Essex RM8 3HT. Tel: (081) 592 2211.
Archaeology and history of the area.

BARNET
(Finchley and Hendon; Barnet, East Barnet and Friern Barnet, formerly part of the old county of Hertfordshire).

A.   Local Studies Libraries and Collection

Barnet Local History Library, Ravensfield House, The Burroughs, Hendon, London NW4 4BE. Tel: (081) 202 5625.

B.   Local Record Office

Archives and Local History Department, Barnet Public Libraries, Central Library, The Burroughs, Hendon, London NW4 4BE. Tel: (081) 202 5625.

C.   Local History Societies

1.   Barnet (and District) Local History Society, Barnet Museum, 31 Wood Street, Barnet, Herts.
2.   Hendon and District Archaeological Society, 78 Temple Fortune Lane, London NW11 7TT (Sec.).
3.   Hertfordshire Family and Population History Society, 6 The Crest, Ware, Herts SG12 0RR (Sec.)
4.   Mill Hill Historical Society, 24 Flower Lane, Mill Hill, London NW7 2JE (Sec.).
5.   North Middlesex Family History Society, 6 Milton Court, 83/87 Hoe Street, Walthamstow, London E17 4SP (Sec.).

D.   Local History Journals

1.   Barnet and District Local History Society Bulletin, 1984 +
2.   Hertfordshire People, No.1, 1977 +
3.   North Middlesex (North Middlesex Family History Society), Vol.1, 1978 +

E.   Museums with Local Studies Collections

Barnet Museum, 31 Wood Street, Barnet, Herts.
Tel: (081) 449 0321 ext.4.

BEXLEY
(Bexley, Erith, Sidcup, formerly part of the old county of Kent)

A.   Local Studies Libraries and Collections

Bexley Libraries and Museums Department, Local Studies Section, Hall Place, Bourne Road, Bexley, Kent DA5 1PQ.
Tel: (0322) 526574 ext.217 and 218.

B.   Local Record Office

Bexley Libraries and Museums Department, Local Studies Section, Hall Place, Bourne Road, Bexley, Kent DA5 1PQ.
Tel: (0322) 526574 ext.217 and 218.

C.   Local History Societies

1.   Bexley Historical Society, 7 Meadowview Road, Bexley, Kent (Sec.).
2.   Crayford Manor House Historical and Archaeological Society, 4 Mayplace Close, Bexleyheath, Kent DA7 6DT (Sec.).
3.   Erith and Belvedere Local History Society, 19 Bladindon Drive, Bexley, Kent (Sec.).
4.   Lamorbey and Sidcup Local History Society, 48 Beverley Avenue, Sidcup, Kent (Sec.).
5.   North West Kent Family History Society, 190 Beckenham Road, Beckenham, Kent (Sec.).
6.   Woolwich and District Family History Society, 4 Church Road, Bexleyheath, Kent DA7 4DA.

D. Local History Journals

1. Bexley Historical Society Newsletter.
2. Crayford Manor House Historical and Archaeological Society Annual Proceedings.
3. North West Kent Family History, No.1, 1978 +
4. Woolwich and District Family History Society Journal.

E. Museums with Local Studies Collections

1. Bexley Museum, Hall Place, Bourne Road, Bexley, Kent DA5 1PQ. Tel: (0322) 526574.
2. Erith Museum, Erith Library, Walnut Tree Road, Erith, Kent DA8 1RS. Tel: Dartford 336582.

BRENT
(Willesden and Wembley)

A.   Local Studies Libraries and Collections

Brent Public Libraries Local History Collection, Grange Museum of
Local History, Neasden House, Neasden Lane, London
NW10 1QB. Tel: (081) 908 7432.

B.   Local Record Office

Grange Museum of Local History, Neasden House, Neasden Lane,
London NW10 1QB. Tel: 081) 908 7432.

C.   Local History Societies

1.   Central Middlesex Family History Society, 155 Harrow View,
Harrow, Middlesex HA1 4SX (Sec.).
2.   Wembley History Society, 117 Church Lane, Kingsbury,
London NW9 8JX (Sec.).
3.   Willesden Local History Society, 45 Doyle Gardens,
London NW10 3DB (Sec.).

D.   Local History Journals

1.   Greentrees (Central Middlesex Family History Society), 1978 +
2.   Wembley History Society Journal.
3.   Willesdon Local History Society Annual Magazine.

E.   Museums with Local Studies Collections

Grange Museum of Local History, Neasden House, Neasden Lane,
London NW10 1QB. Tel: (081) 908 7432.

BROMLEY
(Bromley, Beckenham, Penge, Orpington, Chislehurst, formerly part of the old county of Kent).

A.   Local Studies Libraries and Collections

Bromley Public Libraries Local Studies Library, Bromley Central Library, High Street, Bromley, Kent BR1 1EX.
Tel: (081) 460 9955 ext.261/262.
Branch local studies collections at:
Anerley Library, Anerley Road, Anerley, London SE20 8TH.
Beckenham Library, Beckenham Road, Beckenham,
Kent BR3 4PE.
Orpington Library, The Priory, Church Hill, Orpington,
Kent BR6 0HH.

B.   Local Record Office.

Bromley Public Libraries Archives Section, Central Library,
High Street, Bromley, Kent BR1 1EX.
Tel: (081) 460 9955 ext.261/262.

C.   Local History Societies

1.   Bromley Borough Local History Society, 14 Highland Road,
Bromley, Kent (Sec.).
2.   North West Kent Family History Society, 190 Beckenham Road,
Beckenham, Kent BR3 4RJ (Sec.).
3.   Orpington and District Archaeological Society, 25 Clovelly Way,
off Cotswold Rise, Orpington, Kent BR6 0WD (Sec.).

D.   Local History Journals

1.   Bromley Local Historian, No.1, 1976 +
2.   North West Kent Family History, No.1, 1978 +
3.   Orpington and District Archaeological Society Archives.

E.   Museums with Local Studies Collections

Bromley Museum, The Priory, Church Hill, Orpington BR6 0HH.
Tel: (0689) 31551.

CAMDEN
(St Pancras, Hampstead, Holborn)

A.   Local Studies Libraries and Collections

> Local Studies Library, Holborn Library, 32-38 Theobalds Road,
> London WC1X 8PA. Tel: (071) 405 2705 ext.337.

> Local Studies Library, Swiss Cottage Library, 88 Avenue Road,
> London NW3 3HA. Tel: (071) 586 5989 ext.234.
> *Holds the census returns for the Borough of Camden.*

B.   Local Record Offices

1.   Local Studies Library, Holborn Library, 32-38 Theobalds Road,
      London WC1X 8PA. Tel: (071) 405 2705 ext.337.

2.   Local Studies Library, Swiss Cottage Library, 88 Avenue Road,
      London NW3 3HA. Tel: (071) 586 5989 ext.234.

C.   Local History Societies

1.   Camden History Society, c/o Swiss Cottage Library,
      88 Avenue Road, London NW3 3HA.
2.   Heath and Old Hampstead Society, 34 Princess Road,
      London NW1 8JL (Sec.).
3.   Holborn Society, c/o Bedford House, 35 Emerald Street,
      London WC1N 3QI.
4.   North Middlesex Family History Society, 6 Milton Court,
      83/87 Hoe Street, Walthamstow, London E17 4SP.

D.   Local History Journals

1.   Camden History Review,No.1, 1973 +
2.   Camden History Society Newsletter, No.1, 1970 +
3.   Heath and Old Hampstead Newsletter, No.1, 1970 +
4.   Holborn Society Newsletter, 1969 +
5.   North Middlesex (North Middlesex Family History Society), No.1, 1978/9 +

E.   Museums with Local Studies Collections

Hampstead Museum, Burgh House, New End Square, London NW3 1LT. Tel: (071) 431 0144.

CITY OF LONDON

A.   Local Studies Libraries and Collections

      Guildhall Library, Aldermanbury, London EC2P 2EJ.
   Tel: (switchboard) (071) 606 3030
          (printed books) (071) 260 1868/1870
          (manuscripts) (071) 260 1863
          (prints and maps) (071) 260 1839

B.   Local Record Offices

1.   Corporation of London Records Office, PO Box 270,
    Guildhall,London EC2 2EJ.   Tel: (071) 260 6251 or
    (071) 606 3030 ext.1251.
2.   Guildhall Library Manuscripts Section, Aldermanbury,
    London EC2R 2EJ. Tel: (071) 260 1863.

C.   Local History Societies

1.   City of London Archaeological Society, 11 Chatsworth Avenue,
    Wimbledon Chase, London SW230 8JZ.
2.   City of London Historical Society, 172 Bishopsgate,
    London EC2M 4NQ (Chairperson's business address).
3.   North Middlesex Family History Society, 6 Milton Court,
    83/87 Hoe Street, Walthamstow, London E17 4SA (Sec.).

D.   Local History Journals

1.   City of London Archaeological Society Newsletter.
2.   North Middlesex (North Middlesex Family History Society),
    No.1, 1978/9 +

E.   Museums with Local Studies Collections

Museum of London, London, Wall, London EC27 5HN.
Tel: (071) 600 3699.

CROYDEN
(Croydon, Coulsdon and Purley, formerly part of the old county of Surrey)

A.   Local Studies Libraries and Collections

Croydon Public Libraries Local History Collection, Central
Reference Library, Katharine Street, Croydon, Surrey CR9 1ET.
Tel: (081) 760 5570.

B.   Local Record Office

Croydon Reference Library, Katharine Street, Croydon CR9 1ET.
Tel: (081) 760 5400.

C.   Local History Societies

1.   Bourne Society, 40 Raglan Precinct, Town End, Caterham,
      Surrey CR3 5UG (Sec.).
2.   Croydon Natural History and Scientific Society Ltd.,
      96a Brighton Road, South Croydon CR2 6AD.
3.   East Surrey Family History Society, 370 Chipstead Valley Road,
      Coulsdon CR3 5BF (Sec.).

D.   Local History Journals

1.   Bourne Society Local History Records, No.1, 1962 +
2.   Croydon Natural History and Scientific Society Proceedings,
      Vol.1, 1871 +
3.   East Surrey Family History Journal, Vol.1, 1977

EALING
(Acton, Ealing, Southall)

A.   Local Studies Libraries and Collections

      Local History Library (b), Central Library, Ealing Broadway Centre, Ealing, London W5 5JY. Tel: (081) 567 3656.

B.   Local Record Office

      Local History Library, Central Library, Ealing Broadway Centre, Ealing, London W5 5JY. Tel: (081) 567 3656.

C.   Local History Societies

1.   Acton History Group, 42 Avenue Gardens, London W3 (Sec.).
2.   Central Middlesex Family History Society, 155 Harrow View, Harrow, Middlesex HA1 4SX (Sec.).
3.   Ealing Museum, Art and History Society, Melvin House, Hartington Road, London W13.
4.   Southall Local History Society, c/o Southall District Library Reference Department, Osterley Park Road, Southall, Middlesex.

D.   Local History Journals

1.   Acton Historian, No.1, 1985(?) +
2.   Greentrees (Central Middlesex Family History Society), 1978 +

E.   Museums with Local Studies Collections

      Gunnersbury Park Museum, Gunnersbury Park, London W3 8LQ. Tel: (081) 992 1612.
Local history of the Boroughs of Ealing and Hounslow.

ENFIELD
(Edmonton, Enfield, Southgate)

A.   Local Studies Libraries and Collections

Local History Unit (a), Southgate Town Hall, Green Lanes,
London N13 4XD. Tel: (081) 882 8841/2 ext.2724;
direct line: (081) 982 7453.

B.   Local Record Office

Local History Unit, Southgate Town Hall, Green Lanes,
London N13 4XD. Tel: (081) 882 8841/2 ext.2724;
direct line: (081) 982 7453.

C.   Local History Societies

1.   Edmonton Hundred Historical Society, c/o Local History Unit,
      Southgate Town Hall, Green Lanes, London N13 4XD.
2.   Enfield Archaeological Society, 23 Merton Road, Enfield,
      Middlesex (Sec.).
3.   North Middlesex Family History Society, 6 Milton Court,
      83/87 Hoe Street, Walthamstow, London E17 4SA (Sec.).

D.   Local History Journals

1.   Edmonton Hundred Historical Society Chronicle, 1978-1985.
2.   Enfield Archaeological Society Bulletin, 1959 +
3.   North Middlesex (North Middlesex Family History Society), Vol.1,
      1978/9 +

E.   Museums with Local History Collections

Forty Hall Museum, Forty Hill, Middlesex EN2 9HA.
Tel: (081) 363 8196.

GREENWICH
(Greenwich and Woolwich)

A. Local Studies Libraries and Collections

>   Greenwich Local History Library, Woodlands, 90 Mycenae Road,
>   Blackheath, London SE3 7SE. Tel: (081) 858 4631.

B. Local Record Office

>   Greenwich Local History Library, Woodlands, 90 Mycenae Road,
>   Blackheath, London SE3 7SE. Tel: (081) 858 4631.

C. Local History Societies

1. Greenwich and Lewisham Antiquarian Society, 128
    Evelyn Street, London SE8 5DD (Sec.).
2. Woolwich and District Antiquarian Society, 94 Howarth Road,
    London SE2 0UP (Sec.).
3. Woolwich and District Family History Society, 4 Church Road,
    Bexleyheath, Kent (Sec.).

D. Local History Journals

1. Greenwich and Lewisham Antiquarian Society Transactions,
    1907 +
2. Woolwich and District Antiquarian Society Proceedings, 1896 +
3. Woolwich and District Family History Society Journal.

E. Museums with Local Studies Collections

>   Greenwich Borough Museum, 232 Plumstead High Street,
>   London SE18 1JL. Tel: (081) 855 3240.

HACKNEY
(Hackney, Shoredith, Stoke Newington)

A.   Local Studies Libraries and Collections

Hackney Public Libraries Archives and Local History
Department, Rose Lipman Library, De Beauvoir Road,
London N1 5SQ. Tel: (071) 241 2886.

B.   Local Record Office

Hackney Public Libraries Archives and Local History Department,
Rose Lipman Library, De Beauvoir Road, London N1 5SQ.
Tel: (071) 241 2886.

C.   Local History Societies

1.   East London History Society, 20 Brownfield Street,
London E14 6NE (Sec.).
2.   East of London Family History Society, 178 Burrage Road,
Plumstead, London SE18.
3.   Friends of Hackney Archives, c/o Hackney Archives Department,
Rose Lipman Library, De Beauvoir Road, London N1 5SQ.
4.   Hackney Society, 115 Eleanor Road, London E5 (Sec.).

D.   Local History Journals

1.   Cockney Ancestor (East of London Family History Society),
1978 +
2.   East London Record, No.1, 1978 +
3.   Hackney Society Newsletter, 1987 +
4.   The Terrier, 1985 +

E.   Museums with Local Studies Collections

Hackney Museum, Central Hall, Mare Street, London E8 1HE.
Tel: (071) 986 6914.

HAMMERSMITH AND FULHAM

A.   Local Studies Libraries and Collections

Local History Collections, Fulham Reference Library,
598 Fulham Road, London SW6 5NX.
Tel: (081) 748 3020 ext.3875.

Local History Collection, Hammersmith Reference Library,
Shepherds Bush Road, London W6 7AT.
Tel: (081) 748 3020 ext.3812.

B.   Local Record Office

Hammersmith and Fulham Archives, Shepherds Bush Library,
7 Uxbridge Road, London W12 8LJ. Tel: (081) 743 0910 or
(081) 748 3020 ext.3850.

C.   Local History Societies

1.   Fulham and Hammersmith Historical Society, 56 Palewell Park,
London SW14 8JH (Sec.).
2.   Fulham Family History Society, 143 Harbord Street,
London SW6 (Sec.).
3.   Shepherds Bush Local History Society, 22a Collingbourne Road,
London W12 0JQ (Sec.).
4.   West Middlesex Family History Society, 17 Croft Gardens,
Ruislip, Middlesex HA4 8EY (Sec.).

D.   Local History Journals

1.   Fulham and Hammersmith Historical Society Newsletter.
2.   Shepherds Bush Local History Society Bulletin.
3.   West Middlesex Family History Society Journal.

HARINGEY
(Tottenham, Hornsey, Wood Green)

A.   Local Studies Libraries and Collections

> Haringey Archives Service (includes Local History Collections),
> Bruce Castle Museum, Lordship Lane, Tottenham,
> London N17 8NU. Tel: (081) 808 8772.
> *Small collection at Hornsey Reference Library, Haringey*
> *Park N8 9JA.*

B.   Local Record Office

> Haringey Archives Service, Bruce Castle Museum, Lordship Lane,
> Tottenham, London N17 8NU. Tel: (081) 808 8772.

C.   Local History Societies

1.   Hornsey Historical Society, The Old Schoolhouse,
      136 Tottenham Lane, Hornsey N8 7EL.
2.   North Middlesex Family History Society, 6 Milton Court,
      83/87 Hoe Street, Walthamstow, London E17 4SA (Sec.).

D.   Local History Journals

1.   Haringey History Bulletin, 1973 +
2.   North Middlesex (North Middlesex Family History Society), Vol.1,
      1978/9 +

E.   Museums with Local Studies Collections

Bruce Castle Museum, Lordship Lane, Tottenham,
London N17 8NU. Tel: (081) 808 8772.

HARROW

A.   Local Studies Libraries and Collections

Local History Collection, Civic Centre Library, PO Box 4,
Station Road, Harrow, Middlesex HA1 2UU.
Tel: (081) 863 5611 ext.2055.

B.   Local Record Office

Local History Collection, Civic Centre Library, PO Box 4,
Station Road, Harrow, Middlesex HA1 2UU.
Tel: (081) 863 5611 ext.2055.

C.   Local History Societies

1.   Central Middlesex Family History Society, 155 Harrow View,
Harrow, Middlesex HA1 4SX.
2.   Pinner Local History Society, 24 Melrose Road, Pinner,
Middlesex (Sec.).
3.   Roxeth Local History Society, 171 Arundel Drive, South Harrow,
Middlesex HA2 8PW (Chairperson).
4.   Stanmore and Harrow Historical Society, 4 Whitefriars Drive,
Harrow, Middlesex HA3 5HN.

D.   Local History Journals

1.   Greentrees (Central Middlesex Family History Society), 1978 +
2.   The Pinn, No.1, 1983 +
3.   Roxeth Local History Society Newsletter.
4.   Stanmore and Harrow Historical Society Newsletter.

E.   Museums with Local Studies Collections

Harrow Museum and Heritage Centre, Headstone Manor
Recreation Ground, Pinner View, Harrow, Middlesex HA2 6PX.
Tel: (081) 861 2626.

HAVERING
(Hornchurch, Romford, formerly part of the old county of Essex)

A.   Local Studies Libraries and Collections

Havering Public Libraries Local History Collection, Central
Reference Library, St Edward's Way, Romford, Essex RM1 3AR.
Tel: (0708) 46040 ext.3169/3174.

B.   Local Record Office

Havering Public Libraries Local History Collection, Central
Reference Library, St Edward's Way, Romford, Essex RM1 3AR.
Tel: (0708) 46040 ext.3169/3174.

C.   Local History Societies

1.   East of London Family History Society, 178 Burrage Road,
      Plumstead, London SE18 (Sec.).
2.   Essex Society for Family History, The Cottage, Boyton Cross,
      Roxwell, Chelmsford, Essex CM1 4LP (Sec.).
3.   Hornchurch and District Historical Society, Little Silvers,
      7 Mendoza Close, Hornchurch, Essex RM11 2RP.
4.   Romford and District Historical Society, 14 Thames Close,
      Rainham, Essex RM13 9HP (Sec.).

D.   Local History Journals

1.   Cockney Ancestor (East of London Family History Society),
      1978 +
2.   Essex Family Historian.
3.   Hornchurch and District Historical Society Journal and
      Newsletter.
4.   Romford Record, No.1, 1969 +

E.   Museums with Local Studies Collections

Upminster Tithe Barn Agricultural and Folk Museum, Hall Lane, Upminster.

HILLINGDON
(Hayes and Harlington, Ruislip-Northwood, Yiewsley and West Drayton, Uxbridge)

A.   Local Studies Libraries and Collections

> Hillingdon Local Studies Department (b), Central Library,
> High Street, Uxbridge, Middlesex UB8 1HD. Tel: (0895) 50600.

B.   Local Record Office

> Hillingdon Local Studies Department, Central Library, High Street,
> Uxbridge, Middlesex UB8 1HD. Tel: (0895) 50600.

C.   Local History Societies

1.   Central Middlesex Family History Society, 155 Harrow View, Harrow, Middlesex HA1 4SX (Sec.).
2.   Harefield History Society, Hillside, Park Lane, Harefield, Middlesex (Sec.).
3.   Hayes and Harlington Local History Society, 60 Park Lane, Hayes, Middlesex (Sec.).
4.   Ruislip, Northwood and Eastcote Local History Society, 7 The Greenway, Ickenham, Middlesex (Sec.).
5.   Uxbridge Local History and Archives, 29 Norton Road, Uxbridge, Middlesex (Sec.).
6.   West Drayton and District Local History Society, 36 Church Road, West Drayton, Middlesex (Sec.).
7.   West Middlesex Family History Society, 17 Croft Gardens, Ruislip, Middlesex HA4 8EY (Sec.).

D.   Local History Journals

1.   Greentrees (Central Middlesex Family History Society), 1978 +
2.   Harefield History Society Newsletter.
3.   Hayes and Harlington Local History Society Newsletter, 1970 +
4.   Ruislip, Northwood and Eastcote Local History Society Journal,
       1965 +
5.   Uxbridge Record, 1963 +
6.   West Drayton and District Historian, 1959 +
7.   West Middlesex Family History Society Journal.

HOUNSLOW
(Brentford and Chiswick, Heston and Isleworth, Feltham)

A.   Local Studies Libraries and Collections

Chiswick Public Library (b), Duke's Avenue, Chiswick,
London W4 2AB. Tel: (081) 994 5295.

Feltham Public Library (a), 210 The Centre, Feltham,
Middlesex TW13 6AW.

Hounslow Library Centre (b), 24 Treaty Centre, High Street,
Hounslow TW3 1ES. Tel: (081) 570 9622 ext.296.

B.   Local Record Offices

1.   Chiswick Public Library, Duke's Avenue, Chiswick,
London W4 2AB. Tel: (081) 994 5295.
2.   Hounslow Library Centre, 24 Treaty Centre, High Street,
Hounslow TW3 1ES. Tel: (081) 570 9622 ext.296.

C.   Local History Societies

1.   Brentford and Chiswick Local History Society,
6 Hartington Court, Hartington Road, Chiswick, London W4
(Sec.).
2.   Hounslow and District History Society, Albertine,
Manor House Court, Shepperton, Middlesex (Sec.).
3.   West Middlesex Family History Society, 17 Croft Gardens,
Ruislip, Middlesex HA4 8EY (Sec.).

D.   Local History Journals

1.   Brentford and Chiswick Local History Society Journal, 1980 +
2.   Honeslaw Chronicle, 1978-
3.   West Middlesex Family History Society Journal.

ISLINGTON
(Islington, Finsbury)

A.   Local Studies Libraries and Collections

Finsbury Library Local Collection (Islington Public Libraries),
245 St John Street, London EC1V 4NB. Tel: (071) 609 3051
ext.266 or (071) 278 7343 ext.25.

Islington Collection, Central Reference Library, 2 Fieldway
Crescent, Holloway Road, London N5 1PF. Tel: (071) 609 3051
ext.216/217.

B.   Local Record Offices

1.   Finsbury Library Local Collection (Islington Public Libraries),
245 St John Street, London EC1V 4NB. Tel: (071) 609 3051
ext.266 or (071) 278 7343 ext.25.
2.   Islington Collection, Central Reference Library,
2 Fieldway Crescent, Holloway Road, London N5 1PF.
Tel: (071) 609 3051 ext.216/217.

C.   Local History Societies

1.   Islington Archaeology and History Society,
127 Camberwell Road, London SE5 0HB (Sec.).
2.   Islington Local History Education Trust, 186 Goswell Road,
London EC4 7DT.
3.   North Middlesex Family History Society, 6 Milton Court,
83/87 Hoe Street, Walthamstow, London E17 4SA (Sec.).

D.   Local History Journals

1.   Illustrated Islington History Journal, 1985 +
2.   Islington Archaeology and History Society Newsletter.
3.   North Middlesex (North Middlesex Family History Society),
       Vol.1, 1978/9 +

KENSINGTON AND CHELSEA

A.   Local Studies Libraries and Collections

Chelsea Local Studies Collection, Reference Library, Old Town Hall, King's Road, Chelsea, London SW3 5EZ. Tel: (071) 352 2004 and 6056.

Kensington Local Studies Collection, Central Library, Phillimore Walk, Kensington W8 7RX. Tel: (071) 937 2542/8.

B.   Local Record Offices

1.   Chelsea Local Studies Collection, Reference Library, Old Town Hall, King's Road, Chelsea, London SW3 5EZ. Tel: (071) 352 2004 and 6056.
2.   Kensington Local Studies Collection, Central Library, Phillimore Walk, Kensington W8 7RX. Tel: (071) 937 2542/8.

C.   Local History Societies

1.   Chelsea Society, 39 Old Church Street, London SW3 5BS (Chairperson).
2.   Kensington Society, 18 Kensington Square, London W8 (Sec.).
2.   West Middlesex Family History Society, 17 Croft Gardens, Ruislip, Middlesex HA4 8EY.

D.   Local History Journals

West Middlesex Family History Society Journal.

KINGSTON UPON THAMES
(Kingston, Malden and Coombe, Surbiton, formerly part of the old county
of Surrey)

A.   Local Studies Libraries and Collections

Kingston upon Thames Local History Collection (b), Museum and
Heritage Centre, Wheatfield Way, Kingston upon Thames,
Surrey KT1 2PS. Tel: (081) 546 5386.

B.   Local Record Offices

Royal Borough of Kingston upon Thames Archives,
c/o Surrey Record Office, County Hall, Penrhyn Road,
Kingston upon Thames KT1 2DN. Tel: (081) 541 9064,9065.

C.   Local History Societies

1.   East Surrey Family History Society, 15 Apeldoorn Drive,
     Wallington, Surrey SM6 9LE (Sec.).
2.   Kingston upon Thames Archaeological Society,
     295 West Barnes Lane, New Maldon, Surrey (Sec.).
3.   Surbiton Historical Society, 79 Hamilton Avenue, Tolworth,
     Surbiton, Surrey (Sec.).
4.   West Surrey Family History Society, Bradstone Garden Cottage,
     Christmas Hill, Shalford, Surrey GU4 8HR.

D.   Local History Journals

1.   East Surrey Family History Society Journal, Vol.1, 1977 +
2.   Kingston upon Thames Archaeological Society Newsletter.
3.   Root and Branch (West Surrey Family History Society), Vol.1,
     1974 +

E.   Museums with Local Studies Collections

Kingston upon Thames Museum and Heritage Centre, Wheatfield
Way, Kingston upon Thames, Surrey KT1 2PS.
Tel: (081) 546 5386.

LAMBETH
(Lambeth, Streatham, Clapham)

A.   Local Studies Libraries and Collections

Lambeth Archives Department, Minet Library (b), 52 Knatchbull
Road, Myatt's Field, London SE5 9QY. Tel: (071) 733 3279.

Local Studies Collection (a), Lambeth Reference Library,
Tate Library Brixton, Brixton Oval, London SW2 1JQ.
Tel: (071) 274 7451.

B.   Local Record Office

Lambeth Archives Department, Minet Library, 52 Knatchbull Road,
Myatt's Field, London SE5 9QY. Tel: (071) 733 3279.

C.   Local History Societies

1.   Brixton Society, 82 Mayall Road, London SE24 0PJ (Sec.).
2.   Clapham Antiquarian Society, 58 Crescent Lane,
      London SW4 9PU (Sec.).
3.   East Surrey Family History Society, 15 Apeldoorn Drive,
      Wallington, Surrey SM6 9LE (Sec.).
4.   Southwark and Lambeth Archaeological Society,
      79 Ashridge Crescent, Shooters Hill, London SE18 (Sec.).
5.   West Surrey Family History Society, Bradstone Garden Cottage,
      Christmas Hill, Shalford, Surrey GU4 8HR (Sec.).

D.   Local History Journals

1.   Brixton Society Newsletter.
2.   Clapham Antiquarian Society Newsletter.
3.   East Surrey Family History Society Journal, No.1, 1977 +
4.   The Pump (Streatham Society).
5.   Root and Branch (West Surrey Family History Society), No.1,
      1974 +

LEWISHAM
(Lewisham, Deptford)

A.   Local Studies Libraries and Collections

Lewisham Local History Centre, The Manor House, Old Road, Lee,
London SE13 5SY. Tel: (081) 852 5050 or 7087.

B.   Local Record Office

Lewisham Local History Centre, The Manor House, Old Road, Lee,
London SE13 5SY. Tel: (081) 852 5050 or 7087.

C.   Local History Societies

1.   Greenwich and Lewisham Antiquarian Society,
128 Evelyn Street, London SE8 5DD (Sec.).
2.   Lewisham Local History Society, c/o C.W.Harrison, Lewisham
Local History Centre, The Manor House, Old Road, Lee,
London SE13 5SY.
3.   Woolwich and District Family History Society, 4 Church Road,
Bexleyheath, Kent DA7 4DA.

D.   Local History Journals

1.   Greenwich and Lewisham Antiquarian Society Transactions,
1907 +
2.   Lewisham Local History Society Transactions.
3.   Woolwich and District Family History Society Journal.

MERTON
(Merton and Morden, Mitcham, Wimbledon, formerly part of the old county of Surrey)

A.   Local Studies Libraries and Collections

Local Collection, Mitcham Library, London Road, Mitcham, Surrey CR4 2YR. Tel: (081) 648 4070/6516.
Covers the old parish and pre-1965 Borough of Mitcham.

Local Collection, Morden Library, Crown House, London Road, Morden, Surrey SM4 5DX. Tel: (081) 545 3790.
Covers the old parishes and pre-1965 urban districts of Merton and Morden.

Local History and English Topography Collection, Wimbledon Library, Wimbledon Hill Road, London SW19 7NB.
Tel: (081) 946 7979/7432.
Covers the old parish and pre-1965 Borough of Wimbledon.

B.   Local Record Office

Central Reference Library, Wimbledon Hill Road, London SW19 7NB. Tel: (081) 946 1136.

C.   Local History Societies

1.   East Surrey Family History Society, 15 Apeldoorn Drive, Wallington, Surrey SM6 9LE (Sec.).
2.   Merton Historical Society, 53 Manor Way, Mitcham, Surrey CR4 1EG (Sec.).
3.   Wimbledon Society, Aston Grays, Arterberry Road, London SW20 8AJ (Sec.).

D.   Local History Journals

    1.   East Surrey Family History Society Journal, No.1, 1977 +
    2.   Merton Historical Society Bulletin.
    3.   Wimbledon Society Newsletter.

E.   Museums with Local Studies Collections

        Wimbledon Society Local History Museum, 26 Lingfield Road,
        Wimbledon, London SW19.

NEWHAM
(East and West Ham, Barking, formerly part of the old county of Essex;
Woolwich north of the Thames)

A.   Local Studies Libraries and Collections

Local Studies Library (b), Newham Public Libraries, Stratford
Reference Library, Water Lane, Romford Road, Stratford E15 4NJ.
Tel: (081) 534 4545 ext.25662; evenings and weekends:
534 1305; direct line: 519 6346.

B.   Local Record Office

Local Studies Library, Newham Public Libraries, Stratford
Reference Library, Water Lane, Romford Road, Stratford E15 4NJ.
Tel: (081) 534 4545 ext.25662; evenings and weekends:
534 1305; direct line: 519 6346.

C.   Local History Societies

1.   Docklands History Group, c/o Museum in Docklands Project,
     Museum of London, London Wall, London EC27 5HN.
2.   East London History Society, 20 Brownfield Street,
     London E14 6NE (Sec.).
3.   East of London Family History Society, 178 Burrage Road,
     Plumstead, London SE18 (Sec.).
4.   Newham History Society, 16 Crownfield Avenue, Newbury Park,
     Ilford, Essex IG2 7RR.

D.   Local History Journals

1.   Cockney Ancestor (East of London Family History Society),
     1978 +
2.   East London Record, No.1, 1978 +
3.   Newham History Society Newsletter, 1988 +

E.   Museums with Local Studies Collections

Passmore Edwards Museum, Romford Road, London E15 4LZ.
Tel: (081) 534 4545.

REDBRIDGE
(Ilford, Wanstead and Woodford, small parts of Dagenham and Chigwell, formerly part of the old county of Essex)

A.   Local Studies Libraries and Collections

Local History Room, Redbridge Central Library, Clements Road, Ilford IG1 1EA. Tel: (081) 478 7145.

B.   Local Record Office

Local History Room, Redbridge Central Library, Clements Road, Ilford IG1 1EA. Tel: (081) 478 7145.

C.   Local History Societies

1.   East of London Family History Society, 178 Burrage Road, Plumstead, London SE18 (Sec.).
2.   Ilford and District Historical Society, c/o Central Reference Library, Clements Road, Ilford IG1 1EA.
3.   Seven Kings and Goodmayes Historical Society, 55 Castleton Road, Goodmayes, Ilford, Essex (Sec.).
4.   Wanstead Historical Society, 5 Lorne Gardens, Wanstead, London E11 2BZ (Sec.).
5.   Woodford Historical Society, 39 Smeaton Road, Woodford Bridge, Essex IG8 8BD (Sec.).

D.   Local History Journals

1.   Cockney Ancestor (East of London Family History Society), 1978 +
2.   Woodford Historical Society Transactions.

RICHMOND
(Twickenham; Richmond and Barnes, formerly part of the old county of Surrey)

A. Local Studies Libraries and Collections

Richmond Local Studies Library (b), Old Town Hall,
Whittaker Avenue, Richmond, Surrey TW9 1TP.
Tel: (081) 940 5529 ext.32.

Twickenham Local Studies Library (b), Garfield Road,
Twickenham, Middlesex TW9 3JS. Tel: (081) 891 7271.

B. Local Record Office

1. Richmond Local Studies Library, Old Town Hall,
Whittaker Avenue, Richmond, Surrey TW9 1TP.
Tel: (081) 940 5529 ext.32.
2. Twickenham Local Studies Library, Garfield Road,
Twickenham, Middlesex TW9 3JS. Tel: (081) 891 7271.

C. Local History Societies

1. Barnes and Mortlake History Society, 28 Derby Road,
East Sheen, London SW14 7DP (Sec.)
2. Borough of Twickenham Local History Society,
14a Enmore Gardens, East Sheen, London SW14 (Sec.).
3. Richmond Local History Society, 9 Bridge Road, St Margarets,
East Twickenham (Sec.).
4. West Middlesex Family History Society, 17 Croft Gardens,
Ruislip, Middlesex HA4 8EY (Sec.).

D.   Local History Journals

1.   Borough of Twickenham Local History Society Newsletter.
2.   Richmond History, 1981 +
3.   West Middlesex Family History Society Journal.

E.   Museums with Local Studies Collections

Museum of Richmond, Old Town Hall, Whitakker Avenue,
Richmond, Surrey TW9 1TP. Tel: (081) 332 1141.

SOUTHWARK
(Bermondsey, Camberwell, Southwark)

A.   Local Studies Libraries and Collections

Southwark Local Studies Library, 211 Borough High Street,
London SE1 1JA. Tel: (071) 403 3507.

B.   Local Record Office

Southwark Local Studies Library, 211 Borough High Street,
London SE1 1JA. Tel: (071) 403 3507.

C.   Local History Societies

1.   Dulwich Society, 30 Walkerscroft Road, London SE21 8LJ
(Sec.).
2.   East Surrey Family History Society, 15 Apeldoorn Drive,
Wallington, Surrey SM6 9LE (Sec.).
3.   Southwark and Lambeth Archaeological Society,
79 Ashridge Crescent, Shooters Hill, London SE18 (Sec.).

D.   Local History Journals

1.   East Surrey Family History Society Journal, No.1, 1977 +
2.   Southwark and Lambeth Archaeological Society Newsletter.

E.   Museums with Local Studies Collections

1.   The Cuming Museum, 155-157 Walworth Road,
London SE17 1RS. Tel: (071) 703 3324/5529.
2.   Livesey Museum, 682 Old Kent Road, London SE15 1JF.
Tel: (071) 639 5604.

SUTTON
(Beddington and Wallington, Sutton and Cheam, Carshalton, formerly part
of the old county of Surrey)

A.   Local Studies Libraries and Collections

> Sutton Libraries and Arts Services Local History Collection,
> Central Library, St Nicholas Way, Sutton, Surrey SM1 1EA.
> Tel: (081) 661 5050.

770-4700 LIBRARY   770-4785 1G/ Bookings
770-4782 HERITAGE

B.   Local Record Office

> Sutton Libraries and Arts Services Local History Collection,
> Central Library, St Nicholas Way, Sutton, Surrey SM1 1EA.
> Tel: (081) 661 5050.

C.   Local History Societies

1.   Beddington, Carshalton and Wallington Archaeological Society,
      57 Brambledown Road, Wallington, Surrey SM6 0TF (Sec.).
2.   East Surrey Family History Society, 15 Apeldoorn Drive,
      Wallington, Surrey SM6 9LE (Sec.).
3.   Nonsuch Antiquarian Society, 37 Seymour Avenue, Ewell,
      Surrey KT17 2RS (Sec.).
3.   Sutton Archaeology and Local History Liaison Group,
      29a Benhill Wood Road, Sutton, Surrey (Sec.).

D.   Local History Journals

1.   Beddington, Carshalton and Wallington Archaeological Society
      Newsletter.
2.   East Surrey Family History Society Journal, No.1, 1977 +

E.   Museums with Local Studies Collections

Whitehall, 1 Maldon Road, Cheam, Sutton, Surrey SM3 8QD.
Tel: (081) 643 1236.

TOWER HAMLETS
(Bethnal Green, Poplar, Stepney)

A.   Local Studies Libraries and Collections

Local History Library and Archives (b), Bancroft Library,
277 Bancroft Road, Mile End, London E1 4DQ.

B.   Local Record Office

Local History Library and Archives, Bancroft Library,
277 Bancroft Road, Mile End, London E1 4DQ.

C.   Local History Societies

1.   East London History Society, 20 Brownfield Street,
London E14 6NE (Sec.).
2.   East of London Family History Society, 178 Burrage Road,
Plumstead, London SE18 (Sec.).
3.   Island History Trust (Isle of Dogs), Island House,
4 Roserton Street, London E14 9PG.

D.   Local History Journals

1.   Cockney Ancestor (East of London Family History Society),
1978 +
2.   East London Papers, Nos.1-5, 1958-73.
3.   East London Record, No.1, 1978 +
4.   Island History Newsletter, No.1, 1983 +

E.   Museums with Local Studies Collections

    1.   London Museum of Jewish Life and Research Centre,
        80 East End Road, N3 2SY. Tel: (081) 346 2288.
        History of the Jewish East End.
    2.   Ragged School Museum Trust, 46-48 Copperfield Road, Bow,
        London E3 4RR.
        *History of Dr Barnardo's Free Ragged Schools, and of East End
        families and businesses.*

WALTHAM FOREST
(Chingford, Leyton, Walthamstow, formerly part of the old county of Essex)

A.   Local Studies Libraries and Collections

>   Local History Library, Vestry House Museum, Vestry Road,
>   Walthamstow, London E17 9NH. Tel(081) 527 5544 ext.4391 or
>   509 1917.

B.   Local Record Office

>   Waltham Forest Archives, Vestry House Museum, Vestry Road,
>   Walthamstow, London E17 9NH. Tel: (081) 509 1917 or
>   527 5544 ext.4391.

C.   Local History Societies

1.   East of London Family History Society, 178 Burrage Road,
      Plumstead, London SE18 (Sec.).
2.   Essex Society for Family History, The Cottage, Boyton Cross,
      Roxwell, Chelmsford, Essex CM1 4LP (Sec.).
3.   Chingford Historical Society, 112 Whitehall Road, Chingford
      (Sec.).
4.   Waltham Forest Family History Society, 1 Gelsthorpe Road,
      Romford, Essex RM5 2NB (Sec.).
5.   Walthamstow Historical (previously Antiquarian) Society,
      c/o Vestry House Museum, Vestry Road, Walthamstow,
      London E17 9NH.

D.   Local History Journals

1.   Cockney Ancestor (East of London Family History Society),
      1978 +
2.   Chingford Notes, 1974 +
3.   Essex Family Historian.
4.   Walthamstow Historical Society Newsletter.

E.   Museums with Local Studies Collections

1.   Epping Forest Museum and Queen Elizabeth's Hunting Lodge, Rangers Road, Chingford, London E4 7QH. Tel: (081) 529 6681. *History and natural history of Epping Forest.*

2.   Vestry House Museum, Vestry Road, Walthamstow, London E17 9NH. Tel: (081) 527 5544 ext.4391. *Local history of the Waltham Forest area.*

WANDSWORTH
(Battersea, Wandsworth (without Clapham, now in Lambeth)

A.   Local Studies Libraries and Collections

   Archives and Local History Collection (b),
   Battersea Reference Library, 265 Lavender Hill,
   London SW11 1JB. Tel: (081) 871 7467.

B.   Local Record Office

   Archives and Local History Collection, Battersea Reference
   Library, 265 Lavender Hill, London SW11 1JB. Tel: (081) 871 7467.

C.   Local History Societies

   1.   East Surrey Family History Society, 15 Apeldoorn Drive,
         Wallington, Surrey SM6 9LE (Sec.).
   2.   Wandsworth Historical Society, c/o Wandsworth Museum,
         Putney Library, Disraeli Road, London SW15.
   3.   West Surrey Family History Society, Bradstone Garden Cottage,
         Christmas Hill, Shalford, Surrey GU4 8HR (Sec.).

D.   Local History Journals

   1.   East Surrey Family History Society Journal, No.1, 1977+
   2.   Root and Branch (West Surrey Family History Society),
         No.1, 1974 +
   3.   Wandsworth Historian, 1971 +

E.   Museums with Local Studies Collections

   Wandsworth Museum, Putney Library, Disraeli Road,
   London SW15. Tel: (081) 871 7074.

WESTMINSTER

A.   Local Studies Libraries and Collections

Archives and Local Studies Section, Marylebone Library,
Marylebone Road, London NW1 5PS. Tel: (071) 798 1030.
Covers former Boroughs of Paddington and St Marylebone.
Includes Ashbridge Collection of maps, drawings, watercolours,
engravings and cuttings relating to Marylebone.

Archives and Local Studies Section, Victoria Library,
160 Buckingham Palace Road, London SW1W 9UD.
Tel: (071) 798 2180.
Covers pre-1965 City of Westminster area.

B.   Local Record Offices

1.   Archives and Local Studies Section, Marylebone Library,
Marylebone Road, London NW1 5PS. Tel: (071) 798 1030.
2.   Archives and Local Studies Section, Victoria Library,
160 Buckingham Palace Road, London SW1W 9UD.
Tel: (071) 798 2180.

C.   Local Studies Societies

1.   Central Middlesex Family History Society, 155 Harrow View,
Harrow, Middlesex HA1 4SX (Sec.).
2.   Paddington Society, 30 Westbourne Park Villas,
London W2 5EA (Sec.).
3.   St Marylebone Society, 14 Roxborough Park, Harrow-on-the-Hill,
Middlesex HA1 3BE (Sec.).
4.   Westminster South Local History Society, The Flat,
Royal Horticultural Hall, Greycoat Street, London SW1 (Sec.).

D.   Local History Journals

1.   Greentrees (Central Middlesex Family History Society), 1978 +
2.   Paddington Society Newsletter, 1957+
3.   St Marylebone Society Newsletter, 1948 +
4.   Westminster South Local History Society Newsletter.

MERSEYSIDE

See CHESHIRE
     LANCASHIRE

NORFOLK: old county

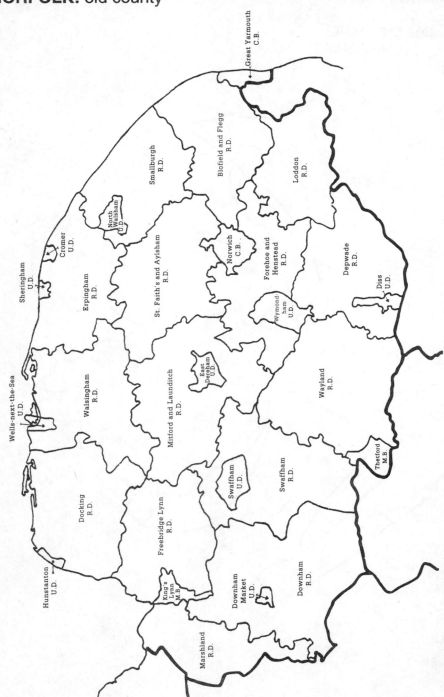

Great Yarmouth C.B.

Smallburgh R.D.

Blofield and Flegg R.D.

Loddon R.D.

North Walsham U.D.

Cromer U.D.

Sheringham U.D.

Norwich C.B.

Forehoe and Henstead R.D.

Depwade R.D.

Erpingham R.D.

St. Faith's and Aylsham R.D.

Diss U.D.

Wymond-ham U.D.

Wells-next-the-Sea U.D.

Walsingham R.D.

East Dereham U.D.

Mitford and Launditch R.D.

Wayland R.D.

Thetford M.B.

Swaffham U.D.

Swaffham R.D.

Docking R.D.

Freebridge Lynn R.D.

Hunstanton U.D.

King's Lynn M.B.

Downham Market U.D.

Downham R.D.

Marshland R.D.

NORFOLK: new county

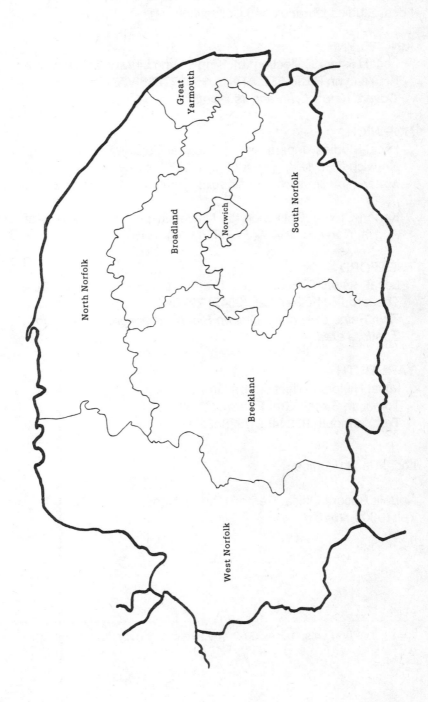

NORFOLK

A.   Local Studies Libraries and Collections

KING'S LYNN
Local History Collection (b), King's Lynn Library, London Road,
King's Lynn PE30 5EZ. Tel: (0553) 772568/761393.
Covers King's Lynn and its vicinity.

NORWICH
Local Studies Department (c), Central Library, Bethel Street,
Norwich NR2 1NJ. Tel: (0603) 611277 ext.29.
Material on Norwich and Norfolk; general collection on East Anglia.

Ketton-Cremer Collection (a), University Library, University of East
Anglia, Norwich NR4 7TJ. Tel: (0603) 56161.

THETFORD
Local History Collection (a), Thetford Library, Raymond Street,
Thetford IP24 2EA. Tel: (0842) 752048.
*Tom Paine Collection, Duleep Singh Collection, material on
Thetford area.*

YARMOUTH
Local History Collection (b), Great Yarmouth Central Library,
Tolhouse Street, Great Yarmouth NR30 2SH.
Tel: Yarmouth 92844551/92842279.

B.   Local Record Office

Norfolk Record Office, Central Library, Norwich NR2 1NJ.
Tel: (0603) 761349.

---

a = under 2000 vols; b = 2000-20,000 vols; c = over 20,000 vols.

C.   Local History Societies

1.   Norfolk and Norwich Archaeological Society, Garsett House,
       St Andrews Hall Plain, Norwich NR3 1AT.
2.   Norfolk and Norwich Genealogical Society, The Whins,
       Chapel Road, Sea Palling, Norwich NR12 0UQ.
3.   Norfolk Industrial Archaeological Society, c/o The Bridewell
       Museum, Norwich NR2 1AQ.
4.   Norfolk Record Society, 425 Unthank Road, Norwich NR4 7QB
       (Sec.).
5.   West Norfolk and King's Lynn Archaeological Society,
       The Willows, 28 Low Road, Congham, King's Lynn PE32 1AE
       (Sec.).

D.   Local History Journals

1.   Norfolk and Norwich Naturalists' Society Transactions, Vol.1,
       1869 +
2.   Norfolk Archaeology, Vol.1, 1847 +
3.   Norfolk Record Society Publications, No.1, 1931 +

E.   Museums with Local Studies Collections

1.   Cromer Museum, East Cottages, Tucker Street, Cromer,
       Norfolk NR27 9HB. Tel: (0263) 513543.
2.   Great Yarmouth: Elizabethan House Museum, 4 South Quay,
       Great Yarmouth, Norfolk NR30 2QH. Tel: (0493) 855746.
       Social and domestic life of the area.
3.   Great Yarmouth: Maritime Museum for East Anglia,
       Marine Parade, Great Yarmouth, Norfolk NR30 2EN.
       Tel: (0493) 842267.
       Maritime history of Norfolk, including the Broads.
4.   Great Yarmouth: Tolhouse Museum, Tolhouse Street,
       Great Yarmouth, Norfolk NR30 2SQ.
       Roman and medieval history of the area.
5.   Iceni Village and Museums, Cockley Cley, nr Swaffham,
       Norfolk PE37 8AG. Tel: (0760) 721339.
       Includes a museum of East Anglian life.

6. King's Lynn: Lynn Museum, Market Street, King's Lynn,
    Norfolk PE30 1NL. Tel: (0553) 775001.
    *King's Lynn Photographic Survey 1900-1913. Sites and
    Monuments Record for West Norfolk.*
7. King's Lynn: Museum of Social History, 27 King's Street,
    King's Lynn, Norfolk PE30 1HA. Tel: (0553) 775004.
    Covers West Norfolk.
8. Norfolk Rural Life Museum, Beech House, Gressenhall,
    Dereham, Norfolk NR20 4DR. Tel: (0362) 860563.
9. Norwich: Bridewell Museum of Norwich Trades and Industries,
    Bridewell Alley, St Andrew's Street, Norwich NR2 1AQ.
    Tel: (0603) 667229.
    Textile industry pattern books, brass rubbings collection.
10. Norwich Castle Museum, Norwich NR1 3JU.
    Tel: (0603) 611277.
    *Natural and social history, archaeology of Norfolk. Natural
    history and archaeology information held on computer.*
11. Norwich: Strangers Hall Museum, Charing Cross,
    Norwich NR2 4AL. Tel: (0603) 667229.
    Domestic life and costume in Norwich from medieval times.
12. Thetford: Ancient House Museum, 21 White Hart Street,
    Thetford, Norfolk IP24 1AA. Tel: (0842) 2599.
    History of Thetford and the Breckland region.

NORTH YORKSHIRE

See YORKSHIRE (East, North, West Ridings)

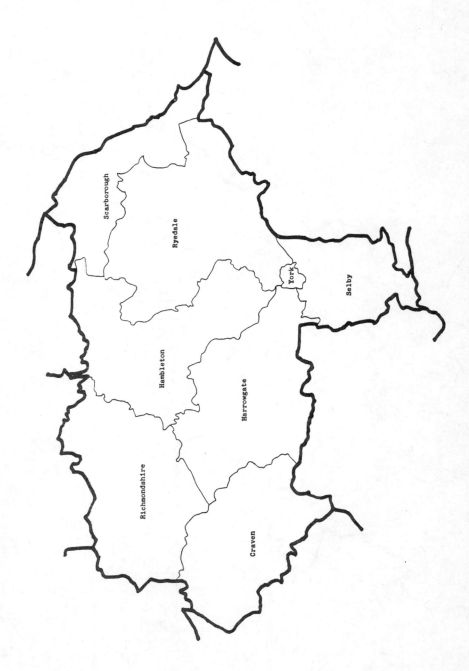

NORTHAMPTONSHIRE AND SOKE OF PETERBOROUGH: old county

NORTHAMPTONSHIRE AND SOKE OF PETERBOROUGH: new county (for Soke of Peterborough after 1974, see CAMBRIDGESHIRE)

NORTHAMPTONSHIRE AND SOKE OF PETERBOROUGH

A.   Local Studies Libraries and Collections

CORBY
Local History Collection, Corby Library, 9 Queen's Square, Corby, Northants. Tel: (05366) 3304.

KETTERING
Local History Collection, Kettering Library, Sheep Street, Kettering, Northants. Tel: (0536) 2315.

NORTHAMPTON
Local History Collection (c), Central Library, Abington Street, Northampton NN1 2BA. Tel: (0604) 33628.
Special collections on John Clare, Charles Bradlaugh, Beeky Thompson Geological Collection; Sir Henry Dryden Architectural Collection.

Nene College Library, Moulton Park, Northampton NN2 7AL.

PETERBOROUGH
Local Studies Collection (b), Central Library, Broadway, Peterborough PE1 1R.

Museum Society Library, Priestgate, Peterborough, Cambridgeshire PE1 1LF. Tel: (0733) 43329.

WELLINGBOROUGH
Local History Collection, Wellingborough Library, Pebble Lane, Wellingborough, Northants. Tel: (0933) 225365.

---

a = under 2000 vols; b = 2000-20,000 vols; c = over 20,000 vols.

B.   Local Record Offices

Northamptonshire Record Office, Delapre Abbey, London Road,
Northampton NN4 9AW. Tel: (0604) 762129.

For post-1965 records for Peterborough:
Cambridgeshire Record Office, Grammar School Walk,
Huntingdon PE18 6LF. Tel: (0480) 425842.

C.   Local History Societies

1.   Northamptonshire Archaeological Society, c/o Central Museum,
      Guildhall Road, Northampton NN1 1DP.
2.   Northamptonshire Family History Society, 11 Wycliffe Road,
      Abington, Northants NN1 5JQ (Sec.)
3.   Northamptonshire Industrial Archaeology Group,
      34 The Crescent, Northampton NN1 4SB (Sec.).
4.   Northamptonshire Natural History Society and Field Club
      (Archaeology Section), 160 The Headland,
      Northampton NN3 2NY (Sec.)
5.   Northamptonshire Record Society, Delapre Abbey,
      Northampton NN4 9AW.
6.   Peterborough and District Family History Society,
      44 The Steynings, Werrington, Peterborough PE4 6QL.

D.   Local History Journals

1.   Northamptonshire Archaeological Society Reports and
      Papers,Nos.1-5,1844-48; Nos.1-42, 1850-1935 (*in Reports and
      Papers of the Associated Architectural Societies*); Nos.43-62,
      1935/6-1975.
2.   Northamptonshire Archaeology (*formerly Bulletin of the
      Northamptonshire Federation of Archaeological Societies*), Vol.1,
      1966 +
3.   Northamptonshire Natural History Society and Field Club
      Journal, 1880 +

4.   Northamptonshire Past and Present, Vol.1, 1948 +
5.   Northamptonshire Record Society Publications, No.1, 1924 +
6.   Peterborough's Past, Nos.1-3, 1983-88.

E.   Museums with Local Studies Collections

1.   East Carlton: Industrial Heritage Centre, East Carlton
      Countryside Park, East Carlton, Market Harborough,
      Leics LE16 8YD. Tel: (0536) 770977.
      History of the Northamptonshire iron industry.
2.   Kettering: Westfield Museum, West Street, Kettering, Northants.
      History of the Kettering area.
3.   Naseby Battle and Farm Museum, Purlieu Farm, Naseby,
      Northants NN6 7DD. Tel: (0604) 740241.
      History of the Battle of Naseby, and social history and
      occupations of the area.
4.   Northampton: Central Museum and Art Gallery, Guildhall Road,
      Northampton NN1 1DP. Tel: (0604) 34881 ext.391.
      Includes history of the local shoemaking industry.
5.   Peterborough Museum and Art Gallery, Priestgate,
      Peterborough, Cambridgeshire PE1 1LF. Tel: (0733) 43329.
      Sites and Monuments Records for Peterborough and environs.
6.   Wollaston Museum, 102-104 High Street, Wollaston,
      Wellingborough, Northamptonshire NN9 7QQ.

NORTHUMBERLAND: old county

NORTHUMBERLAND: new county

Berwick-upon-Tweed

Alnwick

Tynedale

Castle Morpeth

Wansbeck

Blyth
Valley

NORTHUMBERLAND

A.   Local Studies Libraries and Collections

MORPETH
Northumberland County Library Local History Collection (c),
Central Library, Morpeth, Northumberland. Tel: (0670) 512385.

NEWCASTLE UPON TYNE
Library of the Literary and Philosophical Society of Newcastle upon
Tyne, Westgate Road, Newcastle upon Tyne NE1 1SE.
Tel: (0632) 320192.

Library of the Society of Antiquaries of Newcastle upon Tyne,
The Black Gate, Newcastle upon Tyne. Tel: (0632) 27938.

Local Studies Section (c), Newcastle upon Tyne City Libraries and
Arts, Princess Square, Newcastle upon Tyne NE99 1DX.
Tel: (091) 2610619.
Bewick Collection.

NORTH SHIELDS
Local Studies Centre (b), North Tyneside Libraries, Central Library,
Northumberland Square, North Shields, Tyne and Wear
NE30 1QU. Tel: (091) 258 2811 ext.17.

B.   Local Record Offices

1.   Berwick upon Tweed Record Office, Borough Council Offices,
      Wallace Green, Berwick upon Tweed.
2.   Northumberland Record Office, Melton Park, North Gosforth,
      Newcastle upon Tyne NE3 5QX. Tel: (091) 236 2680.
3.   Tyne and Wear Archives Service, Blandford House,
      Blandford Square, Newcastle upon Tyne NE1 4JA.
      Tel: (091) 232 6789.

---

a = under 2000 vols; b = 2000-20,000 vols; c = over 20,000 vols.

C.   Local History Societies

1.   Architectural and Archaeological Society of Durham and
     Northumberland, Department of Archaeology, University of
     Durham, 46 Saddler Street, Durham DH1 3NU.
2.   Association of Northumberland Local History Societies,
     c/o Literary and Philosophical Society, Westgate Road,
     Newcastle upon Tyne NE1 1SE.
3.   Morpeth Northumbrian Gathering Committee, Westgate House,
     Dogger Bank, Morpeth, Northumberland NE61 1RF.
4.   Northumberland and Durham Family History Society,
     10 Melrose Grove, Jarrow, Tyne and Wear NE32 4HP (Sec.).
5.   Northumberland and Newcastle Society, 6 Higham Place,
     Newcastle upon Tyne.
6.   Society of Antiquaries of Newcastle upon Tyne, The Black Gate,
     Newcastle upon Tyne.
7.   Surtees Society, The Prior's Kitchen, The College,
     Durham DH1 3EQ.

D.   Local History Journals

1.   Archaeologia Aeliana, Vol.1, 1822 +
2.   Architectural and Archaeological Society of Durham and
     Northumberland Transactions, Vol.1, 1862 +
3.   Durham and Northumberland Parish Register Society
     Publications, Nos.1-36, 1898-1926.
4.   Journal of the Northumberland and Durham Family History
     Society, 1975 +
5.   Newcastle upon Tyne Records Committee Publications,
     Nos.1-12, 1920-33.
6.   Northumberland Local History Society Newsletter, Nos.1-15,
     1976-77. (*continued as Tyne and Tweed - see below*).
7.   Northumbriana, No.1, 1975 +
8.   Society of Antiquaries of Newcastle upon Tyne Proceedings,
     First Series Vol.1, 1855-5th Series Vol.1, 1956.
9.   Surtees Society Publications, Vol.1, 1835 +
10. Tyne and Tweed, 1977 +

E.   Museums with Local Studies Collections

1.   Berwick Borough Museum and Art Gallery, Berwick Barracks,
      Ravensdowne, Berwick upon Tweed, Northumberland
      TD15 1DG. Tel: (0289) 306332 ext.253.
2.   Middle March Centre for Border History, Manor Office, Hallgate,
      Hexham, Northumberland NE46 3NH.
      Tel: (0434) 604011 ext.259.
3.   Museum of Science and Engineering, Blandford House,
      West Blandford Street, Newcastle upon Tyne NE1 14JA.
      *Mechanical and electrical engineering, mining, shipbuilding,
      manufacturing industries with special reference to the North East
      and the pioneers of Tyneside industry.*
4.   Newcastle upon Tyne: John George Joicy Museum, City Road,
      Newcastle upon Tyne. Tel: (091) 2324562.
      Local history of Newcastle and the area.
5.   Woodhorn Colliery Museum, Ashington, Northumberland
      NE63 9GF. Tel: (0670) 856968.
      *Social history of Ashington, general mining history in
      Northumberland.*
6.   Wylam Railway Museum, Falcon Centre, Falcon Terrace,
      Wylam, Northumberland NE41 8EE.
      History of the local railways.

NOTTINGHAMSHIRE: old county

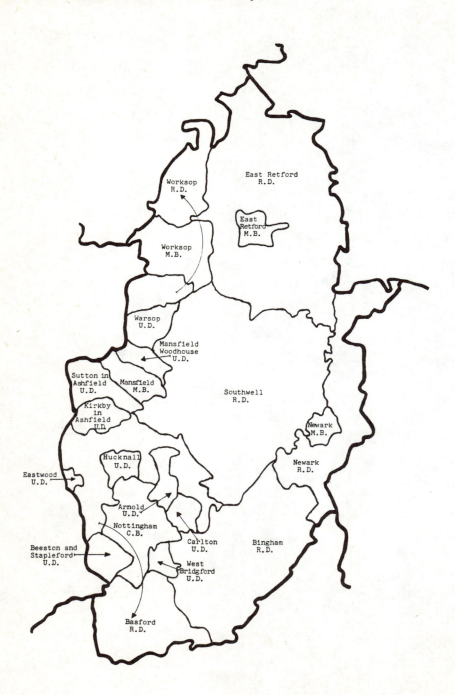

NOTTINGHAMSHIRE: new county

NOTTINGHAMSHIRE

A.   Local Studies Libraries and Collections

NOTTINGHAM
Belper Library, Nottinghamshire Record Office, County House,
High Pavement, Nottingham NG1 1HR. Tel: (0602) 54524.

East Midland Collection, University of Nottingham Library,
University Park, Nottingham NG7 2RD. Tel: (0602) 56101.

Local Studies Library (c), Nottinghamshire County Library,
Central Library, Angel Row, Nottingham, NG1 6HP.
Tel: (0602) 412121.
Also Local Studies Centres in the following 18 locations:
Arnold, Beeston, Bingham, Carlton, East Leake, Eastwood,
Hucknall, Kirby in Ashfield, Mansfield, Mansfield Woodhouse,
Newark, Ollerton, Retford, Southwell, Stapleford, Sutton in Ashfield,
West Bridgford, Worksop.

Nottingham Subscription Library Ltd., Bromley House, Angel Row,
Nottingham. Tel: (0602) 473134.

NEWARK
Newark District County Museum Library, Appletongate, Newark,
Nottingham NG24 1GY. Tel: (0636) 702358.

B.   Local Record Offices   0115 9581634
                                              ~~0115 9506524~~

1.   Nottingham Archives Office, County House, High Pavement,
      Nottingham NG1 1HR. Tel: (0602) 504524.
2.   Nottinghamshire University Library Manuscript Department,
      University Park, Nottingham NG7 2RD. Tel: (0602) 484848
      ext.3440.

---

a = under 2000 vols; b = 2000-20,000 vols; c = over 20,000 vols.

C.   Local History Societies

1.   Mansfield and District Family History Society,
      2 Millersdale Avenue, Mansfield, Notts NG18 5HS (Sec.).
2.   Nottinghamshire Family History Society, 10 Lyme Park,
      West Bridgford, Nottingham NG2 7TR.
3.   Nottinghamshire Local History Association, c/o Bromley House,
      Angel Row, Nottingham NG1 6HL.
4.   Thoroton Society of Nottinghamshire, Bromley House,
      Angel Row, Nottingham NG1 6HL.

D.   Local History Journals

1.   Nottinghamshire Historian, No.13, 1974 +
2.   Nottinghamshire Local History Association Newsletter,
      No.1, 1968 +
3.   Thoroton Society Record Series, No.1, 1903 +
4.   Thoroton Society Transactions, Vol.1, 1898 +

E.   Museums with Local Studies Collections

1.   Mansfield Museum and Art Gallery, Leeming Street, Mansfield,
      Notts NG18 1NG. Tel: (0623) 663088.
2.   Newark: Millgate Folk Museum, Millgate, Newark, Notts
      NG24 4TS. Tel: (0636) 79403.
3.   Newark Museum, Appletongate, Newark, Notts NG24 1JY.
      Tel: (0636) 702358.
      Card files of listed and other buildings and sites, and all aspects
      of town and village life (inspection by appointment only).
4.   Nottingham: Brewhouse Yard Museum, Castle Boulevard,
      Nottingham NG7 1FB. Tel: (0602) 411881 ext.48.
      Daily life in Nottingham from the 17th to the 20th centuries.
      Library of "three-dimensional" material covering social history of
      the area.
5.   Nottingham: Canal Museum, Canal Street,
      Nottingham NG1 7ET. Tel: (0602) 598835.
      History of the River Trent and its tributaries and canal system.

6.   Nottingham: Castle Museum, Nottingham NG1 6EL.
      Tel: (0602) 411881.
      History of Nottingham and district.
7.   Nottingham: The Lace Centre, Severns Buildings, Castle Road,
      Nottingham NG1 6AA. Tel: (0602) 413539.
8.   Nottingham: Lace Hall, High Pavement, Nottingham NG1 1HF.
      Tel: (0602) 484221.
9.   Nottingham Industrial Museum, Courtyard Buildings,
      Wollaston Hall, Nottingham NG8 2AE. Tel: (0602) 284602.
10.   Ruddington Village Museum, The Hermitage, Wilford Road,
      Ruddington, Notts.
      *History of Ruddington, including local archives and library. Card
      index to parish registers, and to census returns.*
11.   Worksop Museum, Worksop Public Library and Museum,
      Memorial Avenue, Worksop, Notts S80 2BP.

OXFORDSHIRE: old county

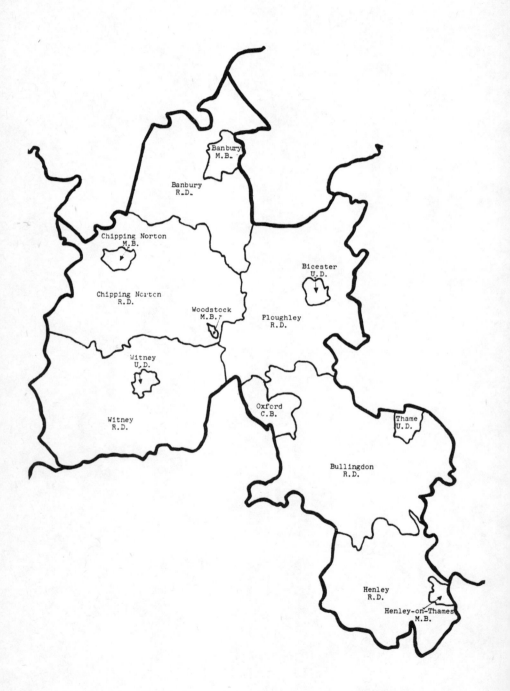

Banbury
M.B.

Banbury
R.D.

Chipping Norton
M.B.

Chipping Norton
R.D.

Bicester
U.D.

Woodstock
M.B.

Ploughley
R.D.

Witney
U.D.

Witney
R.D.

Oxford
C.B.

Thame
U.D.

Bullingdon
R.D.

Henley
R.D.

Henley-on-Thames
M.B.

OXFORDSHIRE: new county

OXFORDSHIRE

A.   Local Studies Libraries and Collections

ABINGDON
Abingdon Library (a), The Charter, Abingdon, Oxon OX14 3LJ.
Tel: (0235) 20374.
Covers local area studies and family history.

BANBURY
Banbury Library (a), Marlborough Road, Banbury, Oxon
OX16 8DF. Tel: (0295) 262282.
Covers local area studies and family history.

HENLEY
Henley Library (a), Ravenscroft Road, Henley-on-Thames,
Oxon RG9 2DH. Tel: (0491) 575278.
Covers local area studies and family history.

OXFORD
Bodleian Library, Department of Printed Books, Oxford OX1 3BG.
Tel: (0865) 277000.
*Contains the Percy Manning Collection of 19th and early 20th
century books on the city, county and university of Oxford, and the
Anthony Wood Collection of 17th century Oxford material.*

Local Studies Library (c), Central Library, Westgate,
Oxford OX1 1DJ. Tel: (0865) 815749.
Oxfordshire local studies and family history.

Oxfordshire Architectural and Historical Society Library (a),
Ashmolean Museum, Beaumont Street, Oxford OX1 2PH.
Tel: (0865) 278000.
*Small society library, open to members only, on the architecture
and local history of the county.*

---

a = under 2000 vols; b = 2000-20,000 vols; c = over 20,000 vols.

WITNEY
Witney Library (a), Welch Way, Witney, Oxon OX8 7HH.
Tel: (0993) 703659.
Covers local area studies and family history.

B. Local Record Office

Oxfordshire Archives, County Record Office, County Hall,
New Road, Oxford OX1 1ND. Tel: (0865) 815203.

C. Local History Societies

1. Oxford Historical Society, The Cottage, Boyton Cross, Roxwell, Chelmsford, Essex CM1 4LP (Sec.).
2. Oxfordshire Architectural and Historical Society, Ashmolean Museum, Beaumont Street, Oxford OX1 2PH.
3. Oxfordshire Family History Society, 10 Bellamy Close, Southmoor, Abingdon, Oxon OX13 5AB (Sec.).
4. Oxfordshire Record Society, c/o Bodleian Library, Oxford.

D. Local History Journals

1. Oxford Historical Society Publications, Nos.1-101, 1885-1936; New Series No.1, 1939 +
2. Oxfordshire Local History, Vol.1, 1980 +
3. Oxfordshire Record Society Series, No.1, 1919 +
4. Oxoniensia, Vol.1, 1936 +
5. Top Oxon, Nos.1-22, 1958-78.

E. Museums with Local Studies Collections

1. Abingdon Museum, The County Hall, Market Place, Abingdon, Oxon. Tel: (0235) 23703.
2. Banbury: Granary Museum, Butlin Farm, Claydon, Banbury, Oxon. Tel: Famborough 258.
   19th and early 20th century material on the social and business life of North Oxfordshire.

3.   Banbury Museum, 8 Horsefair, Banbury, Oxon OX16 8DF.
     Tel: (0295) 59855.
     History of the North Oxfordshire area.
4.   Bloxham Village Museum, The Court House, Bloxham, Oxon.
     Tel: Banbury 72083.
5.   Burford: Tolsey Museum, High Street, Burford, Oxon.
     History of Burford.
6.   Charlbury Museum, Corner House Community Centre,
     Market Street, Charlbury, Oxon.
7.   Chipping Norton Museum, New Street, Chipping Norton, Oxon.
     Tel: Chipping Norton 2754 and 3779.
8.   Cogges Farm Museum, Cogges, nr Witney, Oxon OX8 6LA.
     Tel: (0993) 72602.
9.   Dorchester-on-Thames: Dorchester Abbey Museum, Abbey
     Guest House, Dorchester-on-Thames, Oxon OX9 8HH.
     Tel: (0865) 340056.
10. Oxford: Museum of Oxford, St Aldate's, Oxford OX1 1DZ.
     Tel: (0865) 815559.
     History of Oxford from the earliest times to the present.
11. Oxfordshire County Museum, Fletcher's House, Woodstock,
     Oxon OX7 1SP. Tel: (0993) 40822.
     Archaeology and history of Oxfordshire.
12. Uffington: Tom Brown School Museum, Broad Street, Uffington,
     Faringdon, Oxon SN7 7RA.
     Archaeology, social and agricultural history of the Uffington area.
13. Wallingford Museum, Flint House, High Street, Wallingford,
     Oxon OX10 0DB. Tel: (0491) 35065.
14. Wantage: Champs Chapel Museum, Rosewall, Chapel Square,
     East Hendred, Wantage, Oxon OX12 8JN. Tel: (0235) 833761.
     History of the area.
15. Wantage: Vale and Downland Museum Centre,
     The Old Surgery, Church Street, Wantage, Oxon OX12 8BL.
     Tel: (02357) 66838.
     *Interpretation of the landscape and history of the Vale of the
     White Horse and Wantage town. Photographic collection.*

PETERBOROUGH, Soke of

See NORTHAMPTONSHIRE AND SOKE OF PETERBOROUGH

RUTLAND: old county

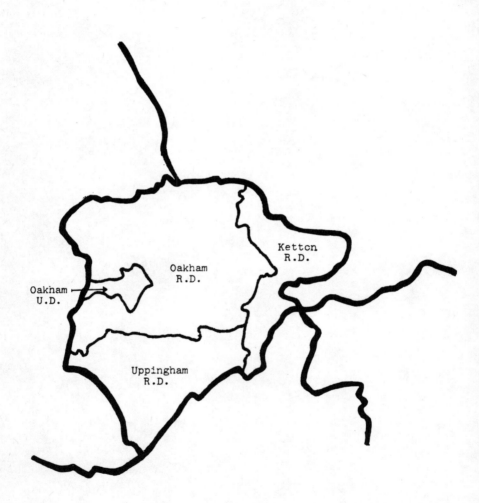

RUTLAND: new status

LEICESTERSHIRE

RUTLAND

A.   Local Studies Libraries

LEICESTER
Leicester University Department of English Local History,
Marc Flitch House, 5 Salisbury Road, Leicester LE1 7QR.
Tel: Leicester 522762 and 522522.
Contains Rutland material in its more general local history collections.

NOTTINGHAM
East Midlands Collection, University of Nottingham Library,
University Park, Nottingham NG7 2RD. Tel: (0602) 484848.

OAKHAM
Oakham Library, Catmos Street, Oakham, Leics LE15 6HW.
Tel: Oakham 722918.
Main collection of Rutland material.

B.   Local Record Office

Leicester Record Office, 57 New Walk, Leicester LE1 7JB.
Tel: (0533) 544566.

C.   Local History Societies

1.   Rutland Local History Society, Rutland County Museum,
Catmos Street, Oakham, Leics LE15 6HW.
2.   Rutland Record Society, Rutland County Museum,
Catmos Street, Oakham, Leics LE15 6HW.

D.   Local History Journals

1.   Leicester and Rutland Heritage, Vol.1, 1988/9 +
2.   Leicestershire and Rutland Magazine, Vols.1-2(3), 1948-50.
3.   Leicestershire and Rutland Notes and Queries, Vols.1-3, 1889-1895.
4.   Rutland Archaeological and Natural History Society Annual Reports, Vols.1-51, 1902/3-1951.
5.   Rutland Magazine and County Historical Record, Vols.1-5,1903-12.
6.   Rutland Record Society: Rutland Record, No.1, 1980 +
7.   Rutland Record Society: Rutland Record Series, No.1, 1980 +

E.   Museums with Local Studies Collections

1.   Normanton Church Water Museum, Rutland Water, Normanton, Oakham, Leics LE15 8PX. Tel: (078086) 321.
       History of Rutland Water reservoir and Normanton Church and Parish.
2.   Rutland County Museum, Catmos Street, Oakham, Leics LE15 6HW. Tel: (0572) 723654.
       History of the county, especially rural life.

SHROPSHIRE: old county

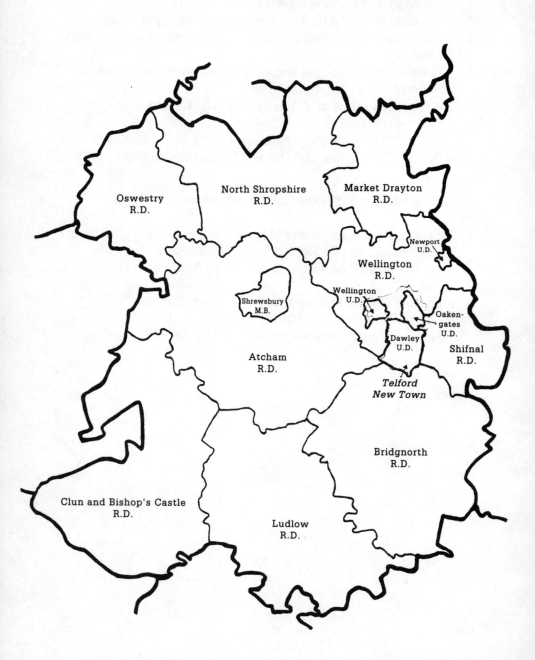

Oswestry
R.D.

North Shropshire
R.D.

Market Drayton
R.D.

Newport
U.D.

Wellington
R.D.

Wellington
U.D.

Shrewsbury
M.B.

Oaken-
gates
U.D.

Dawley
U.D.

Shifnal
R.D.

Atcham
R.D.

*Telford
New Town*

Bridgnorth
R.D.

Clun and Bishop's Castle
R.D.

Ludlow
R.D.

SHROPSHIRE: new county

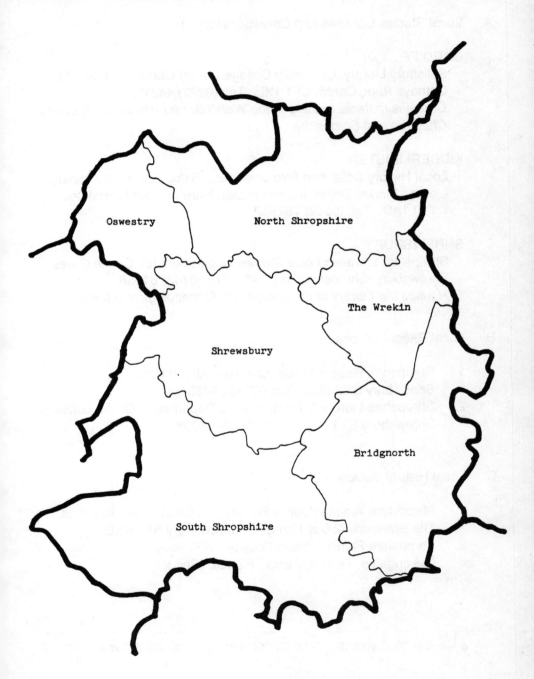

Oswestry

North Shropshire

The Wrekin

Shrewsbury

Bridgnorth

South Shropshire

SHROPSHIRE

A.   Local Studies Libraries and Collections

CARDIFF

Salisbury Library, University College Cardiff Library, PO Box 78
Cathays Park, Cardiff CF1 1XL. Tel: (0222) 44211.
*Contains material relating to the Welsh Border counties, especially
Cheshire and Shropshire.*

KIDDERMINSTER

Local History Collection (Worcester and Salop) (a), Kidderminster
Library, Market Street, Kidderminster, Hereford and Worcester
DY10 1AD. Tel: (0562) 752832.

SHREWSBURY

Shropshire Libraries Local Studies Department (c), Castle Gates,
Shrewsbury, Shropshire SY1 2AS. Tel: (0743) 61058.
Houses the Library of the Shropshire Archaeological Society.

B.   Local Record Offices

1.   Shropshire Record Office, Shirehall, Abbey Foregate,
      Shewsbury SY2 6ND. Tel: (0743 252851/3
2.   Shropshire Libraries, Local Studies Department, Castle Gates,
      Shrewsbury SY1 2AS. Tel: (0743) 61058

C.   Local History Societies

1.   Shropshire Archaeological Society, c/o County Record Office,
      The Shirehall, Abbey Foregate, Shrewsbury SY2 6ND.
2.   Shropshire Family History Society, 15 Wesley Drive,
      Oakengates, Telford, Salop TF2 0DZ (Sec.).

---

a = under 2000 vols; b = 2000-20,000 vols; c = over 20,000 vols.

D.   Local History Journals

1.   Caradoc and Severn Valley Field Club Transations, Vols.1-17,
     1893-1967.
2.   Shropshire Archaeological Society Transactions, Vol.1, 1878 +
3.   Shropshire Notes and Queries, Nos.1-3rd Series 2, 1884-1912.

E.   Museums with Local Studies Collections

1.   Bridgnorth: Northgate Museum, High Street, Bridgnorth,
     Shropshire.
     History of the area for the last 3000 years.
2.   Clun Town Trust Museum, Town Hall, Clun, nr Craven Arms,
     Shropshire. Tel: Clun 576.
3.   Ludlow Museum, The Buttercross, Ludlow, Shropshire.
     Tel: (0584) 3857.
4.   Much Wenlock Museum, High Street, Much Wenlock,
     Shropshire TF13 6HR. Tel: (0952) 727773.
5.   Shrewsbury: Rowley's House Museum, Barker Street,
     Shrewsbury SY1 1QT. Tel: (0743) 61196.
     Geology, natural history and archaeology of Shropshire.
6.   White House Museum of Buildings and Country Life, Aston
     Munslow, nr Craven Arms, Shropshire SY7 9ER.
     Domestic architecture and history of the region.

SOMERSET: old county

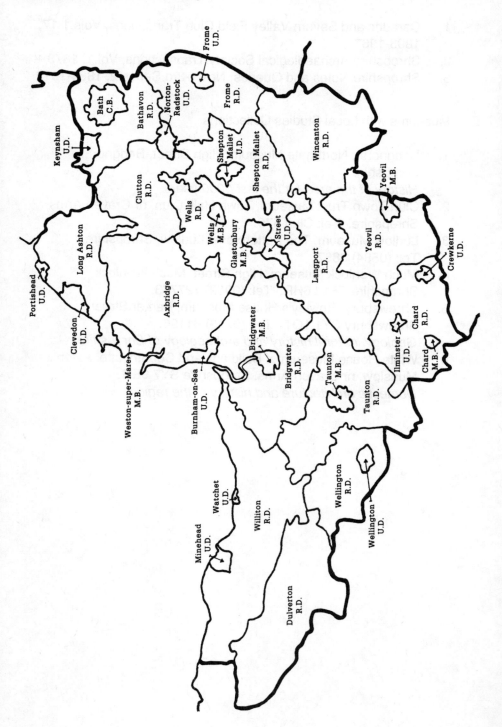

SOMERSET: new county

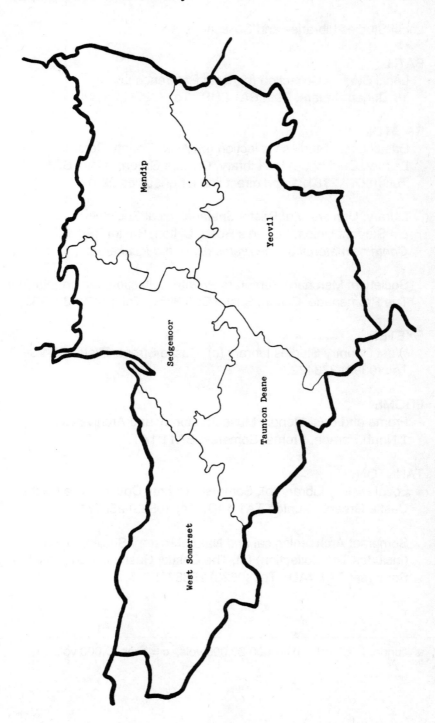

Mendip

Yeovil

Sedgemoor

Taunton Deane

West Somerset

SOMERSET AND BRISTOL

A.   Local Studies Libraries and Collections

BATH
Local Studies Collection (b), Bath Reference Library,
18 Queen Square, Bath BA1 2HP. Tel: (0225) 28144.

BRISTOL
Bristol Local Studies Collection (c), Avon County Reference
Library, County Central Library, College Green, Bristol BS1 5TL.
Tel: (0272) 276121 and direct line for enquiries 299147.

Library, University of Bristol Spelaeological Society,
c/o Student Union, Queen's Road, Clifton, Bristol BS8 1LN.
Contains material on the prehistory of the local area.

Society of Merchant-Venturers Private Collection, Merchants' Hall,
The Promenade, Clifton, Bristol BS8 3NH. Tel: (0272) 38058.

EXETER
West Country Studies Library (c), Castle Street, Exeter EX4 3PQ.
Tel: (0392) 273422.

FROME
Frome and East Mendip Museum Library and Archive Collection,
1 North Parade, Frome, Somerset BA11 1AT.

TAUNTON
Local History Library (b), Somerset County Council, The Castle,
Castle Green, Taunton TA1 4AD. Tel: (0823) 288871.

Somerset Archaeological and Natural History Society Library
(includes Tite Collection) (c), The Castle, Castle Green, Taunton,
Somerset TA1 4AD. Tel: (0823) 288871.

---

a = under 2000 vols; b = 2000-20,000 vols; c = over 20,000 vols.

WELLS
   Local History Library, Wells Museum, 8 Cathedral Green, Wells,
   Somerset BA5 2UE. Tel: (0749) 73477.

WOODSPRING
   Woodspring Central Library, The Boulevard, Weston-super-Mare
   BS23 1PL. Tel: (0934) 624133.
   Local history collection for the Weston-super-Mare area.

YEOVIL
   Tite Bequest of local history material (Somerset County Library),
   The Library, King George Street, Yeovil, Somerset BA20 1PY.
   Tel: (0935) 21910.

B.   Local Record Offices

   1.   Bath City Record Office, Guildhall, Bath BA1 5AW.
        Tel: (0225) 61111 ext.201.
   2.   Bristol Record Office, The Council House, College Green,
        Bristol BS1 5TR. Tel: (0272) 266031 ext.442.
   3.   Somerset Record Office, Obridge Road, Taunton TA2 7PU.
        Tel: (0823) 337600.

C.   Local History Societies

   1.   Avon Local History Association, c/o Avon Community Council,
        209 Redland Road, Bristol BS6 6YV.
   2.   Bath and Camerton Archaeological Society, 1 Meadgate,
        Camerton, Bath.
   3.   Bristol and Avon Archaeological Society, c/o Bristol City Museum
        and Art Gallery, Queen's Road, Bristol BS8 1RL.
   4.   Bristol and Avon Family History Society, 119 Holly Hill Road,
        Kingswood, Bristol BS15 4 DL.
   5.   Bristol and Gloucestershire Archaeological Society,
        22 Beaumont Road, Gloucester GL2 0EJ (Sec.).
   6.   Bristol Industrial Archaeological Society, City Museum and Art
        Gallery, Queen's Road, Bristol BS8 1RL.

7.   Bristol Record Society, c/o M.E.Williams, Council House,
     Bristol BS1 5TR.
8.   Centre for South-West Historical Studies, c/o 7 The Close,
     Exeter EX1 1EZ.
9.   North Somerset Archaeological Research Group,
     32 Brookfield Walk, Clevedon, Avon BS21 6YG (Sec.).
10. Somerset Industrial Archaeological Society, 2 Blake Green,
     Ashcott, Bridgwater, Somerset TA7 9QF (Sec.).
11. Somerset and Dorset Family History Society, PO Box 170,
     Taunton, Somerset TA1 1HF.
12. Somerset Archaeological and Natural History Society,
     Taunton Castle, Taunton TA1 4AD.
13. Somerset Record Society, c/o Local History Library, The Castle,
     Castle Green, Taunton TA1 4AD.
14. South East Somerset Archaeological Society, Furlong,
     Throop Road, Templecombe, Somerset BA8 0HR (Sec.).
15. University of Bristol Spelaeological Society, c/o Student Union,
     Queen's Road, Clifton, Bristol BS8 1LN.
16. West Somerset Archaeological and Natural History Society,
     Glenmoor, Bratton Lane, Woodcombe, Minehead, Somerset
     TA24 8SQ. (Sec.).
17. Weston-super-Mare Family History Society, 92 Elm Tree Road,
     Locking, Weston-super-Mare, Avon BS24 8EJ.
18. Yeovil Archaeological and Local History Society, c/o Brooklands,
     Lower Odcome, nr Yeovil, Somerset (Sec.).

D.   Local History Journals

1.   Avon Past, No.1, 1979 +
2.   Bath History, Vol.1, 1980 +
3.   Bristol and Avon Archaeology, No.1, 1982 +
4.   Bristol and Gloucestershire Archaeological Society Records
     Section Publications,Vol.1, 1952 +
5.   Bristol and Gloucestershire Archaeological Society Transactions,
     Vol.1, 1876 +
6.   Bristol Record Society Publications, No.1, 1930 +
7.   Notes and Queries for Somerset and Dorset, Vol.1, 1890 +
8.   Somerset Archaeology and Natural History, Vol.112, 1968 +

9.   Somerset Levels Papers, Nos.1-15, 1975-89.
10. Somerset Record Society Publications, Vol.1, 1887 +
11. Somerset Archaeological and Natural History Society
     Proceedings, Vols.1-111, 1849-1967 (*continued as Somerset
     Archaeology and Natural History - see above*).
12. University of Bristol Spelaeological Society Proceedings,
     Vol.1, 1919/20 +

E.   Museums with Local Studies Collections

1.   Axbridge: King John's Hunting Lodge, The Square, Axbridge,
     Somerset BS26 2AP. Tel: (0934) 732012.
     *Archaeology and history of Axbridge, including the medieval
     wool and cloth trade.*
2.   Bath: Geology Museum, 18 Queen Square, Bath,
     Avon BA1 2HP. Tel: (0225) 28144.
     *Includes North Somerset fossils, and natural history collections
     of the Bath Royal Literary and Scientific Society.*
3.   Bath Industrial Heritage Centre, Camden Works, Julian Road,
     Bath, Avon BA1 2RH. Tel: (0225) 318348.
     *Archives, photographs and other material on the history of Bath
     firms, including the Bowler Archive and Collection, history of
     Bath stone.*
4.   Bridgwater: Admiral Blake Museum, Blake Street, Bridgwater,
     Somerset TA6 3AR. Tel: (0278) 456127.
     Archaeology, history, industrial history of the Bridgwater area.
5.   Bristol: Blaise Castle House Museum, Henbury, Bristol,
     Avon BS10 7QS. Tel: (0272) 506789.
     *Social history of the Bristol area, local history of Blaise Castle
     and Henbury. Printed files of information on local agriculture and
     Blaise Castle Estate.*
6.   Bristol City Museum and Art Gallery, Queen's Road,
     Bristol BS8 1RL. Tel: (0272) 299771.
     *Topographical drawings and prints of Bristol, including the
     Braikenridge Collection. Field Archaeology Unit maintains a
     local sites and monuments record.*

7.   Bristol Industrial Museum, Prince's Wharf, Prince Street, Bristol, Avon BS1 4RN. Tel: (0272) 251470.
      Manufacturing and transport history of Bristol, York and Keen Collection of shipping photographs, mostly of Bristol City Docks.

8.   Bristol: Maritime Heritage Centre, Gas Ferry Road, Bristol, Avon BS1 5TY.
      Shipbuilding in Bristol for 200 years.

9.   Bristol: St Nicholas' Church Museum, St Nicholas Street, Bristol, Avon BS1 1UE. Tel: (0272) 211365.
      Development of medieval Bristol, 18th and 19th century watercolours of the Bristol area. Treasury for the Diocese of Bristol.

10.   Castle Cary Museum, The Market House, Castle Cary, Somerset BA7 7AL. Tel: (0963) 50277.

11.   Chard and District Museum, Godworthy House, 15 High Street, Chard, Somerset TA20 1QL.
      Chard Museum History and Research Group maintains card files of local information.

12.   Frome and East Mendip Museum, 1 North Parade, Frome, Somerset BA11 1AT.

13.   Glastonbury Lake Village Museum, The Tribunal, High Street, Glastonbury. Tel: (0458) 32949.

14.   Somerset County Museum Service HQ, Weir Lodge, 38 Staplegrove Road, Taunton TA1 1DN. Tel: (0823) 255510.
      Public search facilities by appointment.

15.   Somerset County Museum, Taunton Castle, Taunton, Somerset TA1 4AA. Tel: (0823) 255504.
      Archaeology, social history and natural history of Somerset.

16.   Somerset Rural Life Museum, Abbey Farm, Chilkwell Street, Glastonbury, Somerset BA6 8DB. Tel: (0458) 32903.
      Oral history archive, small library of relevant material.

17.   Watchet Market House Museum, Market Street, Watchet, Somerset TA23 0AN. Tel: (0643) 7132.

18.   Wells Museum, 8 Cathedral Green, Wells, Somerset BA5 2UE. Tel: (0749) 73477.
      Phillips Collection of glass plate negatives of Wells and surrounding area.

19. Weston-super-Mare: Woodspring Museum, Burlington Street,
    Weston-super-Mare, Avon BS23 1PR. Tel: (0934) 621028.
    *Files of information on local archaeological sites, local natural
    history, mining, parishes, Weston-super-Mare.*
20. Wincanton Museum, 32 High Street, Wincanton,
    Somerset BA9 9JF.
21. Yeovil: Museum of South Somerset, Hendford, Yeovil,
    Somerset BA20 1UN. Tel: (0935) 24774.

SOUTH YORKSHIRE

See NOTTINGHAMSHIRE
    YORKSHIRE (West Riding)

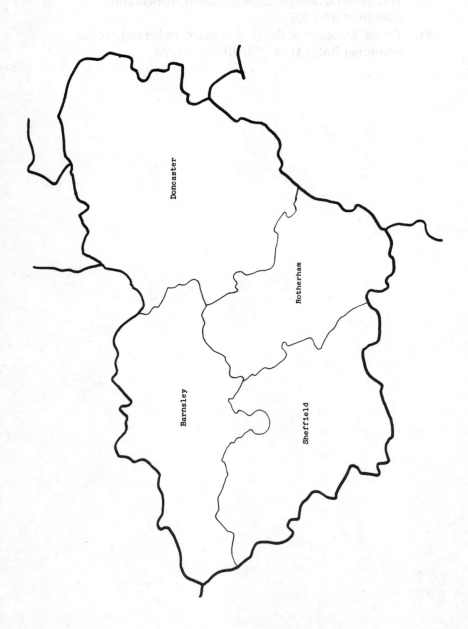

STAFFORDSHIRE: old county

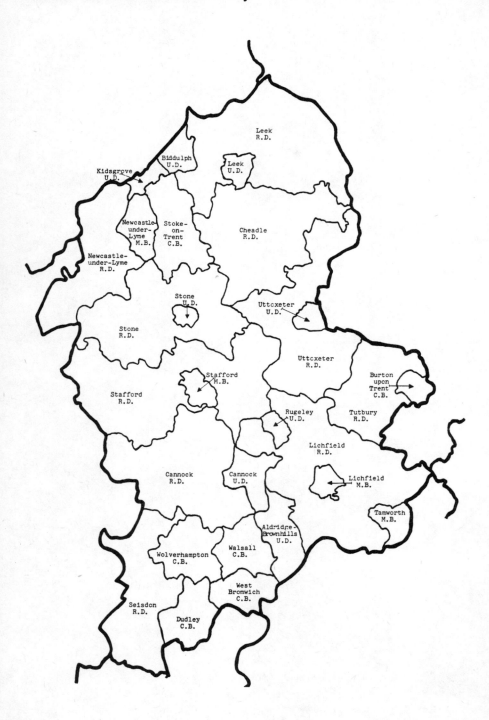

STAFFORDSHIRE: new county

STAFFORDSHIRE

A.   Local Studies Libraries and Collections

BURTON-ON-TRENT
Burton-on-Trent Library, Riverside, Burton-on-Trent,
Staffs DE14 1AH. Tel: (0283) 43271/2.
Covers East Staffordshire area.

HANLEY
Hanley Central Reference Library, Bethesda Street, Hanley,
Stoke-on-Trent, Staffs ST1 3DE. Tel: (00782) 23122/21242.

LEEK
Leek Library, Nicholson Institute, Stockwell Street, Lee ST13 6HQ.
Tel: (0538) 382615.
Covers Staffordshire Moorlands area.

LICHFIELD
Lichfield Library, Bird Street, Lichfield WS13 6PN.
Tel: (0543) 262177.

NEWCASTLE-UNDER-LYME
Newcastle Library, Ironmarket, Newcastle-under-Lyme,
Stoke-on-Trent, Staffs ST5 1AT. Tel: (0782) 618125.

STAFFORD
Stafford Library, The Green, Stafford ST17 4BJ.
Tel: (0785) 42151 ext.8350.
Covers the West Staffordshire area.

William Salt Library (b), Eastgate Street, Stafford ST16 2LZ.
Tel: (0785) 52276.
Main local history collection for Staffordshire

---

a = under 2000 vols; b = 2000-20,000 vols; c = over 20,000 vols.

TAMWORTH
Tamworth Library, Corporation Street, Tamworth, Staffs B79 7DW.
Tel: (0827) 522244.

WALSALL
Local Collection on the Black Country and South Staffs (b),
Walsall Local History Centre, Essex Street, Walsall,
West Midlands WS2 7AS. Tel: (0922) 721305.
*The Centre houses the Borough's photographic and oral history
collections.*

WOLVERHAMPTON
Wolverhampton, Staffordshire and West Midlands Collection (b),
Central Reference Library, Snow Hill, Wolverhampton WV1 3AX.
Tel: (0902) 312025 ext.139/140.

B.   Local Record Offices

1.   Lichfield Joint Record Office, Lichfield Library, Bird Street,
     Lichfield WS13 6PN.   Tel: (0543) 256787.
2.   Staffordshire Record Office, Eastgate Street, Stafford ST16 2LZ.
     Tel: (0785) 223121 ext.8380.
3.   Tamworth Borough Records Collection, Tamworth Castle
     Museum, The Holloway, Tamworth B79 7LR.
     Tel: Tamworth 311222 ext.389, Tamworth 63563 (weekends
     only).
4.   Walsall Archives Service, Local History Centre, Essex Street,
     Walsall WS2 7AS. Tel: (0922) 721305.
5.   Wolverhampton Borough Archives, Central Library, Snow Hill,
     Wolverhampton WV1 3AX. Tel: (0902) 312025 ext.137.

---

a = under 2000 vols; b = 2000-20,000 vols; c = over 20,000 vols.

C.   Local History Societies

1.   Birmingham and Midland Society for Genealogy and Heraldry,
       92 Dimmingsdale Bank, Birmingham B32 1ST (Sec.).
2.   Black Country Society, 15 Claydon Road, Wall Heath,
       Kingswinford, West Midlands DY6 0HA.
3.   City of Stoke-on-Trent Museum Archaeological Society,
       City Museum and Art Gallery, Broad Street, Hanley,
       Stoke-on-Trent ST1 4HS.
4.   South Staffordshire Archaeological and Historical Society,
       c/o Bass Museum of Brewing, Horninglow Street,
       Burton-on-Trent (Sec.).
5.   Staffordshire Catholic History Society, The Dell, Oakmore,
       Stoke-on-Trent ST10 3DJ (Sec.).
6.   Staffordshire Industrial Archaeological Society, 4 Longstaff Croft,
       Lichfield WS13 7DP (Sec.).
7.   Staffordshire Parish Registers Society, 91 Brenton Road, Penn,
       Wolverhampton WV4 5NS (Sec.).
8.   Staffordshire Record Society, c/o William Salt Library,
       Eastgate Street, Stafford ST16 2LZ.
9.   Walsall Local History Society, c/o Central Library,
       Lichfield Street, Walsall.

D.   Local History Journals

1.   The Blackcountryman, Vol.1, 1968 +
2.   Burton-on-Trent Natural History and Archaeological Society
       Transactions, Vols.1-9, 1889-1933.
3.   North Staffordshire Field Club Annual Report and Transactions,
       Vol.1,1865 +
4.   North Staffordshire Field Studies Journal, 1961-1985.
5.   Old Stafford Society Transactions, Vol.1, 1928 +
6.   South Staffordshire Archaeological and Historical Society
       Transactions, Vol.1, 1960 +
7.   Staffordshire Archaeological Studies, No.1, 1984 +
8.   Staffordshire Archaeology, Vol.1, 1972 +
9.   Staffordshire History, Vol.1, 1984 +

10. Staffordshire Record (William Salt Archaeological) Society: Collections for a History of Staffordshire, Vols.1-18, 1880-1897; New Series Vols.1-12, 1898-1909; 3rd Series 1911-1950/51; 4th Series Vol.1, 1957 +

11. Staffordshire Studies, 1989 +

E.   Museums with Local Studies Collections

1.   Bilston Art Gallery and Museum, Mount Pleasant, Bilston, Wolverhampton, West Midlands. Tel: (0902) 49143.
Local crafts, memorabilia of local personalities, local studies exhibitions.

2.   Black Country Museum, Tipton Road, Dudley, West Midlands DY1 4SQ. Tel: (021) 557 9643.

3.   Dudley Museum and Art Gallery, St James's Road, Dudley, West Midlands DY1 1HU. Tel: (0384) 55433 ext.5530.

4.   Leek Nicholson Institute Museum, Stockwell Street, Leek, Staffordshire ST13 6HQ. Tel: (0538) 382721.

5.   Lichfield: Heritage Exhibition and Treasury, St Mary's Centre, Market Square, Lichfield, Staffs. Tel: (0534) 256611.
History of Lichfield. Photographic collection.

6.   Newcastle-under-Lyme: Borough Museum and Art Gallery, The Brampton, Newcastle-under-Lyme, Staffs ST5 0QP. Tel: (0782) 619705.

7.   Shugborough Park Farm Museum, Shugborough Estate, Milford, nr Stafford, Staffs ST17 0XB. Tel: (0889) 881388.
Agricultural history of Shugborough Estate and Staffordshire.

8.   Staffordshire County Museum, Shugborough Estate, Milford, nr Stafford, Staffs ST17 0XB. Tel: (0889) 881388.
Social and agricultural history of rural Staffordshire.

9.   Stoke-on-Trent City Museum and Art Gallery, Bethesda Street, Hanley, Stoke-on-Trent, Staffs ST1 3DE. Tel: (0782) 273173.
Emphasis on the pottery industry of Staffordshire.

10. Tamworth Castle Museum, The Holloway, Tamworth, Staffs B79 7LR. Tel: (0827) 311222 ext.389, and (0827) 63563 (weekends only)

11. Walsall: Canal Boat Museum, Birchills, Walsall.
    Tel: Walsall 640301.
12. Walsall Museum and Art Gallery, Lichfield Street, Walsall,
    West Midlands WS1 1TR. Tel: (0922) 21244 ext.3124/3115.
13. Wednesbury Art Gallery and Museum, Holyhead Road,
    Wednesbury, West Midlands WS10 7DF. Tel: (021) 556 0683.
14. Willenhall: Lock Museum, New Road, Willenhall, West Midlands.
    Tel: Willenhall 634542.
    Collection illustrating one of the principal industries of the area.
15. Willenhall Museum, Willenhall Library, Walsall Street, Willenhall,
    West Midlands.

SUFFOLK: old county

SUFFOLK: new county

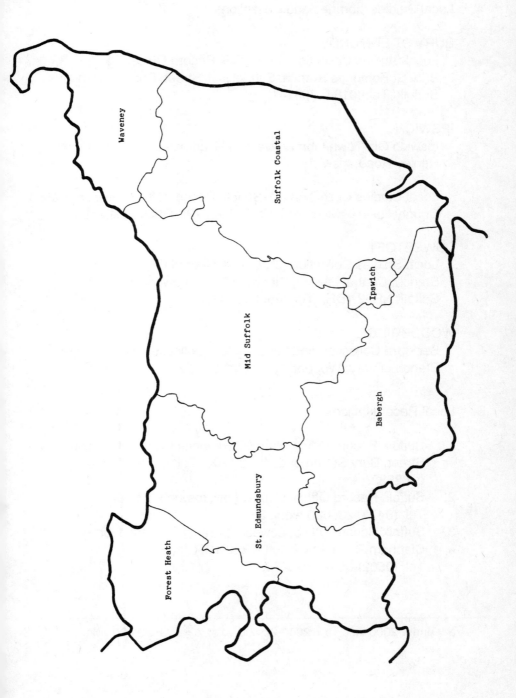

SUFFOLK

A.   Local Studies Libraries and Collections

BURY ST EDMUNDS
Local Studies Collection (b), Suffolk Record Office,
Bury St Edmunds Branch, School Hall Street, Bury St Edmunds,
Suffolk. Tel: (0184) 763141.

IPSWICH
Ipswich Old Town Library, c/o The Headmaster, Ipswich School,
Henley Road, Ipswich.

Local Studies Collection (b), Suffolk Record Office, Ipswich Branch,
County Hall, Ipswich IP4 2JS. Tel: (0473) 230000 ext.2522.

LOWESTOFT
Local Studies Collection (b), Suffolk Record Office, Lowestoft
Branch, Central Library, Clapham Road, Lowestoft,
Suffolk NR32 1DR. Tel: (0502) 66325.

WOODBRIDGE
Seckford Collection and Local History Collection, Woodbridge
Branch Library, Woodbridge, Suffolk.

B.   Local Record Offices

1.   Suffolk Record Office, Bury St Edmunds Branch, Raingate
Street, Bury St Edmunds IP33 1RX. Tel: (0284) 763141
ext.2522.
2.   Suffolk Record Office, County Hall, Ipswich IP4 2JS.
Tel: (0473) 230000 ext.4235.
3.   Suffolk Record Office, Lowestoft Branch, Central Library,
Clapham Road, Lowestoft NR32 1DR.
Tel: (0502) 66325 ext.274.

---

a = under 2000 vols; b = 2000-20,000 vols; c = over 20,000 vols.

C. Local History Societies

1. Felixstowe Family History Society, 5 Marina Gardens, Felixstowe, Suffolk IP11 8HW.
2. Suffolk Family History Society, 30 Gowers End, Glemsford, Sudbury, Suffolk CO10 7UF (Sec.).
3. Suffolk Industrial Archaeology Society, 750 Foxhall Road, Ipswich IP4 5TR (Sec.).
4. Suffolk Institute of Archaeology and History, Oak Tree Farm, Hitcham, Ipswich, Suffolk IP7 7LS.
5. Suffolk Local History Council, Alexandra House, Rope Walk, Ipswich IP4 1LZ.
6. Suffolk Records Society, c/o Green Pightle, Hightown Green, Rattlesden, Bury St Edmunds.

D. Local History Journals

1. East Anglian Magazine, Vols.1-41, 1935-82.
2. Suffolk Charters, No.1, 1979 +
3. Suffolk Fair, 1970-1987.
4. Suffolk Institute of Archaeology and Natural History Proceedings, Vol.1, 1849 +
5. Suffolk Records Society Publications, No.1, 1958 +
6. Suffolk Review, Vols.1-5, 1956-83; New Series No.1, 1983 +

E. Museums with Local Studies Collections

1. Aldeburgh Moot Hall Museum, Moot Hall, Aldeburgh, Suffolk. Tel: (072885) 2158.
    Local history, with emphasis on coastal erosion, shipping and fishing. Collection of historical records, particularly photographs.
2. Beccles and District Museum, Newgate, Beccles, Suffolk NR34 9QA. Tel: (0502) 712628.
3. Bungay Museum, Waveney District Council Offices, Broad Street, Bungay, Suffolk. Tel: (0986) 2176.

4.   Bury St Edmunds: Moyse's Hall Museum, Cornhill,
      Bury St Edmunds, Suffolk IP33 1DX. Tel: (0284) 69834.
      *History of Suffolk. Archaeological locations index on card and
      computer.*
5.   Clare: Ancient House Museum, High Street, Clare, Sudbury,
      Suffolk CO10 8NY. Tel: (0787) 277865.
6.   Dunwich Museum, St James's Street, Dunwich,
      nr Saxmundham, Suffolk IP17 3EA. Tel: Westleton 358.
7.   Framlingham: Lanman Museum, Framlingham Castle,
      Framlingham, Suffolk IP13 8BP. Tel: (0728) 723330.
      History of Framlingham and surrounding villages.
8.   Ipswich: Christchurch Mansion, Christchurch Park, Soane Street,
      Ipswich, Suffolk IP4 2RE. Tel: (0473) 213761/2.
      History of Ipswich and district.
9.   Ipswich Museum, High Street, Ipswich, Suffolk IP1 3QH.
      Tel: (0473) 213761/2.
      Archaeology of Suffolk.
10.   Lowestoft and East Suffolk Maritime Museum, Sparrows Nest
      Park, Whapload Road, Lowestoft, Suffolk NR32 1XG.
      Tel: (0502) 561963.
11.   Lowestoft Museum, Broad House, Nicholas Everitt Park, Oulton
      Broad, Lowestoft, Suffolk NR33 9JR. Tel: (0502) 511457.
12.   Museum of East Anglian Life, Abbot's Hall, Stowmarket,
      Suffolk IP14 1DL. Tel: (0449) 612229.
13.   Southwold Museum, Bartholomew Green, Southwold,
      Suffolk IP18 6HZ.
      Includes collection on Southwold Railway.
14   Woodbridge Museum, Market Hill, Woodbridge,
      Suffolk IP12 4LP. Tel: (0394) 380502.
15   Woolpit Bygones Museum, The Institute, Woolpit,
      Bury St Edmunds, Suffolk.

SURREY: old county

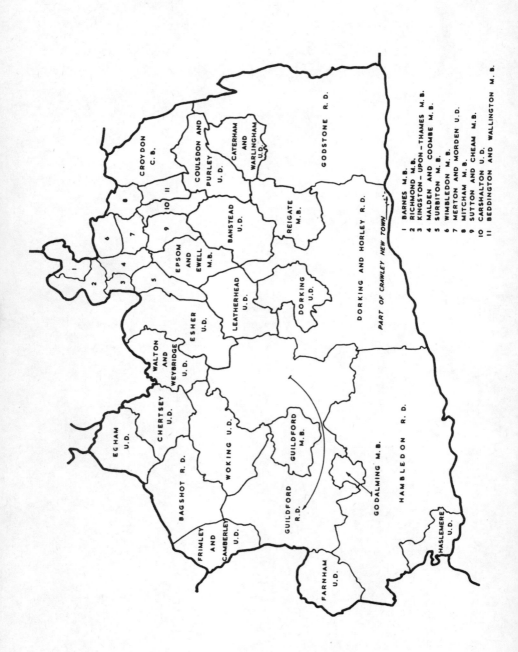

CROYDON C. B.

COULSDON AND PURLEY U. D.

CATERHAM AND WARLINGHAM U. D.

GODSTONE R. D.

BANSTEAD U. D.

REIGATE M. B.

EPSOM AND EWELL M. B.

LEATHERHEAD U. D.

DORKING U. D.

DORKING AND HORLEY R. D.

PART OF CRAWLEY NEW TOWN

ESHER U. D.

WALTON AND WEYBRIDGE U. D.

CHERTSEY U. D.

EGHAM U. D.

BAGSHOT R. D.

WOKING U. D.

GUILDFORD R. D.

GUILDFORD M. B.

GODALMING M. B.

HAMBLEDON R. D.

FRIMLEY AND CAMBERLEY U. D.

FARNHAM U. D.

HASLEMERE U. D.

1 BARNES M.B.
2 RICHMOND M.B.
3 KINGSTON-UPON-THAMES M. B.
4 MALDEN AND COOMBE M. B.
5 SURBITON M. B.
6 WIMBLEDON M. B.
7 MERTON AND MORDEN U.D.
8 MITCHAM M. B.
9 SUTTON AND CHEAM M. B.
10 CARSHALTON U. D.
11 BEDDINGTON AND WALLINGTON M. B.

SURREY: new county

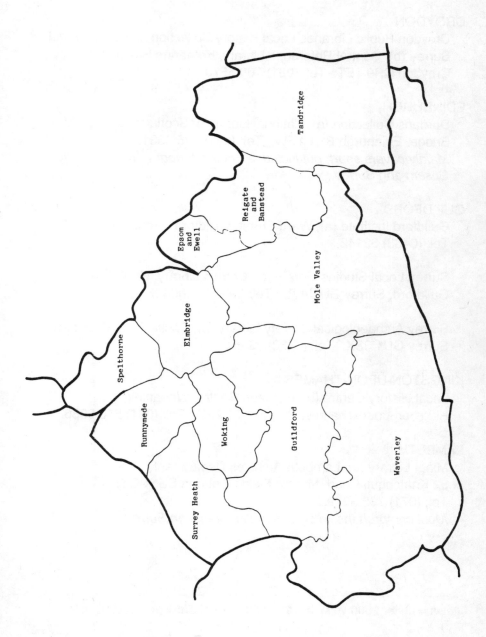

Tandridge

Reigate and Banstead

Epsom and Ewell

Mole Valley

Elmbridge

Spelthorne

Runnymede

Woking

Guildford

Surrey Heath

Waverley

SURREY

A.   Local Studies Libraries and Collections

CROYDON
Croydon Public Libraries Local History Collection on Croydon and
Surrey (b), Central Reference Library, Katharine Street,
Croydon CR9 1ET. Tel: (081) 760 5570.

EDINBURGH
Durdans Collection (a), National Library of Scotland, George IV
Bridge, Edinburgh EH1 1EW. Tel: (031) 226 4531.
*Mainly covers sport, but includes English topography, especially
Epsom and Surrey.*

GUILDFORD
Guildford Institute (a), Ward Street, Guildford, Surrey GU1 4LH.
Tel: (0483) 62142.

Surrey Local Studies Library (c), Branch Library, North Street,
Guildford, Surrey GU1 4AL. Tel: (0483) 34054.

Surrey Archaeological Society Library (b), Castle Arch, Guildford,
Surrey GU1 3SX. Tel: (0483) 32454.

KINGSTON-UPON-THAMES
Local History Centre (b), Heritage Centre, Wheatfield Way,
Kingston-upon-Thames, Surrey KT1 2PS. Tel: (081) 546 5386.

LAMBETH
Minet Library (c), Lambeth Archives Department,
52 Knatchbull Road, Myatt's Fields, London SE5 9QY.
Tel: (071) 733 3279.
Most comprehensive collection of material on Surrey.

---

a = under 2000 vols; b = 2000-20,000 vols; c = over 20,000 vols.

MERTON
Merton Public Libraries Local Collections at:
Mitcham Library, London Road, Mitcham, Surrey CR4 2YR.
Morden Library Local History Collection (b), Crown House,
London Road, Morden, Surrey SM4 5DX. Tel: (081) 545 3790.
Wimbledon Reference Library, Wimbledon Hill Road, London
SW19 7NB.

REIGATE
Holmesdale Natural History Club Library, The Museum, Croydon
Road, Reigate, Surrey.

RICHMOND
Richmond Local Studies Library (b), Central Reference Library,
Old Town Hall, Whittaker Avenue, Richmond, Surrey TW9 1TP.
Tel: (081) 940 5529 ext.32.

SUTTON
Sutton Libraries and Arts Services Local History Collection,
Central Library, St Nicholas Way, Sutton, Surrey SM1 1EA.
Tel: (081) 661 5050.

B.   Local Record Offices

1.   Lambeth Archives Department, Minet Library, 52 Knatchbull
      Road, London SE5 9QY. Tel: (071) 733 3279.
2.   Surrey Record Office, County Hall, Penrhyn Road, Kingston-
      upon-Thames, Surrey KT1 2DN. Tel: (081) 541 9065.
3.   Surrey Record Office, Guildford Muniment Room, Castle Arch,
      Guildford, Surrey GU1 3SX. Tel: (0483) 573942.

---

a = under 2000 vols; b = 2000-20,000 vols; c = over 20,000 vols.

C.   Local History Societies

1.   Bourne Society, 40 Raglan Precinct, Town End, Caterham,
       Surrey CR3 5UG (Sec.).
2.   Croydon Natural History and Scientific Society Ltd.,
       96a Brighton Road, Croydon, Surrey CR2 6AD.
3.   East Surrey Family History Society, 15 Apeldoorn Drive,
       Wallington, Surrey SM6 9LE (Sec.).
4.   Kingston-upon-Thames Archaeological Society,
       295 West Barnes Lane, New Maldon, Surrey KT3 6JE (Sec.).
5.   Merton Historical Society, 53 Manor Way, Mitcham, Surrey
       (Sec.).
6.   Richmond Local History Society, 9 Bridge Road, St Margaret's,
       East Twickenham (Sec.).
7.   Surrey Archaeological Society, Castle Arch, Guildford,
       Surrey GU1 3SX.
8.   Surrey Industrial History Group, Donard, East Street,
       Great Bookham, Leatherhead, Surrey KT23 4QX.
9.   Surrey Local History Council, Jenner House, 2 Jenner Road,
       Guildford, Surrey (Sec.).
10.   Surrey Record Society, 8 Tilehouse Road, Guildford,
       Surrey GU4 8AL (Sec.).
11.   West Surrey Family History Society, Bradstone Garden Cottage,
       Christmas Hill, Shalford, Guildford, Surrey GU4 8HR (Sec.).

D.   Local History Journals

1.   Bourne Society Local History Records, No.1, 1962 +
2.   Croydon Natural History and Scientific Society Proceedings,
       Vol.1, 1871 +
3.   East Surrey Family History Society Journal, No.1, 1977 +
4.   Home Counties Magazine, Nos.1-14, 1899-1912.
5.   Root and Branch (Journal of the West Surrey Family History
       Group), Vol.1, 1974 +
6.   Surrey: the county magazine, No.1, 1970 +

7.   Surrey Archaeological Collections, Vol.1, 1858 +
8.   Surrey Archaeological Society Annual Reports, 1964 +
9.   Surrey Archaeological Society Bulletin, No.1, 1965 +
10. Surrey Archaeological Society Research Volumes, No.1, 1974 +
11. Surrey County Journal, Nos.1-6, 1944-59.
12. Surrey History, No.1, 1973 +
13. Surrey Industrial History Group Newsletters, No.1, 1979 +
14. Surrey Life, Nos.1-5, 1971-77.
15. Surrey Magazine, Nos.1-5, 1899-1905.
16. Surrey Record Society Publications, No.1, 1913 +

E.   Museums with Local Studies Collections

1.   Chertsey Museum, The Cedars, 33 Windsor Street, Chertsey,
     Surrey KT16 8AT. Tel: (0932) 565764.
     History of the Borough of Runnymede and Chertsey Abbey.
2.   East Surrey Museum, 1 Stafford Road, Caterham,
     Surrey CR3 6JG. Tel: (0883) 40275.
3.   Egham Museum, Literary Institute, High Street, Egham,
     Surrey TW20 9EW.
4.   Epsom and Ewell: Bourne Hall Museum, Spring Street, Ewell,
     Epsom, Surrey KT17 1UF. Tel: (081) 394 1734.
     Card file on historic buildings and archaeological excavations
     within the Borough of Epsom and Ewell.
5.   Farnham Museum, 38 West Street, Farnham, Surrey GU9 7DX.
     Tel: (0252) 715094.
6.   Godalming Museum, 109a High Street, Godalming,
     Surrey GU7 1AQ. Tel: (0483) 426510.
7.   Guildford Museum, Castle Arch, Quarry Street, Guildford,
     Surrey GU1 3SX. Tel: (0483) 503497. *01483 444 750*
     Archaeology and history of Surrey, particularly the Guildford
     area.
8.   Kingston-upon-Thames Museum and Heritage Centre,
     Wheatfield Way, Kingston-upon-Thames, Surrey KT1 2PS.
     Tel: (081) 546 5386.
     Local history and archaeology of Surrey, particularly the
     Kingston area. Sites and Monuments Record for Kingston
     Borough.

9. Richmond: Museum of Richmond, Old Town Hall, Whittaker
    Avenue, Richmond, Surrey TW9 1TP. Tel: (081) 332 1141.
10. Surrey Heath Museum, Knoll Road, Camberley,
    Surrey GU15 3HD. Tel: (0276) 686252.
    Includes history of Bagshot Heath.
11. Sutton: Wandle Industrial Museum, 41-47 Hartfield,
    London SW19 3SG. Tel: (081) 542 2406 and (081) 543 4952.
12. Sutton: Whitehall, 1 Malden Road, Cheam, Sutton,
    Surrey SM3 8QD.
    Local history centre, arts and crafts.
13. Weybridge Museum, Church Street, Weybridge,
    Surrey KT13 8DE. Tel: (0932) 843573.
14. Wimbledon Society Local History Museum, Village Club and
    Lecture Hall, Lingfield Road, Wimbledon, London SW19.
    Tel: (081) 946 9529.

SUSSEX: old county

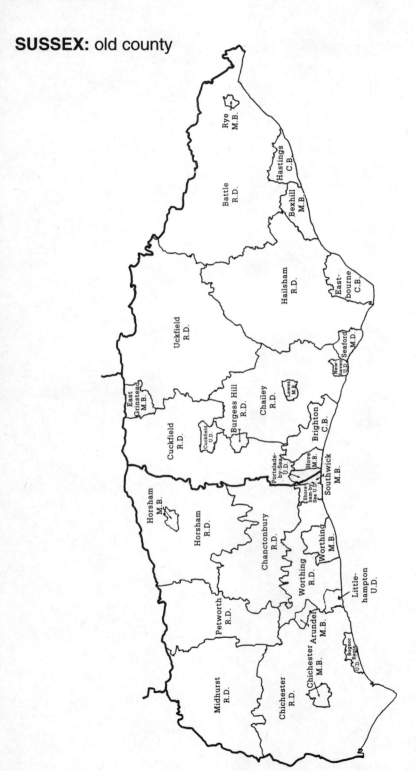

SUSSEX: new counties

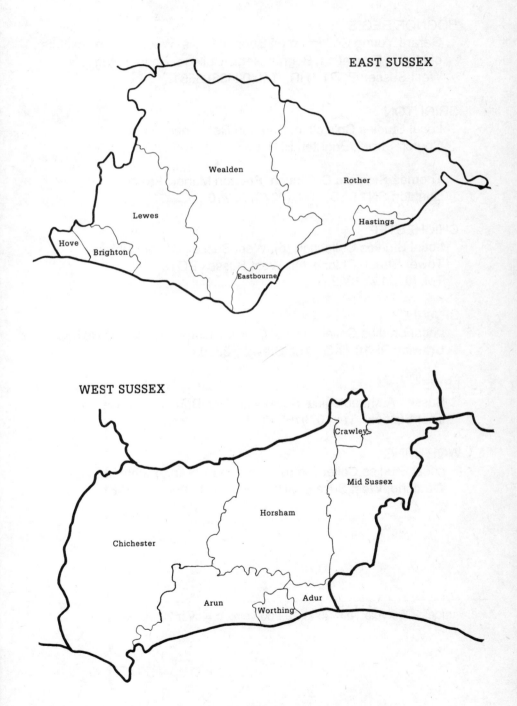

EAST SUSSEX

Wealden

Rother

Lewes

Hastings

Hove

Brighton

Eastbourne

WEST SUSSEX

Crawley

Mid Sussex

Horsham

Chichester

Arun

Adur

Worthing

SUSSEX

A.   Local Studies Libraries and Collections

BOGNOR REGIS
Gerard Young Collection on Bognor Regis, West Sussex Institute
of Higher Education, Bognor Regis College, Bognor Regis,
West Sussex PO21 1HR. Tel:(02433) 5581.

BRIGHTON
Local Studies Collection, Brighton Reference Library,
Church Street, Brighton BN1 1VE. Tel: (0273) 691195/97.

Thomas-Stanford Collection, Preston Manor, Preston Park,
Brighton BN1 6SD. Tel: (0273) 552101.

CHICHESTER
Local Studies Collection (b), West Sussex County Library,
Tower Street, Chichester, West Sussex PO19 1QJ.
Tel: (0234 777352.

CRAWLEY
Local Studies Collection (a), Crawley Library, County Buildings,
Crawley RH10 1XG. Tel: Crawley 35299.

LEWES
Sussex Archaeological Society Library, Barbican House, Lewes,
East Sussex. Tel: (07916) 4379.

WORTHING
Local Studies Collection (b), Worthing Library, Richmond Road,
Worthing, West Sussex BN11 1HD. Tel: (0903) 206961.

---

a = under 2000 vols; b = 2000-20,000 vols; c = over 20,000 vols.

B.   Local Record Offices

    1.   East Sussex County Record Office, The Maltings,
        Castle Precincts, Lewes BN7 1YT.
        Tel: (0273) 475400 ext.12 and 359.
    2.   West Sussex County and Diocesan Record Office,
        Sherburne House, Orchard Street, Chichester.
        Tel: ~~(0243)~~ 533911.

        01243 753600

C.   Local History Societies

    1.   Eastbourne and District (Family Roots) Family History Society,
        22 Abbey Road, Eastbourne, Sussex BN2 8TE.
    2.   Hastings and Rother Family History Society,
        520d South View Court, Old London Road, Hastings,
        East Sussex TN35 5BN.
    3.   Sussex Archaeological Society, Barbican House, Lewes,
        East Sussex BN7 1YE.
    4.   Sussex Family History Group, 44 The Green, Southwick,
        West Sussex BN4 4FR (Sec.).
    5.   Sussex Industrial Archaeology Society, 42 Falmer Avenue,
        Saltdean, Brighton BN2 8FG.
    6.   Sussex Record Society, Barbican House, Lewes,
        East Sussex BN7 1YE.

D.   Local History Journals

    1.   Sussex Archaeological Collections, Vol.1, 1848 +
    2.   Sussex Archaeological Society Newsletter, No.1, 1970 + (*now
        includes material previously appearing in Sussex Notes and
        Queries*).
    3.   Sussex County Magazine, Vols.1-30, 1926-56.
    4.   Sussex Family Historian,Vol.1, 1973 +
    5.   Sussex Genealogist and Local Historian, Vols.1-7(3-4), 1979-86.
    6.   Sussex History, 1976 +
    7.   Sussex Industrial Archaeology Study Group Newsletter, Nos.1-5,
        1968-70. (*continued as Sussex Industrial History - see below*).
    8.   Sussex Industrial History, 1970/71 +

9.   Sussex Notes and Queries, Vols.1-17, 1926-71. (*continued in Sussex Archaeological Society Newsletter - see above*).
10.   Sussex Record Society Publications, No.1, 1901 +
11.   West Sussex Archives Society Newsletter, Nos.1-14, 1974-79. (*continued as West Sussex History - see below*).
12.   West Sussex History, No.15, 1980 +

E.   Museums with Local Studies Collections

East Sussex

1.   Battle and District Historical Museum, Langton House, Battle, East Sussex BN33 0NG.
      Includes history of the Sussex iron industry.
2.   Bexhill Museum, Egerton Road, Bexhill-on-Sea, East Sussex TN39 3HL. Tel: (0424) 211769.
      Includes and archive of photographs and documents.
3.   Eastbourne: Towner Art Gallery and Eastbourne Local History Museum, High Street/Manor Gardens, Old Town, Eastbourne, East Sussex BN20 8BB. Tel: (0323) 21635/25112.
4.   Hailsham Heritage Centre, Ingle Nook, Market Street, Hailsham, East Sussex BN27 2AE.
5.   Hastings: Fishermen's Museum, Rock-a-nore Road, Hastings, East Sussex.
      Display includes "Enterprise", a clinker-built sailing lugger.
6.   Hastings Museum and Art Gallery, John's Place, Cambridge Road, Hastings, East Sussex TN34 1ET. Tel: (0424) 721202.
7.   Hastings: Old Town Museum of Local History, High Street, Hastings, East Sussex TN34 3EW. Tel: (0424) 425855.
8.   Hove Museum and Art Gallery, 19 New Church Road, Hove, East Sussex BN3 4AB.
9.   Lewes: Anne of Cleves House Museum, Southover High Street, Lewes, East Sussex BN7 1JA. Tel: (0273) 474610.
      Wealden iron industry, history of Lewes.
10.   Museum of Sussex Archaeology, Barbican House, High Street, Lewes, East Sussex BN7 1YE. Tel: (0273) 474379.

11. Newhaven Local and Maritime Museum, West Foreshore,
    Newhaven, East Sussex.
12. Pevensey Court House and Museum, High Street, Pevensey,
    East Sussex BN24 5LF.
13. Rottingdean: The Grange Art Gallery and Museum, The Green,
    Rottingdean, East Sussex BN2 7HA. Tel: (0273) 301004.
    History of Rottingdean.
14. Rye: Cherries Folk Museum, Cherries, Playden, Rye,
    East Sussex TN31 7NR. Tel: (0797) 223224.
    Social and domestic life in the area before 1946.
15. Rye: Ypres Tower Museum, Gun Garden, Rye,
    East Sussex TN31 7HE. Tel: (0797) 223254.
    Local history of Rye and the vicinity.
16. Seaford Museum of Local History, Martello Tower,
    No.74 Esplanade, Seaford, East Sussex BN25 1JH.
    Compiles a Housing Register of information on local buildings.
    All correspondence should be addressed to the Hon.Secretary,
    7 South Street, Seaford BN25 1HP, Tel: (03323) 893976.
17. Stanmer Rural Museum, Stanmer Stores, Stanmer Village,
    Brighton, East Sussex. Tel: (0273) 604041.
18. Winchelsea Museum, High Street, Winchelsea, East Sussex.
    History of Winchelsea and the Cinq Ports.

West Sussex

1. Amberley Chalk Pits Museum, Amberley, nr Arundel,
    West Sussex BN18 9LT. Tel: (079) 8831370.
    Open-air museum of regional industry and local narrowgage
    railway. Oral history tapes.
2. Arundel Museum and Heritage Centre, 61 High Street, Arundel,
    West Sussex. Tel: (0903) 882726.
3. Bognor Regis Local History Museum, Hotham Park Lodge,
    High Street, Bognor Regis, West Sussex P021 1HW.
    Large collection of lantern slides.
4. Chichester District Museum, 29 Little London, Chichester,
    West Sussex PO19 1PB. Tel: (0243) 784683.
    Geology, archaeology and history of the district. Archaeology
    Archive: finds, photographs of sites.

5.   Chichester: Guildhall Museum, Priory Park, Priory Road, Chichester, West Sussex. Tel: (0243) 784683.
      Archaeology and social history of Chichester.

6.   Ditchling Museum, Church Lane, Ditchling, Hassocks, West Sussex BN6 8BTB. Tel: (07918) 4744.
      Publications of St Dominic's Press, founded locally by Eric Gill; records, etc., of local artists and craftsmen of 1920s who settled in district.

7.   East Grinstead: Town Museum, East Court, College Lane, East Grinstead, West Sussex RH19 3LT.
      Files of local information for researchers available - contact the Curator, Tel: (0342) 322511.

8.   Henfield Parish Museum, New Village Hall, Henfield, West Sussex BN5 9DB.

9.   Horsham Museum, 9 The Causeway, Horsham, West Sussex. Tel: (0403) 54959.
      Includes the Albery Collection of local history documents and memorabilia.

10.   Littlehampton Museum, 12a River Road, Littlehampton, West Sussex BN17 5BN. Tel: (0903) 715149.

11.   Shoreham: Marlipins Museum, High Street, Shoreham-by-Sea, West Sussex. Tel: (0273) 462994.
      History of Shoreham.

12.   Steyning Museum, 91 High Street, Steyning, West Sussex BN4 3RE.

13.   Weald and Downland Open Air Museum, Singleton, nr Chichester, West Sussex PO18 0EU. Tel: (024363) 348.
      Collection of historic buildings from the area, re-erected, illustrating the history and development of traditional building. Computer file of notable vernacular building being completed.

14.   Worthing Museum and Art Gallery, Chapel Road, Worthing, West Sussex BN11 1HD. Tel: (0903) 39999 ext.121.
      Archaeology, social history of the area. Natural history of the South Downs. Archaeological Sites and Finds Record on card file.

TYNE AND WEAR

See DURHAM
   NORTHUMBERLAND

WARWICKSHIRE: old county

WARWICKSHIRE: new county

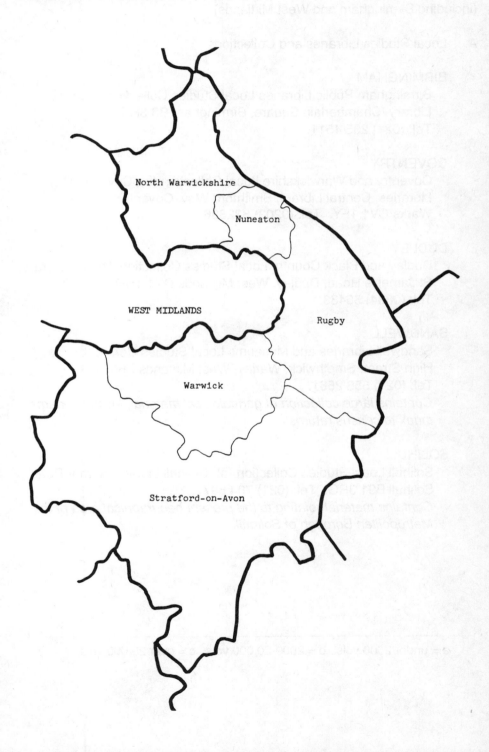

North Warwickshire

Nuneaton

WEST MIDLANDS

Rugby

Warwick

Stratford-on-Avon

WARWICKSHIRE
(including Birmingham and West Midlands)

A.   Local Studies Libraries and Collections

BIRMINGHAM
Birmingham Public Libraries Local Studies Collection, Central
Library, Chamberlain Square, Birmingham B3 3HQ.
Tel: (021) 235 4511.

COVENTRY
Coventry and Warwickshire Local Collection (b), Coventry City
Libraries, Central Library, Smithford Way, Coventry,
Warks CV1 1FY. Tel: (0203) 832336.

DUDLEY
Dudley and Black Country Local Studies Collection, Dudley Library,
St James's Road, Dudley, West Midlands DY1 1HR.
Tel: (0384) 55433.

SANDWELL
Sandwell Libraries and Museums Local Studies Centre (b),
High Street, Smethwick, Warley, West Midlands B66 1AB.
Tel: (021) 558 2561.
*Contains large collection of genealogical material, including name
index to census returns.*

SOLIHULL
Solihull Local Studies Collection (b), Solihull Library, Homer Road,
Solihull B91 3RG. Tel: (021) 704 6977.
*Contains material relating to the present geographical area of the
Metropolitan Borough of Solihull.*

---

a = under 2000 vols; b = 2000-20,000 vols; c = over 20,000 vols.

STRATFORD-UPON-AVON

Shakespeare Birthplace Trust Records Office Library, Shakespeare Centre Library, Shakespeare Birthplace Trust, Henley Street, Stratford-upon-Avon CV37 6QW. Tel: (0789) 4016.
Contains material on topography of Warwickshire, especially the Stratford district, local archaeology and antiquities, biographies of local families.

WALSALL

Local Collection on the Black Country and South Staffordshire (b), Walsall Local History Centre, Essex Street, Walsall WS2 7AS. Tel: (0922) 721305.
Houses the Borough's photographic and sound archive collections.

WARWICK

Warwickshire Collection (b), Warwick Library, Barrack Street, Warwick CV34 4TH. Tel: (0926) 492194.
County local history collection. Smaller collections at Nuneaton, Rugby, Leamington and Stratford.

Warwick County Record Office Library, Priory Park, Cape Road, Warwick. Tel: (0926) 492508.
Contains the library of the Warwickshire Natural History and Archaeological Society.

B.   Local Record Offices

1.   Birmingham Central Library Archives Department, Chamberlain Square, Birmingham B3 3HQ. Tel: (021) 235 4217.
2.   Coventry City Record Office, Mandela House, Bayley Lane, Coventry CV1 5RG. Tel: (0203) 832418.
3.   Sandwell Libraries and Museums Local Studies Centre, High Street, Smethwick, Warley, West Midlands B66 1AB. Tel: (021) 558 2561.

---

a = under 2000 vols; b = 2000-20,000 vols; c = over 20,000 vols.

4.   Shakespeare Birthplace Trust Records Office, Shakespeare
      Centre Library, Shakespeare Birthplace Trust, Henley Street,
      Stratford-upon-Avon CV37 6QW. Tel: (0789) 4016.
5.   Warwick County Record Office, Priory Park, Cape Road,
      Warwick CV34 4JS. Tel: (0926) 493431 ext.2508.

C.   Local History Societies

1.   Birmingham and Midland Society for Genealogy and Heraldry,
      92 Dimmingsdale Bank, Birmingham B32 1ST.
2.   Birmingham and Warwickshire Archaeological Society,
      c/o Birmingham and Midland Institute, Margaret Street,
      Birmingham B3 3BS.
3.   Black Country Society, 49 Victoria Road, Tipton, West Midlands
      DY4 8SW.
4.   Black Country Society Industrial Archaeology Group,
      7 Dudley Street, Cradley Heath, Warley, West Midlands.
5.   Coventry and District Archaeological Society, 20 Harvey Close,
      Allesley, Coventry CV5 9FU.
6.   Dugdale Society, The Shakespeare Centre,
      Stratford-upon-Avon, Warks CV37 6QW.
7.   Warwickshire Local History Society, 28 Lillington Road,
      Leamington Spa, Warks CV32 5YY.

D.   Local History Journals

1.   Birmingham (Birmingham and Warwickshire) Archaeological
      Society Transactions, Vol.1, 1870 +
2.   Birmingham Historian, No.1, 1987 +
3.   Birmingham University Historical Journal, 1947-1970. (*continued
      by Midland History - see below*).
4.   Blackcountryman, Vol.1, 1968 +
5.   Dugdale Society Occasional Papers, No.1, 1924 +
6.   Dugdale Society Publications, No.1, 1921 +
7.   Journal of West Midlands Regional Studies, Vols.1-2, 1967-8.
      (*continued by West Midlands Studies - see below*).

8. Warwickshire and Worcestershire Life, Vol.1, 1951 +
9. Warwickshire History, Vol.1, 1969 +
10. Warwickshire Naturalists' and Archaeologists' Field Club
    Proceedings, 1860-1911.
11. West Midlands Studies, Vol.3, 1969 +

E. Museums with Local Studies Collections

1. Birmingham: City Museum and Art Gallery, Chamberlain Square,
    Birmingham, West Midlands B3 31DH. Tel: (021) 235 4202.
    *Local History Gallery illustrating the origins and growth of
    Birmingham. Historic Buildings Files relating to the City of
    Birmingham and environs, including Sutton Coldfield.*
2. Coventry: Herbert Art Gallery and Museum, Jordan Well,
    Coventry, West Midlands CV1 5RW. Tel: (0203) 832381.
    History of Coventry.
3. Hall Green: Sarehole Mill, Cole Bank Road, Hall Green,
    Birmingham, West Midlands B13 0BD. Tel: (021) 777 6612.
    History of the mill, and of the district of Hall Green.
4. Nuneaton Museum and Art Gallery, Riversley Park, Nuneaton,
    Warwickshire CV11 5TU. Tel: (0203) 376473.
5. Stratford-upon-Avon: New Place and Nash's House,
    Chapel Street, Stratford-upon-Avon, Warks. Tel: (0789) 292325.
    Local history and archaeology of Stratford and district.
6. Warwick: St John's Museum, St John's House,
    Warwick CV34 4NF. Tel: (0926) 410410 ext.2132.
    *Social history of Warwickshire. Card file of information on
    vernacular architecture to 1890s, recorded by parish (description
    and photographs), housed at Field Archaeology Office, The
    Butts, Warwick, Tel: (0926) 412276.*
7. Warwickshire Museum, Market Place, Warwick CV34 4SA.
    Tel: (0926) 410410 ext.2500.
8. Warwickshire Museum of Rural Life, Warwickshire College of
    Agriculture, Moreton Morrell, nr Warwick, Warks.
    Tel: (0926) 410410.
9. Wednesbury Museum and Art Gallery, Holyhead Road,
    Wednesbury, West Midlands. Tel: (021) 556 0683.

WEST MIDLANDS

See STAFFORDSHIRE
WARWICKSHIRE
WORCESTERSHIRE

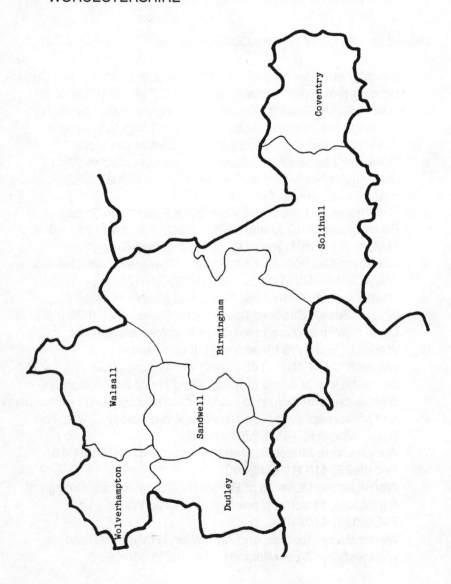

WEST SUSSEX

See SUSSEX

WEST YORKSHIRE

See YORKSHIRE (West Riding)

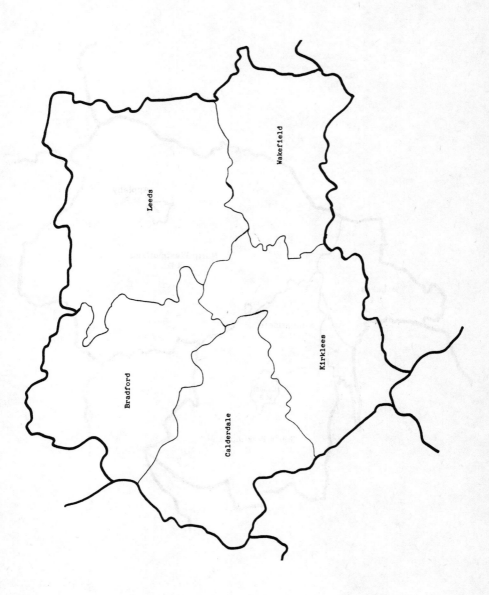

WESTMORLAND: old county

WESTMORLAND: new status

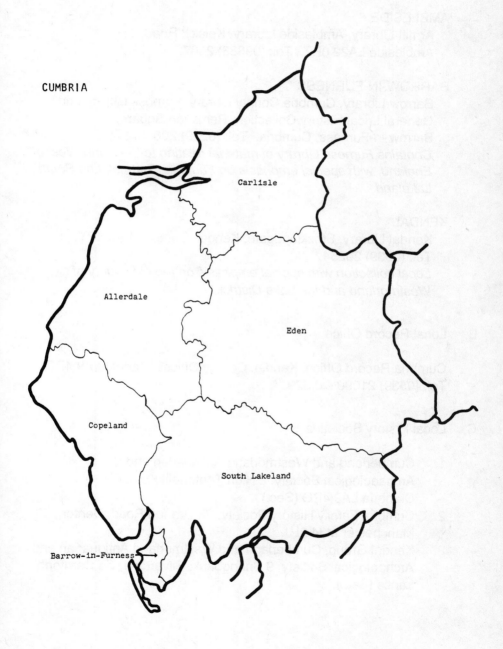

CUMBRIA

Carlisle

Allerdale

Eden

Copeland

South Lakeland

Barrow-in-Furness →

WESTMORLAND

A.   Local Studies Libraries and Collections

AMBLESIDE
Armitt Library, Ambleside Library, Kelsick Road,
Ambleside LA22 0BZ. Tel: (09633) 2507.

BARROW-IN-FURNESS
Barrow Library, Cumbria County Library, Furness Library and
General Local History Collection, Ramsden Square,
Barrow-in-Furness, Cumbria. Tel: (0229) 20650.
*Contains Furness Library of material relating to the North West of
England, with special emphasis on Furness, Cartmel, and South
Lakeland.*

KENDAL
Kendal Library, Stricklandgate, Kendal, Cumbria LA9 4PY.
Tel: (0539) 20254.
*Local collection with special emphasis on the old county of
Westmorland and the Lake District.*

B.   Local Record Office

Cumbria Record Office, Kendal, County Offices, Kendal LA9 4RQ.
Tel: (0539) 21000 ext.329.

C.   Local History Societies

1.   Cumberland and Westmorland Antiquarian and
Archaeological Society, 2 High Tenterfell, Kendal,
Cumbria LA9 4PG (Sec.).
2.   Cumbria Family History Society, 32 Granda Road, Denton,
Manchester M34 2LJ.
3.   Kendal Group, Cumberland and Westmorland Antiquarian and
Archaological Society, 9 Springbank, Silverdale, via Carnforth,
Lancs (Sec.).

D.   Local History Journals

Cumberland and Westmorland Antiquarian and Archaeological
Society:
Transactions, Vols.1-16, 1866-1900; New Series Vol.1, 1901 +
Extra Series, Nos.1-18, 1877-1937.
Record or Cartulary Series, Nos.1-8, 1897-1932.
Tract Series, No.1, 1882 +

E.   Museums with Local Studies Collections

1.   Kendal Museum, Station Road, Kendal, Cumbria LA9 6BT.
     Tel: (0539) 21374.
     Natural history and history of the Lake District and Kendal area.
2.   Museum of Lakeland Life and Industry, Kirkland, Kendal,
     Cumbria LA9 5AL. Tel: (0539) 22464.
     *Collections include: the Arthur Ransome Library,
     W.G.Collingwood Archive, Arts and Crafts Furniture Archive
     (Stanley Davies and Eric Sharpe). Lake District photographic
     archive. Watercolours and some oil paintings on lakeland
     subjects. Files of information on various aspects of the county
     maintained (e.g. agriculture, vernacular architecture, hunting,
     etc.)*

WILTSHIRE: old county

WILTSHIRE: new county

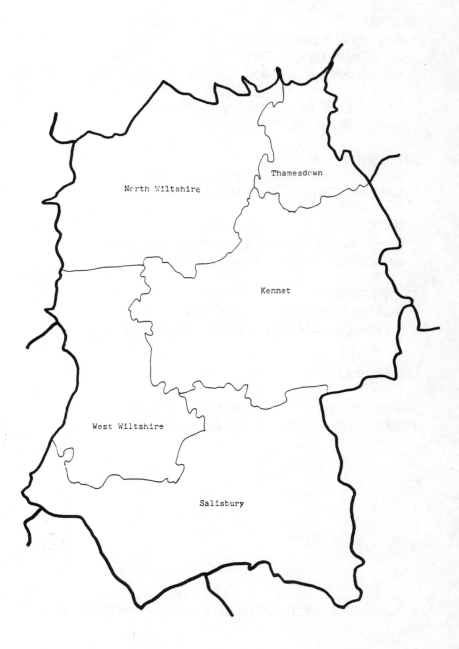

WILTSHIRE

A.   Local Studies Libraries and Collections

DEVIZES
Wiltshire Archaeological and Natural History Society Library (b),
Long Street, Devizes SN10 1NS. Tel: (0380) 727369.
Comprehensive collection of Wiltshire books, prints and drawings.

Devizes Local Studies Library (b), Sheep Street,
Devizes SN10 1DL. Tel: (0380) 726878.

SALISBURY
Salisbury Local Studies Library (b), Market Place,
Salisbury SP1 1BL. Tel: (0722) 411098.

SWINDON
Swindon Local Studies Library (b), Regent Circus,
Swindon SN1 1QG. Tel: (0793) 616277.

TROWBRIDGE
Wiltshire Local Studies Library (b), Bythesea Road,
Trowbridge BA14 8BS. Tel: (0225) 753641 ext.2715.

B.   Local Record Office.

Wiltshire Record Office, County Hall, Bythesea Road,
Trowbridge BA14 8JG. Tel: (0225) 753641 ext.3502.

---

a = under 2000 vols; b = 2000-20,000 vols; c = over 20,000 vols.

C.   Local History Societies

1.   South Wiltshire Industrial Archaeology Society, Sandlewood,
     Portland Avenue, Salisbury, Wilts SP2 8BS.
2.   West Wiltshire Industrial Archaeology Society, Hope Cottage,
     Station Road, Holt, Trowbridge, Wilts (Sec.).
3.   Wiltshire Archaeological and Natural History Society,
     The Museum, Long Street, Devizes, Wilts SN10 1NS.
4.   Wiltshire Family History Society, 65 New Park Street,
     Devizes SN10 1DR.
5.   Wiltshire Folk Life Society, The Great Barn, Avebury,
     Wilts SN8 1RF.
6.   Wiltshire Record Society, c/o Wiltshire Record Office, Bythesea
     Road, Trowbridge BA14 8JG.

D.   Local History Journals

1.   Wiltshire Archaeological and Natural History Society Magazine,
     Vol.1,   1853 +
2.   Wiltshire Archaeological and Natural History Society Records
     Branch Publications, No.1, 1939 +
3.   Wiltshire Family History Society Journal, No.1, 1981 +
4.   Wiltshire Folklife, No.1, 1976 +
5.   Wiltshire List, No.1, 1979 + (*annotated list, compiled by
     Wiltshire Library and Museum Service, of all published Wiltshire
     material*).
6.   Wiltshire Local History Forum Newsletter, No.1, 1985 +

E.   Museums with Local Studies Collections

1.   Avebury: Alexander Keiller Museum, Avebury, nr Marlborough,
     Wilts SN8 1RF. Tel: (06723) 250.
     Archaeology and history of Avebury and district.
2.   Avebury: Great Barn Museum of Wiltshire Folk Life, Avebury,
     nr Marlborough, Wilts SN8 1RF. Tel: (06723) 555.
3.   Chippenham: Yelde Hall Museum, Market Place, Chippenham,
     Wilts SN15 5HL. Tel: 0249) 651488.
     History of Chippenham.

4.   Cirencester: Corinium Museum, Park Street, Cirencester, Glos GL7 2BX. Tel: (0285) 5611.
     Prehistory and Roman history of the Cotswolds. History of Cotswold wool trade.
5.   Devizes Museum, Wiltshire Archaeological and Natural History Society, Long Street, Devizes, Wilts SN10 1NS. Tel: (0380) 77369.
6.   Devizes Wharf Canal Exhibition Centre, The Wharf, Devizes, Wilts SN10 1EB. Tel: (0380) 71279.
     History of the Kennet and Avon Canal.
7.   Malmesbury: Athelstan Museum, Town Hall, Cross Hayes, Malmesbury, Wilts. Tel: (06662) 2143.
     Archaeology and history of the area.
8.   Salisbury and South Wiltshire Museum, The King's House, 65 The Close, Salisbury, Wiltshire SP1 2EN. Tel: (0722) 335659.
9.   Swindon: Museum and Art Gallery, Bath Road, Swindon, Wilts SN1 4BA. Tel: (0793) 26161 ext.3129.
     Wiltshire geology, archaeology, local and natural history.
10. Trowbridge Museum, Town Hall, Trowbridge, Wiltshire BA14 8EQ. Tel: (02214) 65072.
11. Warminster: The Dewey Museum, The Library, Three Horse Shoes Mall, Warminster, Wilts BA12 9BT. Tel: (0985) 216022.

WORCESTERSHIRE: old county

WORCESTERSHIRE: new status

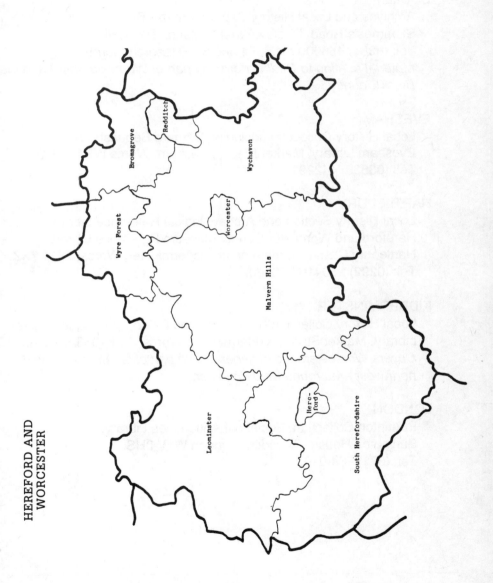

WORCESTERSHIRE

A.   Local Studies Libraries and Collections

DUDLEY
Archives and Local History Department (b), Dudley Library,
St James's Road, Dudley, West Midlands DY1 1HR.
Tel: (0384) 456000 ext.5554 and 5566 (search room).
*Material relating to Dudley (formerly part of Worcestershire) and the
Black Country.*

EVESHAM
Local History Collection (including Barnard Bequest) (a),
Evesham Library, Market Place, Evesham, Worcs WR11 4RW.
Tel: (03836) 442291.

HARTLEBURY
Local History Section and Archaeological Reference Library,
Hereford and Worcester County Museum Reference Library,
Hartlebury Castle, Hartlebury, nr Kidderminster, Worcs DY11 7XZ.
Tel: (0299) 250416/250560.

KIDDERMINSTER
Local History Collection (Worcester and Salop,) (b), Kidderminster
Library, Market Street, Kidderminster, Worcs. Tel: (0562) 752832.
*Covers Worcestershire in general, with particular emphasis on the
northwest area round Kidderminster.*

LONDON
Prattinton Collection, Society of Antiquaries Library,
Burlington House, Piccadilly, London W1V 0HS.
Tel: (071) 734 0193.

---

a = under 2000 vols; b = 2000-20,000 vols; c = over 20,000 vols.

MALVERN

Local History Collection, Malvern Library, Graham Road, Malvern, Worcs WR14 2HN. Tel: (0684) 561223.
Covers Worcestershire in general with emphasis on Malvern area.

WORCESTER

Local Studies Library (b), Worcester City Library, Foregate Street, Worcester WR1 1DT. Tel: (0905) 22154, 24853.
Contains the Willis Bund Collection with many items of local interest.

Worcestershire Archaeological Society Library, The Commandery, Sidbury, Worcester. Tel: (0905) 355071.

B.   Local Record Offices

1.   Dudley Archives and Local History Department, Dudley Library, St James's Road, Dudley DY1 1HR. Tel: (0384) 456000 ext.5554 and 5566.
2.   Hereford and Worcester County Record Office, County Hall, Spetchley Road, Worcester WR5 2NP. Tel: (0905) 763763 ext.3615.
3.   Worcester (St Helen's) Record Office, Fish Street, Worcester WR1 2HW. Tel: (0905) 763763 ext.3616.

C.   Local History Societies

1.   Birmingham and Midland Society for Genealogy and Heraldry, 92 Dimmingsdale Bank, Birmingham, West Midlands B32 1ST.
2.   Black Country Society, 15 Claydon Road, Wallheath, Kingswinford, West Midlands (Sec.).
3.   Hereford and Worcester Architecture Record Group, 56 Dovey Road, Mosely, Birmingham B13 9NX (Sec.).
Holds file of information on 1000 buildings in Worcestershire, at Avoncroft Museum of Buildings, Stoke Prior, Bromsgrove.

4.   South Worcestershire Archaeological Group, 4 Orchard Close,
      Ryall, Upton-upon-Severn, Worcs (Sec.).
5.   Vale of Evesham Historical Society, Almonry Museum, Abbey
      Gate, Evesham WR11 4BG.
6.   Worcester and District Industrial Archaeology and Local History
      Society, 9 Redfern Avenue, Worcester WR5 1PZ (Sec.).
7.   Worcestershire Archaeological Society, 4 Orchard Road,
      Malvern, Worcs (Sec.).
8.   Worcestershire Historical Society, c/o Worcester City Museum,
      Foregate Street, Worcester WR1 1DT.

D.   Local History Journals

1.   Blackcountryman, 1968 +
2.   Journal of West Midlands Studies, Vols.1-2, 1967-8. (*continued
      as West Midlands Studies - see below*).
3.   Warwickshire and Worcestershire Life, Vol.1, 1951 +
4.   Vale of Evesham Historical Society Research Papers,
      Nos.1-7, 1967-79.
5.   West Midlands Studies, Vol.3, 1969 +
6.   Worcestershire: the county magazine, 1987-88.
7.   Worcestershire Archaeological Society Reports and Papers,
      1854-1922(*in Reports and Papers of the Associated
      Architectural Societies*); Transactions, New Series Vols.1-41,
      1923/4-1964; 3rd Series, Vol.1, 1965/7 +
8.   Worcestershire Archaeology and Local History Newsletter,
      1972 +
9.   Worcestershire Countryside, 1949-1951.
10.   Worcestershire Diocesan Architectural and Archaeological
      Proceedings, 1854-1905.
11.   Worcestershire Historical Society Occasional Publications,
      No.1, 1977 +
12.   Worcestershire Historical Society Publications, 1894-1957;
      New Series Vol.1, 1960 +
13.   Worcestershire Parish Register Society Publications,
      Nos.1-5, 1913-1916.

E.   Museums with Local Studies Collections

1.   Bewdley Museum, The Shambles, Load Street, Bewdley,
     Worcester DY12 2AE. Tel: (0299) 403573.
     Traditional crafts and industries of the Wyre Forest area.
     Photographic collection.
2.   Bromsgrove Museum, 26 Birmingham Road, Bromsgrove,
     Worcester B61 0DD. Tel: (0527) 77934.
3.   Evesham: Almonry Museum, Abbey Gate, Evesham,
     Worcester WR11 4BG. Tel: (0386) 6944.
     History of the Vale of Evesham.
4.   Hereford and Worcester County Museum, Hartlebury Castle,
     Hartlebury, nr Kidderminster, Worcester DY11 7XZ.
     Tel: (0299) 250416.
     Life in Herefordshire and Worcestershire from prehistoric times.
     County social history files, Archaeological Sites and Monuments
     Record, County Excavation Archive, parish files.
5.   Malvern Museum, Abbey Gateway, Abbey Road, Malvern,
     Worcester. Tel: (0684) 567811.
6.   Worcester: Tudor House Museum, Friar Street,
     Worcester WR1 2NA. Tel: (0905) 20904.
     Social history of Worcester and district.
7.   Worcester City Museum and Art Gallery, Foregate Street,
     Worcester WR1 10T. Tel: (0905) 25371.
     Geology, natural history and history of Worcester and the Severn
     Valley.

YORKSHIRE, EAST RIDING: old district

Filey
U.D.

Norton
U.D.

Norton
R.D.

Bridlington
R.D.

Bridling-
ton
M.B.

Driffield
R.D.

Driffield
U.D.

Hornsea
U.D.

Pocklington
R.D.

Beverley
M.B.

Holderness
R.D.

Derwent
R.D.

Beverley
R.D.

Howden
R.D.

Kingston
upon Hull
C.B.

Hedon
M.B.

Haltemprice
U.D.

Withernsea
U.D.

YORKSHIRE, EAST RIDING: new county

HUMBERSIDE

North Wolds

Beverley

Holderness

Kingston
upon
Hull

Boothferry

Glanford

Scun-
thorpe

Cleethorpes
Grimsby

YORKSHIRE, NORTH RIDING: old district

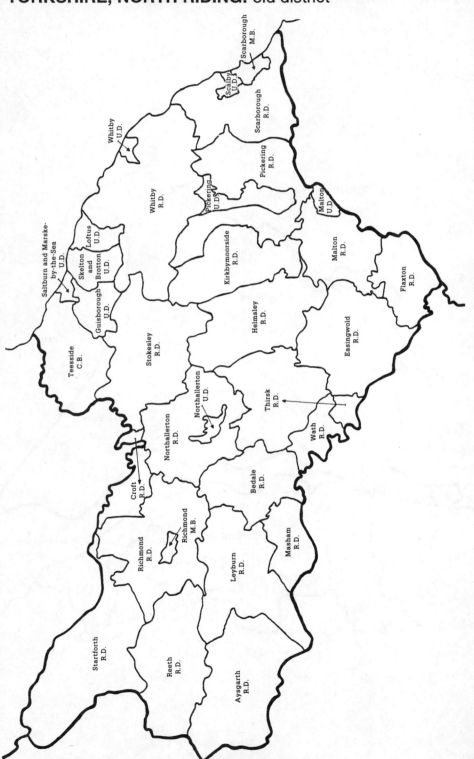

YORKSHIRE, NORTH RIDING: new county

YORKSHIRE, WEST RIDING: old district

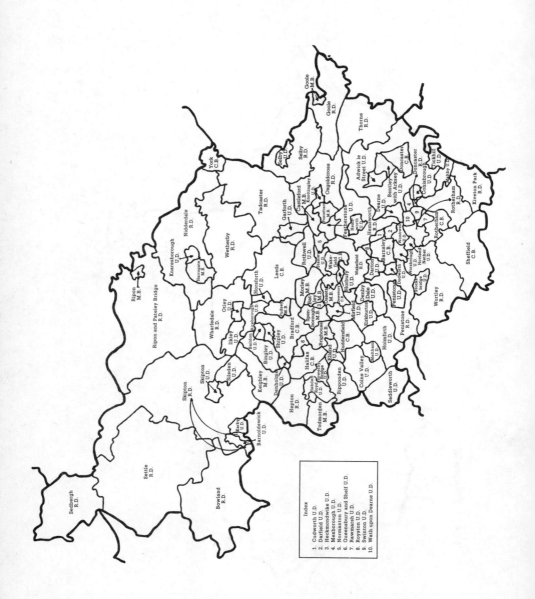

Index

1. Cudworth U.D.
2. Darfield U.D.
3. Heckmondwike U.D.
4. Mexborough U.D.
5. Normanton U.D.
6. Queensbury and Shelf U.D.
7. Rawmarsh U.D.
8. Royston U.D.
9. Swinton U.D.
10. Wath upon Dearne U.D.

YORKSHIRE, WEST RIDING: new counties

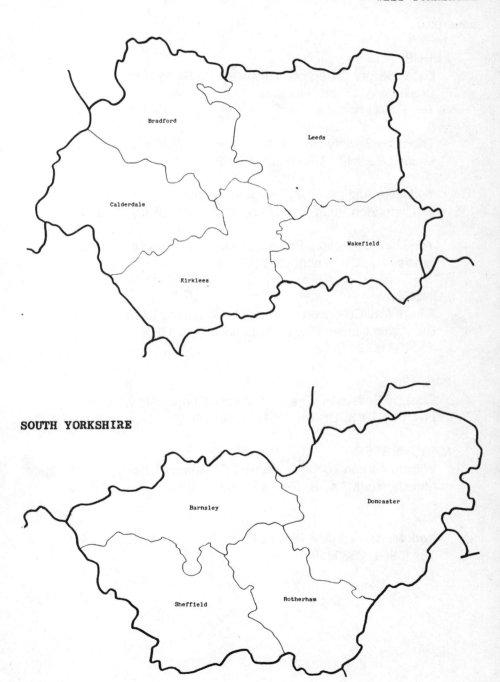

WEST YORKSHIRE

Bradford

Leeds

Calderdale

Wakefield

Kirklees

SOUTH YORKSHIRE

Barnsley

Doncaster

Sheffield

Rotherham

YORKSHIRE

A.   Local Studies Libraries and Collections

General

LEEDS
Local History Collection, Trinity and All Saints' College,
Brownberries Lane, Horsforth, Leeds LS18 5HD.
Tel: (0532) 584341. 0532 837100

Thoresby Society Library, Claremont, 23 Clarendon Road,
Leeds LS2 9NZ. Tel: (0532) 457910.

Yorkshire Archaeological Society Library, Claremont,
23 Clarendon Road, Leeds LS2 9NZ. Tel: (0532) 457910.

Yorkshire Collection, Brotherton Library, University of Leeds,
Leeds LS2 9JT. Tel: (0532) 335513.

LONDON
Albert Way Collection, Society of Antiquaries Library,
Burlington House, Piccadilly, London W1V OHS.
Tel: (071) 734 0193.

LIVERPOOL
Eshelby Collection, The Athenaeum, Church Alley,
Liverpool L1 3DD. Tel: (051) 709 0418.

MANCHESTER
William Ashton Tonge Collection, Chetham's Library, Long Millgate,
Manchester M3 1SB. Tel: (061) 834 7961.

YORK
York Minster Library, Dean's Park, York YO1 2JD.
Tel: (0904) 25308.

East Riding

BEVERLEY
Local Studies Library (b), Beverley Library, Champney Road, Beverley, North Humberside HU17 9BQ. Tel: (0482) 867108. *Covers Beverley and East Riding in depth.*

BRIDLINGTON
Bridlington Collection (b), Bridlington Library, 14 King Street, Bridlington, Humberside YO15 2DF. Tel: (0262) 72917.

HULL
The Hull Collection, Brynmor Jones Library, University of Hull, Hull HU6 7RX. Tel: (0482) 46311.

Local Studies Library (c), Hull Central Library, Albion Street, Hull HU1 3TF. Tel: (0482) 224040 ext.221.

North Riding

MIDDLESBROUGH
Local Collection (c), Middlesbrough Reference Library, Victoria Square, Middlesbrough,Cleveland TS1 2AY. Tel: (0642) 248155 ext.3358/3359.

NORTHALLERTON
Local Collection (b), Northallerton Reference Library, 1 Thirsk Road, Northallerton, North Yorkshire DL6 1PT. Tel: (0609) 6271 ext.150.

REDCAR
Local Collection (b), Redcar Reference Library, Coatborn Road, Redcar, Cleveland TS10 1RP. Tel: (0642) 472162.

---

a = under 2000 vols; b = 2000-20,000 vols; c = over 20,000 vols.

SCARBOROUGH
Local Collection (b), Scarborough Reference Library, Vernon Road, Scarborough, North Yorkshire YO11 2NN. Tel: (0723) 364285.

WHITBY
Local Collection (a), Whitby Library, Windsor Terrace, Whitby, North Yorkshire YO21 1EY. Tel: (0947) 602554.

West Riding

BARNSLEY
Local Studies Collections (b), Central Library, Shambles Street, Barnsley, South Yorkshire S70 2JF. Tel: (0226) 83241.

BRADFORD
Local Collection (c), Reference Library, Bradford Central Library, Prince's Way, Bradford BD1 1NN. Tel: (0274) 753688.

DONCASTER
Local History Library (b), Doncaster Central Library, Waterdale, Doncaster DN1 3JE. Tel: (0302) 734307.

HALIFAX
Horsfall Turner Local History Collection (b), Calderdale Central Library, Northgate House, Halifax HX1 1UN. Tel: (0422) 357257.

HARROGATE
Yorkshire Local Studies Collection (b), Central Library, Victoria Avenue, Harrogate, North Yorkshire HG1 1EG. Tel: (0423) 5022744/504726.

HUDDERSFIELD
Local History Library, Kirklees Libraries and Museums Service, Princess Alexandra Walk, Huddersfield HD1 2SU. Tel: (0484) 513808 ext.206.

---

a = under 2000 vols; b = 2000-20,000 vols; c = over 20,000 vols.

KEIGHLEY
Local Studies Collection (b), Keighley Reference Library,
North Street,'Keighley BD21 3SX. Tel: (0274) 758215.

LEEDS
Local History Collection (c), Central Library, Calverley Street,
Leeds LS1 3AB. Tel: (0532) 462464.

ROTHERHAM
South Yorkshire Archives and Local Studies Section (b),
Central Library, Walker Place, Rotherham S65 1JH.
Tel: (0709) 382121 ext.3616; direct line: 823616.

SHEFFIELD
Local Studies Library, Sheffield City Libraries, Surrey Street,
Sheffield S1 1XZ. Tel: (0742) 734711/3.

SKIPTON
Local Studies (Skipton and Craven) (a), The Library, High Street,
Skipton, North Yorkshire BD23 1JX. Tel: (0756) 2926.

WAKEFIELD
Department of Local Studies and Archives (b), Wakefield
Metropolitan District Libraries, Library Headquarters, Balne Lane,
Wakefield WF2 0DQ. Tel: (0924) 371231.

YORK
York Local Studies Collection, York Reference Library,
Museum Street, York, North Yorkshire YO1 2DS.
Tel: (0904) 654144/655631 ext.37/38.

---

a = under 2000 vols; b = 2000-20,000 vols; c = over 20,000 vols.

B.   Local Record Offices

East Yorkshire

1.   Humberside County Record Office, County Hall, Beverley
      HU17 9BA. Tel: (0482) 867131 ext.3394.
2.   Kingston-upon-Hull City Record Office, 79 Lowgate,
      Hull HU1 2AA. Tel: 222015/6.

North Yorkshire

1.   Cleveland County Archives Department, Exchange House,
      6 Marton Road, Middlesbrough TS1 1DB. Tel: (0642) 248321.
2.   North Yorkshire County Record Office, County Hall,
      Northallerton DL7 8AD. Tel: (0609) 3123 ext.2455.
3.   York City Archives Department, Art Gallery Buildings,
      Exhibition Square,York YO1 2EW. Tel: (0906) 51533.

South Yorkshire

1.   Barnsley Archive Service, Central Library, Shambles Street,
      Barnsley S70 2JF. Tel: (0226) 283241 ext.23.
2.   Doncaster Archives Department, King Edward Road, Balby,
      Doncaster DN4 0NA. Tel: (0302) 859811.
3.   Sheffield Record Office, Central Library, Surrey Street,
      Sheffield S1 1XZ. Tel: (0742) 734756.
4.   South Yorkshire Archives and Local Studies Section, Central
      Library, Walker Place, Rotherham S65 1JH.
      Tel: (0709) 382121 ext.3616; direct line: 823616.

West Yorkshire

1.   West Yorkshire Archives, Bradford, 15 Canal Road,
      Bradford BD1 4AT. Tel: (0274) 731931.
2.   West Yorkshire Archives, Calderdale, Central Library,
      Northgate House, Northgate, Halifax HX1 1UN.
      Tel: (0422) 357257 ext.2626.

3. West Yorkshire Archives, Headquarters and Wakefield
   Registry of Deeds, Newstead Road, Wakefield WF1 2DE.
   Tel: (0924) 367111 ext.2352.
4. West Yorkshire Archives, Kirklees, Central Library,
   Princess Alexandra Walk, Huddersfield HD1 2SU.
   Tel: (0484) 5233808 ext.207.
5. West Yorkshire Archives, Leeds, Chapeltown Road, Sheepscar,
   Leeds LS7 3AS. Tel: (0532) 628339.

C. Local History Societies

.1. Bradford Family History Society, 8 Coates Terrace,
    West Bowling, Bradford BD5 7AB.
2. Bradford Historical and Antiquarian Society, 3 Roundhill Mount,
   Bingley, West Yorkshire BD16 1PG (Sec.).
3. Calderdale Family History Society, 61 Gleanings Avenue,
   Norton Tower, Halifax, West Yorkshire HX2 0NU.
4. City of York and District Family History Society,
   4 Mount Vale Drive, The Mount, York YO2 2DN.
5. Cleveland and Teesside Local History Society,
   11a Orchard Road, Linthorpe, Middlesbrough, Cleveland (Sec.).
6. Cleveland Family History Society, 1 Oxgang Close, Redcar,
   Cleveland.
7. Doncaster Society for Family History, 5 The Brow, Brecks,
   Rotherham, South Yorkshire S65 3HP.
8. East Riding Archaeological Society, 10 Etherington Drive,
   Hull (Sec.).
9. East Yorkshire Family History Society, 367 Main Road, Bilton,
   Hull HU11 4DS.
10. East Yorkshire Local History Society, Beverley Library,
    Champney Road, Beverley, North Humberside HU17 8HE.
11. Halifax Antiquarian Society, 7 Haugh Shaw Road,
    Halifax HX1 3AH (Sec.).
12. Huddersfield and District Family History Society,
    31 Kingshead Road, Mirfield, West Yorkshire WF14 9SJ.
13. Huddersfield Historical Society, c/o Mr P.Greenleaf,
    New College, Huddersfield.

14. Huddersfield Local History Society, 30 Stonecliffe Drive, Middlestown, Wakefield WF4 4QD (Sec.).
15. Hunter Archaeological Society, 37 Chesterwood Drive, Sheffield S10 5DU (Sec.).
16. Ripon and District Family History Group, 17 Knaresborough Road, Bishop Monkton, nr Harrogate, North Yorkshire HG3 3QQ.
17. Sheffield and District Family History Society, 359 Baslow Road, Sheffield S17 3BH.
18. Surtees Society, The Prior's Kitchen, The College, Durham DH1 3EQ.
19. Teesside Archaeological Society, 37 Marske Hill Lane, Saltburn, Cleveland TS12 1HT.
20. Thoresby Society, 23 Clarendon Road, Leeds LS2 9NZ.
21. Wakefield Historical Society, 30 Newland Court, Sandal, Wakefield, West Yorkshire (Sec.).
22. Yorkshire Archaeological Society, Claremont, 23 Clarendon Road, Leeds LS2 9NZ. (*Includes the YAS Family and Population Studies Section*).
23. Yorkshire Architectural and York Archaeological Society, 18 Blake Street, York YO1 2GH.
24. Yorkshire Philosophical Society, The Lodge, Museum Gardens, York YO1 2DR.

D. Local History Journals

1. Bradford Antiquary, Vol.1, 1881 +
2. Bradford Historical and Antiquarian Society Local Record Series, No.1, 1929 +
3. Cleveland and Teesside Local History Society Bulletin, 1979 +
4. East Riding Antiquarian (Archaeological) Society Transactions, 1893-1939; 1949-1967.
5. East Riding Archaeologist, Vol.1, 1968 +
6. East Yorkshire Local History Bulletin, No.1, 1953 +
7. Halifax Antiquarian Society Transactions, Vol.1, 1901 +
8. Hunter Archaeological Society Transactions, Vol.1, 1914/15 +
9. Leeds Philosophical and Literary Society, Literary and Historical Society Proceedings, Vol.1, 1925 +

10. North Riding Record Society Publications, Nos. 1-9, 1884-1892; New Series Nos.1-4, 1894-1897.
11. Old West Riding, Vol.1, 1981 +
12. Ryedale Historian, No.1, 1965 +
13. Surtees Society Publications, No.1, 1835 +
14. Thoresby Society Publications, Vol.1, 1889 +
15. Wakefield Historical Society Journal, No.1, 1974 +
16. York Historian, Vol.1, 1976 +
17. Yorkshire Archaeological Journal, Vol.1, 1869 +
18. Yorkshire Archaeological Society, Records Series, No.1, 1885 +
19. Yorkshire Archaeological Society, Record Series Extra Series, Vol.1, 1914 +
20. Yorkshire Parish Register Society, Vol.1, 1889 +
    From Vol.125, 1961, issued by Yorkshire Archaeological Society Parish Register Section.

E.   Museums with Local Studies Collections

East Riding

1. Beverley Art Gallery and Museum, Champney Road, Beverley, North Humberside HU17 9BQ. Tel: (0482) 882255.
   Beverley Heritage Centre collection on the history of Beverley.
2. Bridlington: Bayle Museum, Bayle Gate, Old Town, Bridlington, North Humberside.
   Social history of Bridlington and district from the middle ages onwards.
3. Bridlington: Sewerby Hall Art Gallery and Museum, Sewerby Park, Bridlington, North Humberside.
   Archaeology, rural, military and natural history of the area.
4. Hornsea Museum of Village Life, 11 Newbegin, Hornsea, North Humberside HU18 1AB. Tel: (0964) 533430/533443.
   Social and industrial history of Hornsea and Holderness.
5. Hull and East Yorkshire Museum, 36 High Street, Kingston-upon-Hull, North Humberside. Tel: (0482) 222737.
   Includes Mortimer Collection on British and Saxon burial mounds in East Yorkshire.

6.   Kingston: Town Docks Museum, Queen Victoria Square,
      Kingston-upon-Hull, North Humberside HU1 3DX.
      Tel: (0482) 222737.
      History of the Hull fishing industry.

North Riding

1.   Bedale Hall, Bedale, North Yorkshire DL8 1AA.
      Tel: (0677) 24604.
      Local bygones, archives and photographs.
2.   Kirkleatham 'Old Hall' Museum, Kirkleatham, Redcar,
      Cleveland TS10 5NW. Tel: (0642) 479500.
      *Social and industrial history of the Borough of Langbaurgh. Card
      file of information on archaeological finds, sites and monuments.*
3.   Malton Museum, Town Hall, Market Place, Malton,
      North Yorkshire YO17 0LT. Tel: (0653) 5136.
      Archaeology of Malton, Norton and Ryedale area.
4.   Newham Grange Leisure Farm Museum, Coulby Newham,
      Middlesbrough, Cleveland. Tel: (0642) 300261/245432.
      History of farming in Cleveland.
5.   Middlesbrough: Dorman Memorial Museum, Linthorpe Road,
      Middlesbrough, Cleveland TS5 6LA. Tel: (0642) 813781.
      Industrial and social history of the area.
6.   Pickering: Beck Isle Museum of Rural Life, Bridge Street,
      Pickering, North Yorkshire YO18 8DU. Tel: (0751) 73653.
      Social and domestic life of the district.
7.   Redcar: Royal National Lifeboat Institution Zetland Lifeboat
      Museum, Old Lifeboat House, Esplanade, Redcar,
      Cleveland TS10 3AG.
      History of Redcar.
8.   Richmondshire Museum, Ryder's Wynd, Richmond,
      North Yorkshire DL10 4JA.
      *History of the Richmond area including the Swaledale
      leadmining industry.*
9.   Ryedale Folk Museum, Hutton-le-Hole,
      North Yorkshire YO6 6UA. Tel: (07515) 367.

10. Swaledale Folk Museum, Reeth, nr Richmond,
    North Yorkshire D11 4RT. Tel: (0748) 84373.
    *Traditional life and occupations in Swaledale and
    Arkengarthdale.*
11. Thirsk Museum, 16 Kirkgate, Thirsk, North Yorkshire YO7 1PQ.
    Tel: (0845) 22755.
12. Upper Dales Folk Museum, Station Yard, Hawes, Wensleydale,
    North Yorkshire DL8 3NT. Tel: (09697) 494.
    Traditional rural life of Wensleydale and Swaledale.
13. Whitby Museum, Pannett Park, Whitby,
    North Yorkshire YO21 1RE. Tel: (0947) 602908.

West Riding

1. Batley: Bagshaw Museum, Wilton Park, Batley,
   West Yorkshire WF17 0AS. Tel: (0924) 472514.
   Local and natural history.
2. Bradford: Bolling Hall Museum, Bowling Hall Road, Bradford,
   West Yorkshire BD4 7LP. Tel: (0274) 723057.
   Local history of Bradford.
3. Bradford Industrial Museum, Moorside Mills, Moorside Road,
   Bradford, West Yorkshire BD2 3HP. Tel: (0274) 631756.
   *History of the wool manufacturing industry. Bradford Heritage
   Recording Unit collection of photographs and tapes.*
4. Bradford and Keighley: Cliffe Castle Art Gallery and Museum,
   Keighley, West Yorkshire BD20 6LH. Tel: (0274) 758230.
   Local and natural history of the Bradford and Keighley districts.
5. Castleford Museum Room, Castleford Library, Carlton Street,
   Castleford, West Yorkshire. Tel: (0977) 559552.
6. Cawthorne Victoria Jubilee Museum, Taylor Hill, Cawthorne,
   Barnsley, South Yorkshire S75 4HH. Tel: (0226) 791273.
   Local and natural history of the area.
7. Craven Museum, Town Hall, High Street, Skipton,
   North Yorkshire BD23 1AH. Tel: (0756) 4079.
   Geology, archaeology and social history of the Craven Dales.
8. Cusworth Hall Museum, Cusworth, Doncaster,
   South Yorkshire DN5 7TU. Tel: (0302) 782342.
   Life in South Yorkshire during the past 200 years.

9.   Gomersal: Red House Museum, Oxford Road, Gomersal,
      West Yorkshire BD19 4JP. Tel: (0274) 872165.
10.   Goole Museum and Art Gallery, Goole Library, Market Square,
      Carlisle Street, Goole, North Humberside DN14 5AA.
      Tel: (0405) 2187.
11.   Halifax: Calderdale Industrial Museum, Winding Road, Halifax,
      West Yorkshire HX1 1PR. Tel: (0422) 59031.
      History of Halifax industries
12.   Harrogate Museums and Art Gallery Service, Royal Pump Room
      Museum, Royal Parade, Harrogate, North Yorkshire.
      Tel: (0423) 503340.
13.   Heptonstall Old Grammar School, Heptonstall, Hebden Bridge,
      West Yorkshire HX7 7LY. Tel: (0422) 843738.
      History of the village and its handloom weaving industry.
14.   Huddersfield: Tolson Museum, Ravensknowle Park, Wakefield
      Road, Huddersfield, West Yorkshire HD5 8DJ.
      Tel: (0484) 530591/541455.
      History and archaeology of Huddersfield and West Yorkshire.
15.   Ilkley: Manor House Art Gallery and Museum, Castle Yard, Ilkley,
      West Yorkshire LS29 9DT. Tel: (0943) 600066.
      Archaeology and history of Ilkley.
16.   Ilkley: White Wells, Wells Road, Ilkley,
      West Yorkshire LS29 9LH.
      Natural history of the district.
17.   Kelham Island Industrial Museum, Kelham Island, off Alma
      Street, Sheffield S3 8RY. Tel: (0742) 22106.
18.   Knaresborough Castle and Old Courthouse Museum, Castle
      Grounds, Knaresborough, North Yorkshire. Tel: (0423) 503340.
19.   Leeds: Abbey House Museum, Abbey Road, Kirkstall, Leeds,
      West Yorkshire LS5 3EH. Tel: (0532) 755821.
      Social history of Leeds.
20.   Leeds Industrial Museum, Armley Mills, Canal Road, Leeds,
      West Yorkshire LS12 2QF. Tel: (0532) 637861.
21.   Nidderdale Museum, Council Offices, King Street, Pateley
      Bridge, Harrogate, North Yorkshire HG3 5LE.
      All aspects of life in the Yorkshire Dales.
22.   Otley Museum, Civic Centre, Cross Green, Otley,
      West Yorkshire. Tel: (0943) 461052.

23. Pontefract Museum, Salter Row, Pontefract,
    West Yorkshire WF8 1BA. Tel: (0977) 797289.
24. Ripon: Wakeman's House Museum, Market Place, Ripon,
    North Yorkshire. Tel: (0423) 503340.
    History of Ripon.
25. Rotherham: Clifton Park Museum, Clifton Lane, Rotherham,
    South Yorkshire S65 2AA. Tel: (0709) 382121.
    *Archaeology, history and natural history of the district, computer
    files of archaeology and natural history information.*
26. Ryburn Farm Museum, Ripponden, West Yorkshire HX4 4DF.
27. Sheffield: Bishop's House, Meersbrook Park, Norton Lees Lane,
    Sheffield S89BE. Tel: (0742) 557701.
    Life in Sheffield in Tudor and Stuart times.
28. Sheffield City Museum, Weston Park, Sheffield S10 2TP.
    Tel: (0742) 27226.
    *History and natural history of the city and district. Bateman
    Antiquarian Manuscripts Collection. Archaeological Sites and
    Monuments Record for South Yorkshire.*
29. Shibden Hall Folk Museum of West Yorkshire, Halifax,
    West Yorkshire HX3 6XG. Tel: (0422) 52246.
    Local History of the Calderdale area.
30. Upper Wharfedale Folk Museum, 6 The Square, Grassington,
    Skipton, North Yorkshire BD23 5HA. Tel: (0756) 752800.
    History of the Yorkshire Dales.
31. Wakefield Museum, Wood Street, Wakefield, West Yorkshire
    WF1 3QW. Tel: (0924) 37)211 ext.7190.
32. York: Jorvik Viking Centre, Coppergate, York,
    North Yorkshire YO1 1NT. Tel: (0904) 643211.
33. York Castle Museum, York YO1 1RY. Tel: (0904) 53611.
    Social and commercial life of York.
34. Yorkshire Museum, Museum Gardens, York,
    North Yorkshire YO1 2DR.
    Archaeology and history of York.